Yvonne BARRETT

A Beautiful Life
Cut Tragically Short

YVONNE BARRETT

A Beautiful Life
Cut Tragically Short

DAMIAN JOHNSTONE

Book cover design and typesetting by WorkingType Design

ISBN: 9-780-6468529-3-5

TABLE OF CONTENTS

1. PREFACE

I first became aware of Yvonne Barrett around the mid-1960s. At that time, I was fourteen and living with my parents and six siblings in Heathcote, a small Victorian country town some ninety minutes' drive from Melbourne. I quickly became a fan of Yvonne's. I have to admit that I also developed a schoolboy crush on her, but I'm sure I wasn't the only one who felt that way. Yvonne was not only a very talented singer. She was also very attractive!

After leaving school, I started a job in June 1969 in the Commonwealth public service in Maribyrnong, an inner Melbourne suburb north-west of the city. Little did I know at that time that Yvonne lived in the western suburb of Braybrook, let alone that her home was only a short drive from where I worked. Moreover, I discovered during my research for this biography that Yvonne was very proud to have grown up in Braybrook.

Yvonne's sister Tricia developed a love of dancing at an early age, and it wasn't long before Yvonne started going along with her to dancing lessons. Dancing soon became a passion of Yvonne's. That passion resulted in Yvonne winning a number of dancing competitions. Yvonne also appeared in a number of pantomimes, before going on to achieve success as a cast member of the famed *Swallows Juniors* television show. She subsequently appeared in highly successful stage shows such as *Sound of Music, Stop The World I Want To Get Off* and *A Funny Thing Happened On The Way To The Forum*.

Yvonne then turned to full time singing and she became a regular cast member of the pop music TV program the *Go!! Show* in 1965. That in turn led to her being signed to Go!! Records. Yvonne also did a lot of session work which included radio jingles and TV commercials.

In 1965 Yvonne toured Vietnam as part of the first Australian Government sponsored entertainer's tour of that country. She completed a second tour in 1968.

Yvonne subsequently went on to appear regularly on TV on numerous music shows in the late 1960s and 1970s including *Uptight, Bandstand,* the *Happening 70's* series, *In Melbourne Tonight, The Penthouse Club, The Mike Walsh Show, The Ernie Sigley Show,* and Ernie Sigley's and Barry Ion's *Adelaide Tonight* shows, *The Graham Kennedy Show,* and *The Don Lane Show* during this period. She also made numerous appearances in clubs throughout Australia.

I will never forget the day I met Yvonne for the first and only time in June 1969. I had gone into 3UZ's studios at 45 Bourke Street, Melbourne to collect the latest 3UZ Top 40 Chart. Just as I was leaving 3UZ, I happened to look across to the other side of Bourke Street, and lo and behold, I noticed Yvonne coming out of a shop. I immediately ran across the road as quick as I could so that I could meet her.

During the brief chat we had, she asked me where I came from. I told her I grew up in Heathcote, and that I'd just started working in Melbourne in the Commonwealth public service. I also mentioned that I was in the city this particular day attending a training course.

Yvonne left a lasting impression on me that day. We only spoke for a few minutes, but I have never forgotten how friendly, unassuming and gracious she was. Back then I loved collecting autographs, but all I had for Yvonne to sign that day was a Brashs' record paper bag. That didn't bother Yvonne one bit. She very kindly signed the bag, and after our brief chat we both went our separate ways.

I subsequently wrote to Yvonne and thanked her for her kind gesture. To my great surprise a short time later she sent me a personalised autographed photo of herself. I have treasured that photo and the Brashs' bag autograph ever since. Yvonne was one of the few Australian singers who replied to my many letters to singers during my teenage years. Johnny O'Keefe, Noeleen Batley, Pat Carroll and Laurel Lea also replied to my letters, and each sent me much appreciated and treasured autographed photos.

Much to my delight, I learnt during my research for this biography that Yvonne had also been an autograph collector in her youth. Among her collection were the autographs of Johnny O'Keefe, his band The Dee Jays, The Mouseketeers (who toured Australia in 1959) and numerous Melbourne television personalities and performers.

In late 1969 I saw Yvonne perform live on stage at Bendigo's Pacific Ballroom. Unfortunately, I didn't get to speak to her on that occasion, as she had to rush off to another commitment that same night. My memories of meeting Yvonne and seeing her sing on stage will live with me forever.

Yvonne's biography is my third. The first was *The "Wild One"*

— *The life and times of Johnny O'Keefe*. As well as telling Johnny's life story, it is also the story of the arrival of the cult of the teenager, of pop radio in the age of payola and the birth of TV, of bodgies and widgies[1], and mods and rockers.

This was followed up by *A Race to Remember* which is a biography of Peter Norman, the silver medal-winning Australian athlete who stood on the Olympic dais and proudly wore a civil rights badge in support of the silent protest made by two African American athletes at the 1968 Mexico City Olympic Games.

These biographies share one thing in common. In my early teens I took a strong interest in the subject of each biography, and I wrote to each of them during that period. In each instance, I received a letter and an autographed photo back from them, and much to my delight, I eventually met each of them. In short, the seeds for each biography started with the letters I received from those three people, who cared enough to respond to my letters.

Writing someone's life story is an intimidating and all-consuming endeavour. To do it justice not only requires great sacrifice on the biographer's part, but also on their family. In my case, my wife Therese has made tremendous sacrifices. Always a great encourager and supporter, she was even more so through this exercise. She has shown me incredible love and support during the past 45 years, and I love her heaps. She has contributed in so many ways over the past five years during the research and writing of Yvonne's biography.

---

1   Bodgies and widgies refer to a youth subculture that existed in Australia and New Zealand in the 1950s, similar to the rocker culture in the UK or Greaser culture in the United States. The males were called bodgies and the females were called widgies. https://en.wikipedia.org/wiki/Bodgies_and_widgies

Thank you, Therese, for your belief in me, your constant encouragement and sacrifice, and for "pumping up my tyres" so to speak, when I doubted myself. Above all, thank you for your undying love.

Our children: Glenn, Clare and Karen, and their respective spouses Louise, Dave and Rick, have been gigantic supporters of this project from day one. Your support, encouragement and love mean a great deal to me. Our adorable grandchildren, Alec, Levi, Samadhi, Zinn and Ethan also mean a great deal to me. They provided welcome relief from the book when I've needed to take breaks from writing. I've loved all you beautiful people from the moment I set eyes on you, and I always will!

I will always be eternally grateful for the love and support of my late and very dear mother Carmel and father Harold. They encouraged my letter writing and reading of books in my younger years, and they did the same with the interests of each of my six siblings: Michael (deceased), Maree, Geraldine, Loreto, Kathryn and Brendan. They also sacrificed a great deal to educate and support all of us. We all turned out okay, thanks to the wonderful example they set us.

I dedicate Yvonne's biography to her sister Tricia Barrett. This biography could not have been written without the unconditional and total support that I received from Tricia. Much to my regret, Tricia's brother Peter declined to be interviewed for Yvonne's biography.

My sincere thanks to you Tricia for being so open and frank with me, for loaning me scrapbooks and photos, and for always making yourself available whenever I needed another batch of questions answered. I'm sure that it was a joy for you to discuss your happy memories of Yvonne, but I also know that other discussions undoubtedly evoked feelings of great hurt and sorrow, and resurrected memories previously locked away. I also extend my thanks to Tricia's daughter Martine who I met and spoke to in the early days of this project. Your support was much appreciated Martine.

This book would not have been possible without the following people, who gave their time freely for interviews — several of them on numerous occasions — for which I am most grateful. Thanks to: Gavan Anderson, Sam Anglesey, Helen (Reid) Barr, Martine Barrett, Tricia Barrett, Margie Bayes, Geraldine Bourke, Ronnie Burns AM and Maggie Stewart, Carmel Chayne & Kel Monaghan, Johnny Chester, Liz Dennis, Jamie Dillon, Robert Driver, Denise Drysdale, Maureen Elkner, Pat Farrar, Jan & Lyn Field, John Finn, Ron Fletcher, Lionel Gell, Diane Glenn, Sandy Glenny, Ron Golding, Brenda Halman, Mick Hamilton, Ted Hamilton OAM, Barry Hirst, Frank Howson, Jan Hunter, Peter James, Kaye Johnston, Marcie Jones, Lesley & Ian Kirk, Rhonda Kneebone, Jeff Lander, Clarrie Lemme & Jeffrey Ahern, Marc Leon & Glenys Hewett, Ken Leroy, Kevin McCabe, Robin Malone, Gordon Marsh, Geoff Mayne, Stanley Middleton, Ron Moore, Kaye Murray, Patti Newton, Loretta O'Brien, Kathryn O'Toole, Robert Reid, Marie Ryan, Di Senn, Wendy Stapleton, Bruce Stewart, Denis Tucker, John Vallins, Terry Walker, Ross D. Wyllie and Brendan Zinn.

My thanks also go to the following people, who all helped in various ways: Emma Anglesey, Lloyd Arnstey, Dominic Barbuto, Bill Bauernfeind, Janice Chambers, Mick Connelly, Mick Credlin, Helen Dillon, Harvey Duff, Brendan Fagin, Neville Fox, Susie Gamble (I highly recommend Susie's wonderful *GO!! Show* Facebook page. Susie is a great promoter of Yvonne and many other *GO!! Show* favourites), Scott Garnett, Cheryl Gould, Liz Hawley, John Hosie, Ron Iddles, Roman Kozlovski, Kristine Jeremiah, Loreto & Brendan Johnstone, David Kusznir, Clare Lombardi, Jillian McCandlish, Paul McHenry, Tasso Matheas, Ken Mather, Margaret Mikkelsen, John Newhill, Jim Nugent, Cheryl O'Brien, Maree Petchell, Greg Plank, Judy Quarantotto, Mick Robbins, Gill Smith, Vince Spiteri, Luke Taiapa, and Jen Williams.

Special mention must be made of the contribution given to me by my Wisconsin, USA based friend Bill Bauernfeind. Bill has been a close friend of mine for many years. He and I initially connected through our love of the music of the late and great Buddy Holly. Bill has been a teacher of writing. He has also proofed and edited a number of writings, including a play, a book, and many essays and short stories

Bill hadn't heard of Yvonne until I mentioned this year that I was writing her biography. He quickly found himself involved in Yvonne's story. He offered his support after watching several of Yvonne's music clips on the internet. He has helped me in numerous ways, including reading several versions of the manuscript, as well as offering numerous insightful observations. Thank you Bill for all your support. It has been very much appreciated.

Damian Johnstone

2. 'YVONNE CAME OUT DANCING AND NEVER STOPPED'

During the 1920s, new immigration agreements were introduced between State and Commonwealth governments within Australia, between the British and Australian governments, and between government and non-government organisations. The Commonwealth assumed the selection, medical examination and transport of prospective immigrants. The states requisitioned the numbers and categories they wanted and arranged settlement and after-care.

The Joint Commonwealth and States Scheme of 1921 formalised these arrangements and the Empire Settlement Act 1922 was a landmark in the history of Australian immigration, especially for its encouragement of child and youth migration. Under the Empire Settlement Act, an annual expenditure ceiling was set at £1.5 million in 1922, and £3 million for each of the fourteen years thereafter. Treasury was authorised to approve all schemes and the maximum British contribution in any instance was half. Approximately 221,000 new settlers received passage assistance to Australia between 1921 and 1929, the majority going to New South Wales and Victoria.[2]

Ted Barrett was one such new settler. Ted was born Albert

2   'Good British Stock: Child and Youth Migration to Australia', http://guides.naa. gov.au/good-british-stock/chapter1/index.aspx.

Edward Barrett in Leeds in the United Kingdom on October 24th 1904. Details of Ted's childhood are scarce because he very rarely talked about it with his family. Ted sang in the famed Leeds Cathedral Choir as a youth and he played piano by ear.[3] He was also a talented dancer. Ted had two siblings, his older brother Bill and sister Dolly, who was also a fine singer.

Tragedy struck Ted's life at the age of seventeen when his mother died in his arms.[4] Her death had a profound effect on Ted, so much so that he migrated to Australia soon after his mother's death[5] to join his brother Bill who had migrated some time earlier. Ted's father[6] and sister Dolly remained in the UK. On his arrival in Australia, Ted settled in Geelong and found work as a textile worker at the Godfrey Hirst Woollen Mills.[7] While working in Geelong, Ted met Sheila Mary Smith. It wasn't long before a romance developed.

Sheila Mary Smith was born on May 30th 1917 at Royal Women's Hospital in Melbourne. Sheila's mother was from Ararat[8] and her father came from a very wealthy sheep and farming family in western Victoria. Sheila's parents never married because Sheila's mother's family wouldn't allow Sheila's mother to marry the non-Catholic father. As a result,

---

3 Playing by ear is the ability of a performing musician to reproduce a piece of music they have heard, without having seen it notated in any form of sheet music.

4 The cause of her death is not known.

5 Details of exactly when Ted arrived in Australia are not known, but it is thought he arrived early in 1922.

6 Ted's father died during the bombing of London in the Second World War.

7 The company was founded in the late 1800's by Godfrey Hirst. He was an immigrant from Yorkshire, which was the centre of textile manufacturing in England. Hirst's ability to manufacture first quality textiles helped eliminate Australia's dependence on England for cloth.

8 Ararat is some 198 kilometres west of Melbourne.

Sheila was placed by her mother[9] in a Geelong orphanage. Sometime later Sheila and four other girls named Eily, Gwenny, Cassie and Rita were subsequently fostered out of the orphanage by two Geelong-based 'maiden aunts'.

The five girls were never adopted. Instead they were raised as sisters by the two maiden aunts, one they called "Mum", and the other "Aunty". Yvonne's sister Tricia understands that the families of the five girls paid for their upkeep, but their lives weren't talked about. 'I know that my mother's mother paid money to the "Aunts", but I don't know to what extent. We knew nothing about my father's or my mother's early lives because we didn't sit around and talk families.'[10]

Tricia found out years later that "Mum" and "Aunty" were sisters. She also learnt at that time that the two sisters had another sister. 'That sister had adopted a child, so they probably visited her occasionally. We became quite close to that girl in our childhood. "Mum" and "Aunty" had passed away by then.'

Tricia remembers her mother Sheila telling her that the five girls had very simple, peaceful and happy lives. All they ever did was go to school, play outside after school, and go to church on Sundays. There were no presents at Christmas because the girls didn't really belong to them. Instead they'd get something like an orange for Christmas. 'That was sad. The five girls might have had nasty moments too, but we were never told about them.'

---

9   Tricia Barrett ultimately met her grandmother when she was about twelve. 'I took an instant and total dislike to her. She was an old bitch. Even though I was her granddaughter, I was never told that she was my grandmother till she died. I only ever knew her as Aunty May. She was a very nervy and edgy person. I think it took a toll on her mentally, possibly because she was afraid that her then husband would find out that she was seeing the daughter that she had given up.'

10   Tricia is still close to her only cousins.

Liz Dennis (nee Perkins) recalls that her mother Eily was taken away at a very young age from her alcoholic mother and made a ward of the state because her father had died when she was very young. 'Mum never felt she was treated badly, but she said the two "Aunts" were really strict. The girls didn't have mothers, so they had no one to love them or to put their arms around them or show them any affection. The two women didn't do it for the love of the children. They did it for an income.

'The government paid the aunts for bringing up the five girls. Clothing, shoes, and school uniforms were also provided while the girls were educated at Geelong's St Mary's Star of The Sea school. Mum said the other school kids would get all new things, whereas the five girls were treated differently. They were given hand-me-down things from the school or from the government.'

Once the girls turned fourteen, the government stopped their financial support. The girls were then considered old enough to leave their foster home and fend for themselves.[11] Having turned fourteen, Sheila went into service as a housekeeper, cleaning and cooking for a doctor and his wife in Kew. Tricia recalls Sheila telling her that the doctor was a lovely man, but his wife was very cruel. 'She treated our mother very badly, so she left as soon as she could. I don't know what she did for work after that, as she only ever talked about that first job.'

Liz Dennis remembers her mother telling her that she had a nasty experience while working for a doctor's family in Geelong. 'Then she went to work on a farm for a beautiful

---

11   The five girls kept in contact over ensuing years.

family. She was doing all the house work. The mother took mum under her wing and taught her how to set the table, etc., but she wasn't getting much money.'[12]

The 1930s was not a happy period for countless Australian families. Although not hit as hard as America, Britain, Germany and other Western economies, Australia nevertheless suffered severely from the rippling effects of the Wall Street Crash in October 1929.[13] Billions of dollars of investments were wiped out in a matter of days, heralding the beginning of the Great Depression. Australia's economy relied heavily on overseas loans and the sale of its primary products. Share prices plummeted and, as the value of money dwindled, businesses closed, farms were abandoned and people who could not pay their rent were forced out of their homes. Thousands of Australians were out of work by 1930, and those lucky enough to have a job were battling for a living as wages were cut and permanent jobs became part time or casual.[14]

Nevertheless, nineteen-year-old Sheila Smith and thirty-one-year-old Ted Barrett married in Geelong on April 23rd 1936. Ted was still working at the Godfrey Hirst Woollen Mills in Geelong at that time. Wanting to win the favour of Sheila's

---

12   Liz Dennis remembers her mother being a very strong woman. 'She was thirty one when she got married. She was lucky with Dad. He was a fine man. Sheila was a very strong woman too. Rita had a handicapped and disabled child. She looked after her till she was 80. She had other children who were fine. Cassie had a sad life due to a tumultuous marriage. All the sisters kept in touch. Each had a story which affected them. Out of all the five girls and their families, my family and Yvonne's family were the closest because we had more in common.'

13   The Wall Street Crash, also known as the Stock Market Crash, started on October 24 ("Black Thursday") and continued until October 29th 1929 ("Black Tuesday"), when share prices on the New York Stock Exchange collapsed. https://en.wikipedia.org/wiki/Wall_Street_Crash_of_1929.

14   Peter Luck, David Salter, and Carolyn Noad: 'This Fabulous Century', Circus Books, 1979.

maiden aunts, he came up with the idea of telling them before the wedding that he was born in Ireland, knowing that they were Irish. Tricia Barrett opines that 'this went over much better because he said he was an Irish Catholic. I don't know if he was Catholic, but he said he was!'

Australia's recovery from the Depression was slow and full employment did not return until the outbreak of the Second World War in 1939. During the war there was rationing of petrol, cooking appliances, household drapery, tea, beer, sugar, butter, tobacco, chocolate, meat and clothes, so family life was still pretty tough. Pressure was also strong on young Australians to enlist in the services to fight in Europe, North Africa, South East Asia, and Papua New Guinea. Closer to home there was a legitimate, though exaggerated fear of invasion from Japan, and demands to work hard to sustain the nation and economy in a time of great need.[15]

Ted and Sheila Barrett moved to the New South Wales town of Orange in 1940. By now the twenty-three-year-old Sheila was pregnant. She subsequently gave birth to a daughter named Mary. Sadly, Mary lived for only ten minutes. Shortly after Mary's burial in the Orange cemetery, the heartbroken couple moved to Melbourne. After finding accommodation in a small single-fronted house in Stafford Street, Abbotsford, Ted obtained employment in Abbotsford as a textile worker at the Yarra Falls Woollen Mills.

Sheila subsequently gave birth prematurely to Patricia Anne Barrett[16] in the Barrett family home in Abbotsford

---

15   Garry Disher, Australia Then and Now, Oxford University Press, Melbourne, 1987, pp. 141, 145.

16   Patricia is now known as Tricia Barrett.

on November 9th 1941. Peter Edward Barrett was also born prematurely at the family home on November 13th 1943. Yvonne Frances Barrett completed a trio of premature births, when she too was born at home in Abbotsford on July 1st 1946. As was the case following her siblings' births, Yvonne was immediately taken to the nearby Maristowe Private Hospital in Fairfield to be checked by a doctor. Tricia Barrett recalls her mother often speaking of Yvonne's birth and saying that 'Yvonne came out dancing and never stopped!'

Radio had been a great comfort to Australian families during the Second World War, both for news and entertainment. Some of the better known programs through the 1940s included *The Argonauts Club, Dad and Dave, The Quiz Kids, Australia's Amateur Hour, Blue Hills* and *McCackie Mansion*.[17] Music was also big on radio. Every kind of popular music was featured from crooning, band recitals, hymns, community singing, hillbilly music, jazz and jive through to big-band music.[18]

Dancing was a 'big thing' for Tricia Barrett from an early age and it didn't take long for Yvonne to follow suit. Yvonne lived for dancing from the age of two and a half. 'Our childhood was just dancing,' remembers Tricia. 'Our mother would have loved to have danced, but she had no rhythm whatsoever. She watched us dance all our lives and she still had no rhythm. I think we were sent to dancing school because of Shirley Temple.[19] I was learning dancing so Yvonne came along with me. We would walk up to the cathedral hall, near Gertrude street and St Vincent's hospital

---

17   Jacqueline Kent, Out of the Bakelite Box, Angus & Robertson, Sydney, 1983, pp. 266-8.

18   Ibid.,p.73.

19   Tricia, Peter and Yvonne all had Shirley Temple curls as very young children.

in Fitzroy, where Edna Hardy's dance studio was. We all then walked home after the lessons.

'Anything I ever did, like a little solo, Yvonne copied it from me. We had "cobbler competitions"[20] at the end of dancing. It would be Yvonne and me battling it out at the end. I couldn't let her win and she wasn't about to let me win. Half the time Edna Hardy would stop us because we were getting a bit intense. We'd both get an ice cream then. I think Yvonne won more times than me.'

Tricia recalls Yvonne being gorgeous as a child. 'She was beautiful, happy, bright, bubbly, and loving. She just loved singing, dancing and animals. We always had cats and a dog. At one stage we also had a rabbit, a duck and a cockatoo called Big Julie.'

Life in Australia in the early 1950s was more stable than it had been for many years. Robert Menzies's Liberal government had assumed power in 1949 and within a few years the worst effects of the Second World War had receded. Australia's economy was on an even keel and growing steadily. There was a boom in industrial development, foreign investment (particularly from America) and mineral discoveries. Families were gradually achieving a higher standard of living.

The influence of the United States became increasingly apparent as Australians drifted away from the old British values of thrift and prudence to the American way of the pursuit of happiness through consumption. As well as catering for food, clothing, doctors' bills, school fees and the like, family budgets were now expected to cover the purchase of household appliances such as a refrigerator and a washing

---

20   Tricia likens the cobbler to the Russian Cossacks action where the dancer goes down in a squat and begins kicking one leg in front of the other.

machine. Many families purchased such items on hire purchase (or on a "buy now, pay later" premise).

The early 1950s also saw a large population increase, from both the post-war baby boom (an increase in births with the return of Australian servicemen home from the War) and immigration. After the War the Commonwealth Government, as part of its economic plan for national development, embarked on a policy of population growth through immigration. Between 1945 and 1952 some 720,000 immigrants arrived in Australia, including approximately 360,000 British and some 170,000 displaced persons, mostly from eastern Europe.[21] Employment was high and home ownership increased. In rural areas, farmers' incomes grew significantly following high demand for wool and foodstuffs. At first, many were sceptical about the boom lasting. After all, it was all too easy to look back a few short years to the war, and the Depression before that. But the decade continued to roll along smoothly and the scepticism gradually disappeared.

In the meantime, five-year-old Yvonne Barrett participated in a Fancy Dress Children's Ball held at the Collingwood Town Hall on May 22nd 1952. Its aim was to raise funds for the then Opportunity Clubs charity organisation. The next day the Sun News-Pictorial newspaper featured photos of Yvonne taken the previous night. The first photo showed Yvonne dressed in a short cowgirl outfit and cowgirl boots. Her hair was in long ringlets and she was wearing a cowgirl hat. Her male partner, five-year-old "Captain" Lloyd Evans was dressed up as a pirate. He had cast aside his wicked cutlass and was seen approaching

---

21   Stella Lees and June Senyard, *The 1950s*, Hyland House, Melbourne, 1987, p.106.

his prize — the lovely cowgirl who was sucking a dubious finger.

Another photo showed Yvonne and "Captain" Evans dancing. The newspaper caption read: 'She smiles. The prize is won. On with the dance.' The last photo revealed "Captain" Evans with his arm across the cowgirl's back. That caption read: 'The bold, but not really bad, pirate spied the fair damsel with the long ringlets and the sweet country air, curled his moustache in decision and changed course to capture her.' [22]

Edna Hardy subsequently opened her own dance school in Footscray with her husband Bill Ross. Yvonne undertook ballet lessons there for a short period. When Tricia was nearing the age of fourteen and Yvonne nine, Edna closed her school and began teaching for May Downs at her dance studio in Melbourne's Russell Street.[23] Yvonne and Tricia subsequently took lessons from Edna Hardy at May Downs's studio.

Born in 1891, May Downs took to the stage as a young girl playing live variety theatre in Melbourne, including The Tivoli, and on tour throughout Australia. She lost her job when she turned twenty-one and qualified for adult pay, so she began a teaching career that made her name famous in show business.[24] Her school is still Australia's longest established dance academy.

May Downs was known to be a very hard taskmaster. Tricia Barrett recalls that 'May set very high standards and she was pretty tough on her students. She used to sit with her legs wide open and she'd have a cigarette hanging out

---

22 "Here's How The Pirate Captured The Cowgirl", "Sun News Pictorial", May 23rd 1952.

23 It was an appropriate move as Edna had initially learnt dancing from May.

24 'May Kicked On', Australasian Post, June 12th 1969.

of her mouth. If she didn't like something that a student did, she'd whack that person as they went past. Mothers certainly wouldn't put up with that now!'[25]

Yvonne's dancing improved under Edna Hardy's tutelage and she began entering dance competitions and appearing in pantomimes. There were no Barrett family holidays because school holidays were always devoted to Yvonne's dancing competitions and Christmas holidays saw her appearing in pantomimes.

It was always financially difficult for Ted and Sheila Barrett to fund dancing lessons for their two daughters, piano lessons for Tricia, as well as expenses associated with Peter Barrett being a Queens Scout and learning a musical instrument. School fees also had to be paid. Tricia, Peter and later Yvonne went to the Abbotsford convent which was run by the Good Shepherd nuns. 'We were day pupils at the tiny little school,' says Tricia, 'but I thought it was huge at the time.'

'I didn't know we were poor at that time,' contends Tricia. 'I thought we were just like everybody else, until I couldn't go to Genazzano Convent in Kew.[26] Two girls I played the piano with went there, so I wondered why I couldn't go there and why Peter couldn't go to Xavier College.[27] Then I found out we didn't have much money. We didn't want for anything though.

---

25 Denise Drysdale was some two and a half years younger than Yvonne. Denise started dancing lessons at May Downs studio at the age of three and a half. Her opinion of May differs from Tricia's. Denise opines that May was 'the best dancing teacher ever put on earth! She taught you discipline and her discipline stayed with me.'

26 Genazzano was founded in 1889 by the Catholic Order of Sisters, the Faithful Companions of Jesus (FCJ).

27 Xavier College is a Roman Catholic, day and boarding school predominantly for boys, founded in 1872 by the Society of Jesus, with its main campus located in Kew, an eastern suburb of Melbourne.

All we wanted was to dance. I would have been there two nights a week and all day Saturday.'

Tricia remembers Sunday mass being very important to her mother. 'We always had money for the collection plate at church on Sundays, but it didn't always go on the plate. I had it so that I could buy something with sixpence[28] on the way home. Other than mass on Sundays, our lives revolved around dancing and ballet lessons.'

Tricia enjoyed playing the piano. Because the Barrett family didn't own a piano, Tricia took piano lessons at the Abbotsford Convent. 'I used to have to stay after school and practice with the nuns. When you learnt anything from the nuns, you learnt it well!'

Tricia went on to win prizes for her playing. In two of her exams she scored the highest in Victoria, and she won a talent competition on a 3XY radio show. She then began entertaining patients by playing the piano in hospitals. She subsequently played piano for a local marching girls' group while they practised. 'They took me to the Sunbury mental home to play for them, but I didn't cope with all the patients there. It was horrible, so I dropped out of that. I only ever played classical music. It got a bit boring, so I stopped playing when I was about fourteen because I'd become interested in rock'n'roll music — and in boys.'

Tricia ultimately stopped taking dance lessons at May Downs studio in 1956 because her parents couldn't afford lessons for both daughters. Tricia was happy for Yvonne to stay on at May Downs. 'I loved dancing, but I wasn't that good.

---

28 After decimalisation on February 14th 1966, the sixpence continued to circulate at the value of 5cents.

I was too short and I didn't have long legs, whereas Yvonne had beautiful long legs.'

Ted and Sheila Barrett were not the only parents struggling financially at the time, but help came their way and the way of other parents from a patron of the Melbourne Arts. The patron was an old friend of May Downs. Known at the time as "Uncle Frank", he covered costs associated with dancing lessons and costumes for several students whose families were struggling financially. Tricia recalls "Uncle Frank" covering some of Yvonne's expenses at the time. 'Back then he looked about sixty. I don't know his surname, but he was a great help to my mother and others.'

Liz Dennis remembers meeting Sheila, Tricia and Yvonne for the first time in Bourke Street, Melbourne. 'My mother and I were walking down Bourke Street from Spring Street. Aunty Sheila was coming up Bourke Street with two beautiful girls. Yvonne was in a pink, frilly, fluffy dress and Tricia was in blue. They both had beautiful blue eyes. They were probably about five and nine at the time.'

After that initial meeting, Liz saw a lot of the Barrett family in her pre-teen years. 'My family and Yvonne's family were the closest out of the families of the five "sisters" because the two families had more in common.[29] We lived in West Melbourne, so Aunty Sheila would often call in with Yvonne and Tricia on the way home from dancing class at May Downs.[30] We also had lots of fun together at parties over the years. My

---

29 Liz Dennis recalls that Rita had a handicapped and disabled daughter. 'She looked after her till she was 80. She had other children who were fine. Cassie had a sad life due to a tumultuous marriage. My mum Eily was 31 when she got married. She was lucky with Dad. He was a fine man.' Details on Gwenny are not known.

30 Liz learnt dancing for a short time at Olive Wallace's dance studio.

Dad played the fiddle and his friend played the squeezebox.[31] Aunty Sheila would come over with the kids and we'd dance and sing.'

Liz recalls that Yvonne was a year younger than her. 'She loved to perform. She wasn't embarrassed in front of a crowd of people. I remember the little routines that we did together. It was all very serious! We'd go into another room and work out what each of us was going to do. One of the songs we used to do with all the actions was "All Me Life I Wanted To Be A Barrow-Boy."[32] Another one was "Little Mister Baggy Britches." I was the boy, and Yvonne was the girl, because she was so petite and lovely. They were fun times!

'Yvonne slept the night at my place on one of my birthdays. I remember she gave me a box of dominoes. I said to her when we got in bed, "What do I do with these?" She said, "Don't worry. You don't need them. Let's sing a song." I've never used the dominoes. They are still in the box.'

Around 1953 to 1954, the Barrett family moved to a Housing Commission home in Dodd Street, Braybrook, a western suburb of Melbourne, because homes in Abbotsford were being demolished at the time.[33] Ted Barrett initially found work at Bester Bros Chocolates in Ballarat Road, Braybrook. He ultimately gained employment as a storeman at the Braybrook ETA factory.[34] Ted was well thought of at ETA because of

---

31 The term "squeezebox" is a colloquial expression for an accordion or a concertina.

32 The song was made famous during and after World War II by Flanagan and Allen, a British singing and comedy double act.

33 A number of homes were initially declared unfit for human habitation. Others were assessed as being repairable, but a large majority of homes were demolished.

34 ETA Foods had been instrumental in the development of the peanut growing industry in Queensland in the 1920s. The ETA brand subsequently became a household name of the post-war era.

his good work ethic. When he hurt his back at work, ETA management transferred Ted to a position of gatekeeper at the factory. Tricia recalls that Ted never missed a day of work 'even with the back injury, but he was never on big money.'

Ted and Sheila, Ted's brother Bill and his wife Dorrie, and their respective families were close while Ted and his family lived in Abbotsford. The brothers were always on good terms until such time as they'd had a few drinks. Neither could hold their drink and a row would soon break out. Things would settle down for a time until another drinking session resulted in another disagreement. 'We didn't see them as much when we moved out to Braybrook,' relates Tricia. 'They didn't have a car and they didn't travel on public transport much, so we drifted apart. That was sad because they were our only true relatives!'

Tricia contends that Ted Barrett was a very loving father — until he started drinking when she was about seven.[35] 'It ruined our childhood. I remember having to run from our Abbotsford home to the Collingwood police station to get the police. A policeman would dink[36] me home on his bike. I got a two wheeler bike when I was nine and I rode that to the police station. Yvonne never really saw that side of our father. She wasn't home the nights he was bad because she was at dancing school two nights a week. Because she didn't have those memories in Abbotsford or Braybrook, Yvonne remained close to our father.

'It was no secret that our father was a heavy drinker. Our

---

35 It is thought that Ted began drinking sometime late in 1948 or in the early months of 1949.

36 To "dink" someone means to give another person a ride on your bike by allowing that person to sit on the crossbar bar of the bicycle while the bike owner pedals the bike.

neighbours and friends knew. That affected Peter. He didn't get a lot of support in boy's things, like the scouts. I always went to his scout functions. Our father never did though because he was always drinking.'

Following the family's move to Braybrook, Ted Barrett became a regular drinker at Braybrook's Ashley Hotel. He was known to play the bagpipes on his throat and also sing his favourite song "Danny Boy" to the bar staff and hotel patrons. It's said by those patrons that there was never a dull moment when Ted was in the pub. He fancied himself as a pool shark.

Gordon Marsh played pool with Ted on occasions. He remembers that Ted couldn't hit a ball if you paid him to, until he had something like a half-dozen pots. 'That's when he'd turn into a very good player. Once he'd got a few shots in, he'd start playing cagey shots off the sides.' Tricia remembers Ted being a good pool player. 'He used to win at the Ashley Hotel, so they'd buy him drinks. So that was good for him.'

Ted and Sheila Barrett separated several times because Sheila didn't take too kindly to Ted's heavy drinking. She gave him numerous chances to stop his excessive drinking, but Ted kept at it, so Sheila told him to leave the family home, and the couple separated for good.

'Ted moved into the Ashley Hotel when my mother finally put him out,' Tricia remembers. 'He lived there for years. Yvonne remained close with him. She would have a drink with him at the Ashley. That was the last thing I would have ever done. I never did make my peace with him, which I'm ashamed of now. That's a regret that I live with. My brother Peter and I had trauma with our home life, but Yvonne didn't. She wasn't there for the bad times with alcohol. She didn't go through every Saturday night's drama because she was at work. She saw very little of it which was good luck for her. They say that children in families have different lives within the family. We certainly did.'

Following the family's move to Braybrook, Tricia went into Grade 7 at Our Lady's Catholic School in Sunshine. 'I hated it because the nuns were horrible. I wagged school[37] for a couple of weeks, so my mother sent me back to the Abbotsford convent. Peter went to the Christian Brothers College in North Melbourne.'

Yvonne went into Grade 3 when she started at Braybrook State School. Yvonne liked the school. She was happy there and did well academically. Tricia recalls a period of time when Yvonne began taking some of her school friends home at lunchtime. 'She'd cook them fried onions on toast for their lunch. She did this until our mother found out. Mum was working in a cake shop and she put a stop to it for fear of Yvonne getting burnt or something worse happening.'

John Finn recalls Yvonne being two grades ahead of him at the state school. 'Yvonne lived in the street behind me. She was a very nice looking girl. All the boys wanted to carry her bag home from school for her. But I never had much to do with her because she was an upper class sort of bird!'

Yvonne left Braybrook State School after completing Grade 5 in 1956. She began the 1957 school year in Grade 6 at Braybrook's Christ The King School, which was run by the Religious Sisters of the Sacred Heart. Yvonne settled in well at her new school

---

37   To wag school means that students are absent from school without their parents' knowledge or permission.

because the nuns cultivated her talent. They allowed Yvonne to sing "Give Me The Simple Life"[38] at a school carnival.

The nuns were very happy for Yvonne to have time off from school for anything to do with singing or dancing. This was in direct contrast to Tricia's experience with the nuns at the Abbotsford convent. Tricia recalls 'You were not really liked or welcome at the convent if you were a dancing kid. They didn't like dancing kids at all, whereas they were really good to Yvonne at Christ The King!'

Di Senn knew Yvonne growing up in Braybrook. She recalls Yvonne being sweet, shy and unassuming at the time. She also remembers Yvonne singing at her school's carnivals every year. 'Yvonne had a great voice and I can still hear her singing "Give Me The Simple Life" at the school carnival when she was about ten years old.' It is generally accepted that Yvonne's music talent came via her father.

Di recalls that her father used to have the occasional drink with Ted Barrett. 'My Dad told me that Ted used to regale staff and customers at the Ashley Hotel with stories of Yvonne.'

In Form 1, Yvonne befriended Marie Ryan, a new student at Christ The King. Marie was born the same year as Yvonne and she and Yvonne were in the same class. Marie recalls their teacher, Mother Mary McGivern, being a 'real sweetheart'. 'Yvonne and I were two of her pets. We were both meticulous in our school work and neat when wearing our school uniform, which consisted of a grey tunic, blue blouse, red tie and blazer with the school's emblem on the blazer pocket.'

Marie remembers Yvonne being a very good student, but she was not allowed to do a lot of socializing at school as her

---

38 Yvonne had learnt the song at May Downs dancing school.

mother always dropped her off and picked her up from school in a green Morris Minor. 'Yvonne's mother had big ambitions for her and had her involved in dancing, gymnastics and ballet. She didn't want Yvonne wasting her time with school friends. If we called into her house her Mum would tell us Yvonne was busy. Sometimes I would meet Yvonne at the dance studio in our local shopping centre in Nicholson Street, Footscray. I'd be quite enthralled watching her pirouetting around in her pretty pink ballet shoes. But her mother would always pick her up, so we never got an opportunity to have a milkshake together. We both had strict mothers, and we wouldn't dare disobey them.'

On February 3rd 1961 a devastating fire saw the Christ The King school gutted. Thanks to the efforts of Braybrook's parish priest Father Thomas Murray, the Victorian state government agreed to give the school temporary access to buildings in Melbourne's showgrounds located in Ascot Vale. Yvonne, Marie and hundreds of students were bussed daily to and from the showgrounds. At the end of July 1961, the school moved back to their original site when portables were rented from the state government.

Liz Hawley (nee Vendille) grew up in Braybrook. She started in Form 1 at Christ The King school and she was also in the same grade as Yvonne. Liz recalls some of Yvonne's antics while travelling on the bus to the showgrounds. 'Yvonne and I were close friends. I really liked her. She was funny and always mucking around doing stupid things on the bus, such as pulling a window down and putting her arms right out the window. One time she cut the brim off her school hat and she wore the bit that sat on her crown.'

Judy Quarantotto recalls being in Yvonne's class in Form 3 at Christ The King. Judy describes Yvonne as being friendly. 'She used to show us a little tap dancing sometimes, and she would sing "Steam Heat"'[39].

Tricia opines that Sheila was a really good mother and she was wonderful about looking after babies and children of friends. 'She loved little kids, but she didn't cope with teenagers. She didn't cope with me getting older either. I think it was because she was born out of wedlock. Her main worry in life was that I might have had a child out of wedlock.'

Tricia, Peter and Yvonne all knew they were loved by their parents, but they were never shown physical affection by them. Moreover, there was certainly no praise extended to them. Tricia believes that Sheila 'didn't know how to do that because praise wasn't heaped on her when she was brought up in the foster home. Yet two other fostered girls that Sheila grew up with were different to her as mothers.'

Liz Dennis recalls her mother reacting the same way as Sheila. 'There were no cuddles or affection from my mother. Moreover, you weren't allowed to love yourself or be vain. It was a case of "Get away from the mirror and get on with things!"'

Tricia describes her family life as being pretty fractured. 'We've never talked about any of it. My father, my husband and my brother were the three men in my life, but none of them ever talked to me about it. No one ever said, "How bad was it?" or "How did you cope?" or "Good on you girl for what you did!"'

Rhonda Kneebone (nee McCabe)'s family moved to Braybrook some eighteen months after the Barrett family.

---

39   Steam Heat" is a show tune from the 1954 Broadway musical The Pajama Game. It
      was also a hit record for Patti Page.

Rhonda was approaching two years of age when her family moved into a housing commission home on the corner of Balmoral and Dodd Streets, thereby becoming the Barrett family's next-door neighbours. It didn't take long for Sheila and Rhonda's mother Vali[40] to become very close friends.

Rhonda recalls the Barrett family being 'nice, down to earth people. We lived next door to Yvonne's family for most of my childhood. We had a lot to do with them. Mrs Barrett was very friendly and helpful to her neighbours. She had a phone, whereas we didn't. On the odd occasion we needed to ring someone up, we'd use their phone which sat on top of an old-style stool in their passage. We used to pay Mrs Barrett a shilling to use the phone.

'My mother and Yvonne's mother were very good friends until the day my mother died in 1994. After that happened, Mrs Barrett and I kept in contact. She'd ring me and I'd ring her. She'd always end her calls with "God bless. Love you."

'Mr Barrett had his ups and downs, but he was a nice man. He had a great mop of white hair. It didn't seem to ever thin out. He had a great sense of humour and he always dressed nicely and always wore a hat when he walked up the street. He took my sister and I to the pictures in the city to see the movie *Pollyanna*[41]. He and Yvonne were very close. She loved her dad and he idolised her.'

Rhonda recalls Yvonne being some seven years older than her. 'She wasn't stuck up or anything like that. She was just a normal, easy-going girl. What you saw is what you got with

---

40   Short for Valerie.

41   *Pollyanna* was a 1960 Walt Disney Productions film, starring child actress Hayley Mills, Jane Wyman, Karl Malden, and Richard Egan. It is a story about a cheerful orphan (Mills) changing the outlook of a small town.

Yvonne! I had more to do with her mother growing up because Yvonne seemed to be very busy when she was performing. She was in and out all the time through the day and busy at night. So we didn't get to see a lot of her.'

Rhonda's younger brother Kevin McCabe recalls that Yvonne's cockatoo Big Julie would walk along the fence that divided their properties. 'Sheila made my play lunch for school every morning. She'd make me a little cake or something else. She used to yell out to me "Kevin come and get your play lunch". The cockie would be yelling out "Kevin!" all the time while sitting on the back fence.'

The nuns at Christ the King's willingness for Yvonne to take time off from school for singing and dancing pursuits would soon prove to be instrumental in Yvonne's plans to seriously pursue a career in show business.

3. SWALLOWS JUNIORS

Television's arrival in Australia in September 1956 opened up a whole new world, not only with its programs, but with advertising, much of which was aimed at teenagers. Commercial television in particular was very much American focused. In content and message, television portrayed the image of America as the centre of the universe.

Rock'n'roll music would soon benefit from exposure on Australian television, but in the meantime the release of the 1956 movie "*Rock Around The Clock*" [42] did much to bolster rock'n'roll in Australia. The movie loosely told of the so-called rags to riches rise of Bill Haley & His Comets. It also featured nine of Haley's best recordings and its success encouraged other film studios to turn out similar films. The title tune had by now sold in excess of 200,000 copies in Australia since its release a year earlier on the Festival Records label.

It was said at the time that Bill Haley gave birth to rock'n'roll in Australia with "Rock Around The Clock", but until Elvis Presley broke in Australia with his "Heartbreak Hotel" record, no one really knew what rock'n'roll looked like. Presley offered the total package. He not only sounded good,

---

42   "Rock Around the Clock" featured Bill Haley & His Comets, disc jockey Alan Freed, The Platters, Tony Martinez and His Band, and Freddie Bell and His Bellboys.

but he looked good too. The release of the "Hound Dog"/ "Don't Be Cruel" single cemented Presley's popularity in Australia. Haley was thirty years of age, rotund and balding, whereas Presley was twenty-one and in great physical shape. Presley brought together rhythm and blues with country and western, or "hillbilly music", but also added that most powerful of ingredients — sex appeal.

The "Rock Around The Clock" record and the movie of the same name enhanced Sydney-based singer Johnny O'Keefe's determination to achieve success in the music business. By 1956 Australia was ready for rock'n'roll. The impact of Haley and then Presley did much to help Johnny's cause. In January 1958 Johnny O'Keefe and his group The Dee Jays recorded "Wild One", which not only became the first Australian recording to reach the Top 40 music charts, but also provided Johnny with a nickname that soon became synonymous with him. From that time on, wherever he travelled Australia, it was always Johnny O'Keefe 'the Wild One'. Johnny's ongoing success was a fillip for many young Australian performers who would eventually follow in his footsteps.

By now Australians had more money and free time than ever before. Families were able to afford such labour-saving devices as washing machines with spin dryers, vacuum cleaners and refrigerators that didn't need constant cleaning, and Victa lawn mowers were gaining popularity. Cars were more readily available. Magazines like *Weekend*, *Pix*, *People* and *Women's Weekly* had large circulations. Comics were popular with the young, who now had more money in their pockets.

Teenagers as a social group in Australia arose with the emergence of the rock'n'roll culture in the 1950s. By now teenagers straight out of school were virtually guaranteed jobs. Advertisers were quick to realise that teenagers were now an untapped market for consumer goods. Moreover, they wielded considerable buying power, particularly in clothes and music.

On November 4th 1956, HSV7 Melbourne became the first television station to broadcast to viewers in Melbourne. Liz Dennis recalls an event that occurred soon after that broadcast. 'Aunty Sheila (Barrett) and Yvonne met my mum and me in Lonsdale Street and we went into the Myer store where we saw Brian Naylor sitting on a chair on a stage. A Channel 7 camera was focussed on Brian. He was inviting people to talk to him, so that they could see themselves on television, because it was just all new.

'My mum pushed me to go up onto the stage, but I was too shy, whereas Yvonne didn't flinch. She went straight up onto the stage. She was ten at the time. Aunty Sheila had Yvonne dressed like a doll. She had a white Breton hat on. It was like a sailor's hat. She was also wearing white lace gloves. She looked beautiful on camera and she was natural with the way she spoke. She was only on camera for about five minutes, but she enjoyed every minute of it.'

Little did Yvonne know at the time that she would appear countless times on television in future years, let alone that she would also appear in a television show with Brian Naylor. But for now, she focussed on her dancing as well as rehearsing for her appearance in the Garner H. Carroll & David N. Martin's presentation, at Melbourne's Princess Theatre, of the 'lavish laughter pantomime' "*Jack & Jill.*" The pantomime, which featured an all-star cast of eighty people, including

Australia's most lovable boy "Smiley" Colin Petersen[43], Lucky Grills, Heather Horwood, Irene Bevans and the talented children from May Downs' School of Dancing[44], ran twice daily from December 31st 1956 through to February 4th 1957.[45]

While enjoying pantomimes, Yvonne absolutely lived for dancing. By now she had quickly progressed to the point where she could lift her legs higher than anyone else in her dancing class. She also began to win a number of song and dance competitions held in Melbourne's western suburbs during school holidays.

On May 26th 1958, eleven-year-old Yvonne won three events performing song and dance acts at the annual festival of the Commonwealth Society of Dancing Teachers (CSDT) at the Fitzroy Town Hall. She won competitions performing "The Joint Is Really Jumpin' Down at Carnegie Hall" which was a song made famous by Judy Garland in 1943. As part of her performance, Yvonne would lean backwards, touch the floor with her hands, and then stand up straight again.

Shortly after that, Yvonne won a trip to Tasmania in a television talent quest. She also appeared twice on the TV variety series *Studio A*. In the latter part of 1958, the now twelve-year-old Yvonne won fifty pounds[46] in a contest held on HSV7's *Swallows Juniors* which aimed 'to find a typical "Mammy's Little Baby" eating shortnin' bread.'

---

43 At the age of nine, Colin Petersen starred in the American-British DeLuxe Color film. Set in Australia, the film tells the story of a young Australian boy who is determined to buy a bicycle for four pounds. Along the way he gets into many misadventures. https://en.wikipedia.org/wiki/Smiley_(1956_film)

44 Including Yvonne and Patti McGrath.

45 A photo of Yvonne and three other pantomime children appeared in The Argus newspaper on January 15th 1957.

46 This would be equivalent to $100 today.

Swallows Juniors began on Melbourne radio station 3DB in 1950. It was initially hosted by the station's breakfast announcer John Eden. Brian Naylor[47] subsequently joined 3DB and worked there with Ernie Sigley as an announcer. Brian also took over hosting *Swallow's Juniors* on 3DB before it moved to television in November 1957.

With the advent of television in Melbourne, Brian moved from 3DB to its new sister station HSV7 as host of *Swallow's Juniors*.[48] At the time it was the only TV show entirely devoted to presenting young variety acts. Yvonne saw this as a great opportunity to push her chances of ultimately becoming a regular on *Swallows Juniors*.

Born on February 4th 1945, Patti McGrath had been a regular on the radio version of *Swallows Juniors* since the age of six. She automatically became a cast member on the television program. She remembers cast members 'getting something like two shillings and six pence'[49] per show at that time.

Yvonne and Patti first met at May Downs' dancing school. They did a lot of classes together because they were in the same type of dancing troupes. They also competed at the Fitzroy and Ballarat dancing competitions. 'It wasn't just Yvonne and I,' recalls Patti. 'There was a whole troupe of us. We would spend our school holidays in Ballarat doing competition work. Our mums would come as well. We had a wonderful time because we were all staying in a hotel. That was fun and a bit of a treat.

'Yvonne and I became good mates. She used to come to my

---

47 Naylor was born in January 1931. After leaving school, he took up a job as a production cadet at the Australian Paper Manufacturers. Shortly thereafter he joined a blinds manufacturing company. This led to a two-year stint as the presenter of the company's radio program on 3AK.

48 The Swallows Biscuit Company continued to sponsor the television program.

49 This would be equivalent to 25 cents today.

place at times for the weekend after we'd finished dancing on Saturday. We used to sunbake in our bathers in our big backyard. Yvonne loved my big white Alsatian "Snowball" and the cat and the menagerie that I had. Mum and Dad would take us to the movies in the night time at the Crystal Palace Theatre in Caulfield.

'My parents thought the world of Yvonne, as did Pat Carroll's mum and dad. Pat and Yvonne were very close friends. They used to dance together at May Downs' and in lots of competition work. Yvonne used to stay a lot with Pat too. Pat's mum and dad were a lovely couple. Mrs Carroll was a dressmaker. If she made Pat a dress, Pat would say "Can you make a dress for Yvonne too?" Mrs Carroll would make one for Yvonne so they'd both have the same dresses.'

Pat Carroll was born six weeks earlier than Yvonne on May 18th 1946. Pat recalls meeting Yvonne at May Downs' dancing school. 'It was May's decision that Yvonne and I work together. She thought we looked good together as we were the same height and the same kind of build. So we started doing our double act. Yvonne and I won a talent competition on the *Young 7* television show soon after we first met. We won a trip on TAA[50] to Adelaide[51] as well as other prizes. We stayed in Adelaide with my aunt.'

Pat opines that May Downs and her daughter Tuppy were extremely influential in their careers. 'They were really good teachers. They taught us everything and encouraged us to audition for shows. Yvonne was already a permanent member on *Swallows Juniors* when I went on the show as a guest once or twice. Before they asked me to join permanently, I performed a couple of things I was already doing in competition.'

---

50   Trans Australia Airlines (TAA) was one of two major Australian domestic airlines between its inception in 1946 and its merger with Qantas in September 1992.

51   They flew to Adelaide on March 7th 1959 and returned home two days later.

Tricia Barrett recalls the Barrett's neighbour Vali McCabe being very good to Yvonne and Sheila. 'Vali was a talented seamstress and had a lot of input into Yvonne's costumes. My mother was self-taught so Vali would always help her with things that she couldn't manage.' Tricia remembers that her mother made most of Yvonne's stage costumes and Vali made some of Yvonne's costumes for television.

Pat recalls Yvonne spending a lot of time at the Carroll home in Brunswick when she and Yvonne were kids. 'Yvonne and I were very close friends from when I was about ten till sixteen or seventeen. Dancing was the common denominator. Yvonne was a lot of fun and we had a lot of fun together. She loved my parents and she practically lived at our house. Yvonne also used to spend weekends at a place we had at Port Arlington.[52] She had a great sense of humour. I related to her humour. For example, Yvonne lived in a commission house in Braybrook, but she always said she lived in the Paris end of Braybrook!'

Tricia remembers Pat's parents being very good to Yvonne. 'They took Yvonne away with them on holidays in Port Arlington until she started doing pantomimes. Patti McGrath used to go to Port Arlington too with her family. They were also very good to Yvonne.' Tricia recalls that her brother Peter became very good friends with Pat's brothers John and Terry. Tricia opines that 'the Carroll's home was always the house where everybody gathered because it was such a happy house and the Carroll family were such good people.'

Pat Carroll used to stay overnight at Yvonne's home from time to time. She didn't get to know Yvonne's father Ted very well, but she remembers Yvonne's mother being a lovely lady.

---

52   Tricia Barrett recalls that Yvonne learnt to swim while staying with the Carroll family at Port Arlington.

'Mrs Barrett was a terrific woman. My mother and Mrs Barrett loved the dancing we did and they devoted a lot of time to travelling with us to competitions and concerts. I remember going to Ballarat quite a lot with our mums. Mrs Barrett used to drive us up there. My mother made all the costumes for Yvonne and me and also for most of the kids at the dancing school. The parents couldn't afford it so she did it for them.'

Sheila Barrett initially took Yvonne into dancing classes at May Downs' school two nights a week and on Saturdays via public transport. At one stage, Yvonne began to notice her mother leaving the dancing school for an hour on those nights. That got Yvonne wondering where her mother was going.

Sheila was actually having driving lessons. She ultimately got her driver's licence and bought herself a Morris Minor so that she could drive Yvonne to Channel 7 and other places, as Yvonne was too young to drive.

'Doing that and making Yvonne's clothes was Mum's role,' says Tricia. 'We didn't have a phone in the early days. I worked on reception at Dyecraft in Ballarat Road, Braybrook before I became the manager's personal assistant, so I used to get Mum's phone calls. As I was working only five minutes from home, I would run home with messages for Mum to ring different people. When she got a phone of her own, she took the phone messages. It was a lot of work and a lot of driving for Mum. She'd drive Yvonne to Ballarat for the competitions and to other events during the school holidays. She'd also be at Channel 7 with Yvonne all day Saturday. Mum did a good job. She didn't get any support from her husband Ted.'

Yvonne appeared in the *Puss In Boots* pantomime which ran at the Melbourne's Tivoli Theatre from December 24th 1958 to February 2nd 1959. This pantomime starred Syd and Max Harrison, Terry Scanlon, Heather Horwood and David Steele.

In May 1959, much to her delight, Yvonne attended the West Melbourne Stadium (aka Festival Hall) along with other cast members of *Swallows Juniors* to see Walt Disney's Mickey Mouse Club cast members The Mouseketeers. Led by songwriter and Head Mouseketeer Jimmie Dodd, the group consisted of Bobby Burgess, Cubby O'Brien, Karen Pendleton, Doreen Tracey, Sharon Baird, and Tommy Cole. They performed a variety of musical and dance numbers in their show. The very popular vocal group The Diamonds, consisting of lead singer Dave Somerville[53], Mike Douglas, Evan Fisher and John Felten,[54] were also on the bill.[55] Yvonne was an avid autograph collector at the time, so after the show she went backstage and obtained the autographs of all the Mouseketeers. She also went home with a pair of Mouseketeer ears, which were very popular souvenirs sold at the shows.

Tricia Barrett was a big fan of the "Wild One" Johnny O'Keefe and much to her delight Yvonne was able to obtain free tickets for Tricia to see Johnny and other rock'n'roll stars perform at various stadium shows. 'I never had to pay for tickets,' says Tricia, who also went backstage at some of the shows.

In September 1959, Yvonne excelled at the Royal South Street Society competitions in Ballarat.[56] She won the 58 Tapping Solo — 12 Years and Under 15 event by one point[57],

---

53   Dave Somerville was a Canadian born singer operating primarily in the United States. He was best known as the co-founder, and original lead singer, of The Diamonds, one of the most popular vocal groups of the 1950s.

54   Douglas, Fisher and Felten were not original members of The Diamonds.

55   The Diamonds' biggest hits were "Little Darlin" and "The Stroll" (both in 1957).

56   The competitions have been held every year since June 1891.

57   Second place was taken by Pat Carroll.

the 77 Song and Dance Solo — 12 Years and Under 15 event by two points, and she teamed with Pat Carroll to win the 81 Song and Dance Duo — Under 15 Years event by three points.

Yvonne subsequently appeared in the *Robinson Crusoe On Ice* pantomime at the Tivoli Theatre from December 24th 1959 to February 1st 1960. This pantomime starred Bill French and Jackie Clancy. Yvonne played a member of Blackbeard's villainous crew. Jackie Clancy was very impressed with Yvonne's performance, so much so that he wrote in Yvonne's autograph book: 'To Yvonne with many thanks for helping to make this show the great success it is.'

Yvonne achieved further success in the 1960 and 1961 Royal South Street Society competitions. In September 1960 Yvonne and Pat Carroll finished second in the 81 Song and Dance Duo event. Yvonne won the 77 Song and Dance Solo — 12 years and under 15 event. In September 1961 Yvonne won the 59 Girls Tapping Solo — 15 Years and Over event, and the 84 Song and Dance Solo — 15 Years and Over event, both by a margin of only half a point.[58]

Around this time Yvonne participated in an act on the trapeze with Meryvn Ashton and other members of "The Flying Ashton's" which was one of the finest trapeze acts in the world at the time.[59] Yvonne enjoyed the experience, but she told Mervyn that she preferred to stick to dancing.

Yvonne was also keen to develop her singing further. She hadn't had many singing lessons at this point in time, whereas Pat Carroll and Patti McGrath had. Tricia Barrett opines that

---

58 After Yvonne's passing, the South Street Dancing competition introduced a memorial trophy that was awarded in Yvonne's memory.

59 The Ashton Circus was the biggest and most well-known circus in Australia at the time.

Yvonne 'got through on guts, but she never felt good enough because she didn't have the professional training like her peer group. I think she thought she probably wasn't as good a singer as everyone else because of this. Later on, she had singing lessons with Mabel Nelson who played the piano for *Swallows Juniors*. She also had a few singing lessons with Jack White.'[60]

Tricia contends that Yvonne's interest in singing developed purely and simply through dancing. 'When we went to dancing classes, we used to have to learn songs from songbooks that had the words to the songs. We'd sing things from the musical *Singing In The Rain* and from other musical shows. So, our interest in music came from there. Back then it wasn't songs by Elvis or any of the rock'n'roll singers. They came later. Yvonne later discovered she could sing and the rest of the stuff was fun. If I ever had to sing in church or anywhere else, I mimed!'

Sheila Barrett, Eunice McGrath and Pearl Carroll were all good friends as too were their daughters. Patti McGrath recalls that she and Yvonne and Pat were close friends. 'We would get together for lunches and gatherings for all sorts of things. Our mothers used to sit and watch us at May Downs' school and they would also sit in the audience and watch *Swallows Juniors* being broadcast live to air on Channel 7. During the week you were given a song to sing and you learnt it. You were also probably given a routine by May Downs and then you went in on Saturday and did it on the show. The show had a very low budget. We initially got paid a pound, then it went up to two pounds.'

Patti remembers that there were times when she and Yvonne would 'go into another studio at Channel 7 and

---

60   White was based at the Suttons Building in Elizabeth Street, Melbourne.

watch shows such as *The Hit Parade*, *Teenage Mailbag* and *The Teenage Show* with Ernie Sigley, Heather Horwood and Gaynor Bunning[61] when we were there to do *Swallows Juniors*.

Patti has never forgotten the night she and Yvonne entered Bert Newton's dressing room at Channel 7, which he shared with Brian Naylor. 'He was cleaning his teeth at the time. Yvonne and I just stood there thinking "Isn't this fabulous! He's on tele and he's being so normal cleaning his teeth." Bert then swallowed his toothpaste. Yvonne and I thought that we were the only people in the world to know that Bert Newton didn't spit toothpaste out. Instead he swallowed it. I think he only did that because he didn't want to be rude and spit his tooth paste out in front of us.'[62]

Margie Bayes remembers being with Patti and Yvonne that night. 'We all went into Bert's dressing room and watched him clean his teeth. It was so romantic! We were all little girls staring at him. Little did we know that one of us would marry him.'[63]

Margie had joined the cast of 3DB's radio program *Swallows Juniors* in 1950 when she was five. John Eden was the compere at that time. Margie recalls that she sang her first song two weeks after she joined the show. 'Ernie Sigley and I sang "Tell Me A Story" which had been a hit song by Frankie Laine and Jimmy Boyd.'

Margie's real name was Margaret and she was known by that name on the show until Brian Naylor took over the role

---

61 Ernie Sigley, Heather Horwood and Gaynor Bunning started their singing careers on the radio version of "Swallows Juniors".

62 In 1958 Bert wrote the following message in Yvonne's autograph book: 'To Yvonne one of my favourite "Swallows Juniors" Love Bert Newton HSV7'. Tricia Barrett recalls that Yvonne did her first interview with Bert Newton at the age of 14.

63 Patti McGrath married Bert Newton on November 9th 1974.

of compere. He felt that it was too confusing to have two cast members named Margaret on the show[64], so he decided to rename Margaret Bayes as Margie Bayes. The name has stuck ever since.

Margie opines that it didn't take long for her and Yvonne to become good mates. 'I took to Yvonne straight away. I loved her singing. We had similar backgrounds. She lived in Braybrook and I lived in Richmond. Our Mums were similar and got on really well. There were a number of show business mums, but Mrs Barrett wasn't one, nor was my mum Doris. Mrs Barrett didn't talk about Yvonne all the time and I knew my mum wouldn't be talking about me.

'Yvonne used to come and stay at my house at weekends and I used to stay at her house. I wasn't a Catholic but I would go to mass on a Sunday with Yvonne and Patti when they came to my place. I couldn't take communion, but I used to sit with them in the church.

'When I'd go to Yvonne's to stay, her mum would take us from the show. When Yvonne came to my place, we'd come to my home straight from the show. I got to know Tricia and Peter Barrett. They were nice, just like Von.[65] I met her dad a lot of times, but I never got to know him that well. He would be watching TV, whereas Yvonne and I would either be in her room playing records or we'd go out to a milk bar to get a malted milk. Sometimes we'd go to the Pictures at The Grand Theatre in Footscray, or if they'd have a rock'n'roll dance over that way on a Saturday night, we'd go to that.

'We were never prudish, nor were we cheap. We were just

---

64 Margaret Lewis was the second Margaret.

65 Margie often refer to Yvonne as Von or Vonnie.

happy girls. Yvonne's parents were ordinary working class people like mine. They took the same attitude that my parents took, namely that just because we were in show business and on the stage, it didn't mean that we classed ourselves better than anybody else. Vonnie never changed, nor did I.'

Margie Bayes was a cast member on *Swallows Juniors* for thirteen and a half years, from the time she was five till she was eighteen and a half. In that time, she only missed two shows. Margie recalls that all cast members had to supply their own make up and put it on themselves when they first appeared on the TV version of *Swallows Juniors*. 'We also had to do our own hair and supply all our own costumes. We got paid ten shillings then. Then it went up to a pound, and that pound became two dollars when decimal currency was introduced on February 14th 1966.

'I was the longest one in the show when I left in March 1964. After I'd joined, Actors Equity moved in and the age became seven-years-old to start and sixteen-years-old to leave. So nobody could have ever beaten my record. I sang more songs than anyone else on *Swallows Juniors*, not only because I was the longest one in it, but because I was quick to learn the songs. The show was such a big part of my life. Mabel Nelson selected the songs we sang on the show. She would give me all the Judy Garland songs to sing.'

Margie recollects that Yvonne didn't sing a lot of solos when she first joined the cast of *Swallows Juniors*. 'She was mainly used for her dancing at that time.' In 1959 Yvonne began to sing on the show. On March 21st 1959 she sang the Sophia Loren song "Bim Bang Bong"[66]. On November 14th 1959 she

---

66   Sophie Loren sang this song in the 1958 Paramount film "Houseboat" which also starred Cary Grant.

sang the Spike Jones song "Popcorn Sack" and on December 19th 1959 she sang the Perry Como and Fontane Sisters hit "It's Beginning To Look A Lot Like Christmas."

Yvonne was allocated more songs to sing during 1960. On January 2nd 1960 Yvonne, Patti McGrath and Warren Gibbs sang the Lloyd Price hit song "Personality". In ensuing months throughout 1960 Yvonne sang such songs as Nancy Lee and the Hilltoppers's "In A Little Red Barn", Dean Martin's "Just A Little Bit North of Carolina", Tommy Steele's "Little White Bull", Bing Crosby's "Give Me The Simple Life", Debbie Reynolds's "Tammy", Judy Garland's "Minnie From Trinidad", Pee Wee King and Redd Stewart's "Slowcoach".

Patti opines that Tommy Steele's 1959 hit song "Little White Bull," which Yvonne sang on *Swallows Juniors* on April 30th 1960[67] was 'Yvonne's big song'. 'It was one of the best and the most memorable songs she did on the show.' Yvonne's neighbour Rhonda Kneebone (nee McCabe) and her family were regular viewers of *Swallows Juniors*. Rhonda remembers Sheila Barrett taking her and her brother Kevin into Channel 7 the night that Yvonne sang "Little White Bull" to her rabbit on the show.

The songs performed on *Swallows Juniors* were primarily those that were in the hit parade at the time. 'They'd pick out the songs for say four or five soloists on a particular night,' says Patti. 'The next week there was every chance you didn't do a solo. Most of the songs were too old for young kids to be singing. It's quite funny when you think about it now, because it didn't really make sense for me to sing Emile Ford's big hit "What Do You Want To Make Those Eyes At Me For?".'

Patti remembers that you could make suggestions, like

---

67   That same night Patti sang "What Do You Want To Make Those Eyes At Me For?"

"There's a new song that's just come out and I'd love to do it."
'They might say we've had that in mind for Yvonne, so we're
going to get her to do that. So during that week, in her solo
dance lesson at May Downs', Yvonne would go through her
song and the teacher would give her a few movements to do
while she sang the song. There was no choreography, so we
were all learning together in television's early days.

'The singers who could dance got a lot of the numbers
where they could do a bit of production with the song. The
singers who couldn't dance would sit on a stool and sing the
quieter songs, so they didn't have to move much. The backing
was provided by the lovely Mabel Nelson on piano, Shirley
Radford on the organ, and John Hyde on the drums. It was a
funny combination, but it worked at the time!

'We'd go to the 3DB studios on a Saturday morning and we'd
rehearse in one of the rooms with Mabel on piano. We'd almost
learn the song on that day and we'd then go to the Channel 7
studio A. There we'd learn where we were standing and we'd
have a camera run through. Then we'd go live to air at 6:30PM.
It was a long day, but it was only one day a week. Before a lot of
people had television sets, they used to go to the local milk bar
and watch the show. My Nana used to watch the show at the
local milk bar too so that she could see me on tele.'

1961 saw Yvonne singing multiple songs live on *Swallows
Juniors*, including: Flanagan & Allen's "Down Forget-Me-Not
Lane", Col Joye's "Oh Yeah Uh-Huh", Ella Fitzgerald's "Gypsy
In My Soul", "Steam Heat" from *The Pajama Game* musical,
Tommy Steele's "Handful of Songs", Dean Martin's "Let It
Snow" and "I'm Gonna Wash That Man Right Out Of My Hair"
from the *South Pacific* musical.

Swallows Juniors cast member Margaret (nee Lewis) Mikkelsen recalls one memory of Yvonne that sticks in her mind. 'I was very impressed with the way Yvonne sang a song entitled "Let's Face the Music and Dance".'[68]

Margie Bayes' brother turned twenty-one in September 1961.[69] Margie recalls that her parents said she could ask a girlfriend and a boy to the party. 'So I asked Yvonne who was my best mate at the time, and I also asked John, the boy I eventually married. John brought a friend for Yvonne, but Yvonne wasn't a bit interested in him. I didn't blame her. We had a terrific night jiving together.

'Jack Dyer was at the party.[70] My dad knew him. My brother was a footballer and Jack Dyer Jnr was one of my brother's best mates. Old Jack owned a milk bar and a pub at the time. He was a card[71] and he was such a mountain of a man. He said to Yvonne and me at the party "Little girls I wanna sing with ya." We said, 'Do you Mr Dyer?' He said "Call me Jack." He then said, 'Do you know "All Me Life I've Wanted To Be A Bower Boy?"'? We said, "Do we ever!"

'So Jack extended his arms out. Yvonne was on one arm and I was on the other and we went into the song. Kenny, one of my brother's friends, started talking and Big Jack let Yvonne and me go and he went over to Kenny. He got hold of him and he lifted Kenny up and said "Don't talk while I'm performing

---

68   "Let's Face the Music and Dance" was written in 1936 by Irving Berlin for the film" Follow the Fleet". The song is introduced in the film by Fred Astaire and it is featured in an Astaire and Ginger Rogers dance duet.

69   Margie turned sixteen the week after that.

70   Jack "Captain Blood" Dyer is an Australian Rules football legend. He retired after playing 312 games with Richmond. An enormously colourful character, Dyer subsequently made himself a huge reputation in the football media as a television and radio commentator and writer following his retirement.

71   This meant Jack had a real sense of humour.

with the little girls!" By this time Kenny was trembling, so Jack put him down. Then we just went on as if nothing had happened. Yvonne and I often laughed about that.'

Yvonne's school friend Marie Ryan recalls Yvonne appearing on *Swallows Juniors*. 'Naturally we all watched her sing and dance on the show. She was a very pretty blonde and she was the girl next door type. She was never "up herself" so to speak. She was kind-hearted too and she often brought heaps of Swallows biscuits to school for us. She was also very well liked and admired at school.'

Tricia Barrett describes her sister as being 'just gorgeous, happy, bright, bubbly, and loving. She loved animals. At one stage we had a dog named Prince, several cats all called Tabby, a cockatoo, a rabbit, a duck and a budgie. Yvonne took them all into *Swallows Juniors* one time for a farm act on the show.'

Margie Bayes remembers that all cast members loved compere Brian Naylor. 'He loved us too. He made us feel important and he never showed any favouritism. That was one of his endearing qualities. He treated every kid as an equal, whether they were really popular with the people, or whether they were just one of the minority that were in the show.'

Patti McGrath[72] echoes Margie's thoughts. 'Brian was a wonderful man. We all loved him. He had a boat and we went out on it sometimes. Once he took us for a big picnic on the Yarra and we had a run around on his boat. It was a very happy and good time for all of us. We were all still at school, but we

---

72   Patti McGrath left "Swallows Juniors" to go into theatre. 'I remember the night I left. I was very upset because it was something that was very much part of my life. I didn't really want to leave, but I wanted to appear in the "Bye Bye Birdie" stage show.'

had something else as well. In those days it was quite special to be on tele when you were young.'

Yvonne's neighbour's son Kevin McCabe had just started school at the Braybrook State School when Yvonne had a publicity photo taken of herself singing. Kevin remembers a couple of kids going to Yvonne's home one particular day to get Yvonne's autograph. 'Eventually about 50 kids were lined up out the front of her home,' says Kevin. 'They were piling in the front door and out the back door after getting an autograph.'

Yvonne had a real fan in Kevin. When Kevin was five years of age, Yvonne described him to a reporter as being 'her most ardent admirer.' She added that Kevin goes to see her in shows, and if anyone asks where he lives, he replies 'next door to Yvonne Barrett!'[73]

Patti McGrath[74] recalls having a lot of parties for her mother as the years went on. Patti would invite other *Swallows Juniors* mums who were still good friends with her mother. 'Mrs Barrett was always one of them. She and Tricia Barrett often came to the gatherings.'

Yvonne gained a great deal of experience, and confidence in her ability, from appearing on *Swallows Juniors*. She also gained a number of close friends from that show such as Patti McGrath, Pat Carroll, and Margie Bayes. *Swallows Juniors* would be the catalyst for Yvonne to begin auditioning for roles in musicals.

---

73   'A Great Future', Footscray Advertiser, February 12, 1964.

74   Patti would ultimately marry TV personality Bert Newton.

4. "THERE'S NO BUSINESS LIKE SHOW BUSINESS"

Yvonne auditioned for a part in the *Bye Bye Birdie*[75] musical that ran at Melbourne's Her Majesty's Theatre from March 4th 1961 to July 1st 1961. Yvonne was offered a role in the musical, but much to her disappointment she couldn't accept that offer. Education authorities denied her application to leave school as she wasn't due to turn fifteen until the last day of the Melbourne season. Moreover, she would not have been able to rehearse during the day, let alone appear in matinees during the week, as she would have been at school at those times.

Patti McGrath, Pat Carroll, and Ian Turpie appeared in *Bye Bye Birdie*. Patti recalls that she and Pat both left *Swallows Juniors* to go into the musical. 'We were all young kids at the time. It was the first professional theatre show any of us had ever done. Yvonne used to come around to the theatre to see us. Her friend Joanie Stuart would come too and we'd all sit around the dressing room having a wonderful time.'

Yvonne turned fifteen on July 1st 1961. Much to her delight, permission was granted for her to leave school.

On September 4th 1961,[76] Yvonne, and Patti McGrath and

---

75   *"Bye Bye Birdie"* tells the story of a rock'n'roll singer who is about to be inducted into the army.

76   Further auditions were held on September 5th and 6th 1961.

some two hundred other children auditioned at Melbourne's Princess Theatre for director Charles Hickman, for a part in the Garnett H. Carroll and Australian Elizabethan Theatre Trust's production of *The Sound of Music*.

A photo of Yvonne appeared on the front page of The Sun News-Pictorial newspaper on the following day. The caption under Yvonne's photo read 'With the light shining in her hair Yvonne Barrett, of Braybrook, 15, sings for the part of Eliza of the Trapp Family Singers, around whom the musical was formed.' In fact, there was no such role as Eliza in the musical. Yvonne hoped to win the role of "Louisa von Trapp" the second eldest child of the Trapp Family Singers. The harassed director Charles Hickman was quoted in the same newspaper as saying 'I won't fill any of these parts till I have seen every available child. But if a child has a strong Australian accent, it is no good to me.'

Set in Austria in 1938, *The Sound of Music* sees Maria (played by June Bronhill) preparing to become a nun, but she struggles to accept her abbey's strict rules and regulations. Maria is subsequently sent to be a temporary governess to the seven children of Captain Georg von Trapp, played by English musical-comedy star Peter Graves. Embittered by the death of his wife, von Trapp has disciplined his children in naval fashion, making them wear uniforms and answer to a whistle. Maria gradually transforms the family home by teaching the children to sing and enjoy life. Their music ultimately touches their father's heart. He quarrels with his wealthy fiancée over her support of the Nazis. He ultimately falls in love with Maria and they marry. The family then flees from Austria.

Patti McGrath recalls that 'kids weren't allowed to do eight performances a week, so you had to have a couple of people do the same role. The younger you were, the less performances you could do. For the little Gretel, they had three Gretels.'

Patti and Yvonne were both ultimately chosen to share the role of Louisa von Trapp. Patti recalls that 'Yvonne and I were old enough, so they only needed the two of us to play Louisa. So we rehearsed together.' Having been selected first for the role, Patti was chosen to perform on opening night and all major nights. She and Yvonne rotated performances beyond those nights. Patti remembers advising the show's English producer that she wouldn't be able to appear in the Wednesday matinees because she had television commitments that day. 'He just said, "Okay you two swap. Yvonne you come forward and Patti you go back. You can have that day off Patti and you can choose the other days you want to do the show."'

Sheila Barrett was delighted with Yvonne's selection as she had a great love of theatre and had always wanted one of her children to appear on stage.

Shortly before opening night, Yvonne's confidence received a real boost following glowing comments from TV star Bert Newton. Bert asserted that he had never considered himself a star finder, or a star maker, 'but I must mention a young girl with much potential and star qualities. She is young Yvonne Barrett who is to appear in *The Sound of Music* at the Princess Theatre. We had Yvonne on IMT[77] some weeks ago and she performed so well that I hope I can have her back to appear

---

[77] *"In Melbourne Tonight"*, also known as "IMT", was a highly popular nightly Logie award winning variety television show produced at GTV-9 Melbourne from May 1957 to 1970.

with me on a Thursday night soon.'[78] Yvonne subsequently appeared on IMT and sang "Give Me The Simple Life" to Bert.[79]

The Sound of Music had its Australian premiere at the Princess Theatre on October 20th 1961. Theatre goers gave 'an enthusiastic reception to the much awaited musical.'[80] On December 16th 1961, Yvonne appeared with June Bronhill and other *The Sound of Music* cast members on the Christmas edition of the BP Super Show on GTV9. They sang the 'special number' "12 Days of Christmas."[81] On December 23rd 1961, the principals of *The Sound of Music* combined with stage staff to arrange a Christmas party at the Princess Theatre for the children in the show. 'They provided a Christmas tree for the stage, Father Christmas to hand out presents for all, and party fare. There were eighteen children associated with *The Sound of Music*, but at their own request, they were joined by 35 under-privileged children.'[82] *The Sound of Music* continued at the Princess Theatre right through December 1961 and into 1962. Additional matinee performances were held through the school holiday period.

Rhonda Kneebone remembers Sheila Barrett taking her and her sister and her brother to see Yvonne in *The Sound of Music*. 'Mrs Barrett took an interest in my brother because he was the youngest one. So, she took him to meet June Bronhill.'

Jan Hunter wasn't in the entertainment business, but she had a school friend who had a cousin named Joy Paten who lived near Pat Carroll. Jan remembers being invited to go over

---

78   'On Camera with Bert Newton', TV Times, mid-1961.

79   'Envoy of Christmas Cheer', The Age, December 5th 1965.

80   'Family that loved music,' The Australian Women's Weekly, December 27th 1961.

81   The Age — TV & Radio Guide, Dec. 14th 1961.

82   'Christmas Party,' The Age, December 23rd 1961.

to Joy Paten's home every weekend. 'I met Yvonne through the Paten family when Yvonne and I were both fifteen. Yvonne went out with Joy Paten's brother Ray for a couple of years. Yvonne was always so nice to me. I got to know her mum and her brother Peter quite well and I was also friends with Tricia and her family.

'I was an only child and my life style was completely different. I saw all of Yvonne's theatre shows. It was exciting for me even though I had never learnt dancing or singing. Yvonne didn't care about that. She seemed to love everybody. She treated me exactly the same as she treated everyone else, whether it be Olivia Newton John or Pat Carroll. She thought I was special too!

'Yvonne was so funny and she was always the most fun to be around. We'd go to all the parties in the 1960s and if Yvonne was going, it would be a good party. She was stunning-looking with her blue eyes, and she was much prettier than she photographed. I thought out of all those girls, including Olivia and Pat, that Yvonne was the most talented. She had so much natural talent and we all loved her.'

Yvonne subsequently dated Peter Reid for some six months. Peter lived in Braybrook and worked in a local paint store. He was approximately two years older than Yvonne at the time.[83] Peter's younger brother Robert recalls Yvonne being a very nice girl. 'She was never a snob.' Robert remembers going with Peter to see Yvonne perform at Leggett's Ballroom in Prahran. He also saw her perform at the Heidelberg Town Hall and the Footscray YMCA. Robert describes Peter as being outgoing and very generous. 'He never said a bad word about anyone

---

83 Peter suffered a massive heart attack and died on September 1st 1997.

and he didn't have a mean streak in his body. He was always happy, but he would never have had any money because he was a bit of a spendthrift.'

On March 15th 1962 Yvonne appeared in a photo, in The Age newspaper, along with other so-called 'juvenile members' of *The Sound of Music* cast. The photo showed Yvonne and the young cast members sitting in a 1913 Mercedes as a promotion for the Motor Show which started at the Melbourne Exhibition Building that same day.

On May 11th 1962, Yvonne appeared on the front page of The Sun News-Pictorial for the second time. The caption read '*The Sound of Music* became the "sound" of sewing at the Princess Theatre yesterday when June Bronhill, star of the show, which tells the story of the Trapp Family Singers, got members of the cast to help her with her entry for The Sun-Myer Doll Pageant. The members of the "family" were Julie Day (who plays the part of Leisl), Noel Styler (Friedrich), Yvonne Barrett (Louisa), Nancy Hawthorn (Briggita), David Phillips (Kurt), Ann Heales (Marta), Angela Davies (Gretyl) and June Bronhill.

On June 14th 1962, forty children from the Yooralla School for Crippled Children were entertained by Yvonne and other *The Sound of Music* cast members and Princess Theatre staff. The next day a photo of a ten-year-old Yooralla school boy named Noel, together with 'the four pretty daughters' of the Trapp family, namely Yvonne, Gayle Kinzel, Jenny O'Çonnor, and Angela Kendall appeared in the Age newspaper.[84]

The Sound of Music closed in Melbourne on September 22nd 1962. The production then moved to Sydney. Yvonne loved appearing in *The Sound of Music*, but as she noted in an

---

84　'Noel Meets The Trapp Family', The Age, June 15th 1962. Gayle Kinzel, Jenny O'Çonnor and Angela Kendall were alternate cast members.

interview she was not able to play the part of Louisa in the Sydney production. 'We had a wonderful time, but I was only able to play in Melbourne as I was under age and could not travel with the rest of the cast interstate.'[85]

Yvonne was a very popular cast member, so much so that the entire *The Sound of Music* cast either autographed her program or wrote glowing comments about her. For example, June Bronhill wrote 'There are lots of things I could say about Yvonne, but I won't. The most important one is "Don't grow up too quickly." Fondest love June.' Peter Graves wrote 'Good luck Yvonne. With love Peter.' Norman Yemm wrote 'To dear Yvonne with love & best wishes for the future. May all your dreams come true.' Patti McGrath wrote 'Lots of love Yvonne. I hope I work with you again soon.'

Yvonne went on to appear in J.C.W's magical musical *Carnival*, which ran at Melbourne's Her Majesty's Theatre from October 19th 1962 to February 18th 1963. Starring Kevin Colson, Jill Perryman, Kevan Johnston, and David Hutcheson, *Carnival* told the story of Lili, a lonely orphan, who was enchanted by a traveling carnival troupe. Lili joins the troupe and ends up working with a puppet act. Meanwhile, both the puppeteer, Paul, and the magician, Marco the Magnificent, fall in love with Lili. The two men subsequently engage in a fierce rivalry for Lili's affections.

Yvonne played the "Bear Girl" in the production. She was also a member of the "Bluebird Girls" as too were Pat Carroll and Joan Stuart.[86] *Carnival* cast member Brenda (Long) Halman recalls that the entire *Carnival* cast performed

---

85   'Broadway's Her Goal', The Australian Women's Weekly, July 22nd 1964.

86   Pat Carroll recalls that she and Yvonne took dancing classes with choreographer Betty Pounder at Her Majesty's Theatre during the "*Carnival*" season.

a charity concert at an elderly citizen's home during the Melbourne season. 'Yvonne and her Braybrook friend Joan Stuart dressed as tramps and performed "We're A Couple Of Swells." I was fifteen at the time and I did some airy-fairy thing.' Yvonne and Pat Carroll subsequently appeared in the Sydney season of *Carnival* which ran at the Theatre Royal from February 21st 1963 to March 27th 1963.

Yvonne next appeared as a singer and dancer[87] in the Garnett H. Carroll Management and the Australian Elizabethan Theatre Trust presentation of the *Wildcat* musical comedy at Melbourne's Princess Theatre.[88] Starring Toni Lamond and Gordon Boyd, the musical focussed on a woman named "Wildcat" Jackson who dreams of striking oil, but has neither the capital nor the know-how to help her accomplish her goal. *Wildcat* ran from July 19th 1963 to September 14th 1963. Press adverts stated that the "tune-filled and laugh-packed musical was a sure cure for the blues, flu or whatever ails you...We'll make you feel warm all over. Your spine will tingle with excitement and your heart will beat time with pleasure."[89]

In the meantime, Tricia Barrett had married Alan Mallatt on June 5th 1963. Tricia chose Yvonne to be her bridesmaid[90] and Pat Carroll's mother made Yvonne's bridesmaid's dress and headgear. 'I was originally going to have Yvonne as bridesmaid and Alan's two nieces as flower girls,' Tricia remembers. 'At the time I was estranged from my father, and I was for most of my life. Friends brought him to my very small wedding. He didn't give me away because we weren't ever close. He had

---

87   Yvonne was also an understudy for the second lead part in the production.
88   The original production opened on Broadway in 1960 starring Lucille Ball.
89   The Age, July 29th 1963.
90   Yvonne was also a bridesmaid at Peter & Jan Barrett's wedding in 1970.

ruined my twenty-first birthday in November 1962, because of the drink, so I wasn't having him give me away.

'My mother stood outside the non-Catholic church during the wedding. She didn't come into the church because I was marrying out of the church because of the horrible priest I had to deal with. My mother was very religious back then and what the church said went! We didn't get on for five or six years after that, but when I had my children, she was the most wonderful grandmother. They loved her to death.[91]

'The wedding party was held at the home of Alan's brother-in-law Jack Edwards. He was on television at the time in a football sports show and Yvonne was rehearsing for the *Wildcat* show at the time. So the wedding party was held on a night when Jack and Yvonne could both be there.'[92]

On February 4th 1964 a photo of Yvonne appeared on the front page of The Sun News-Pictorial newspaper announcing the fact that Yvonne was the first Sun Moomba Queen entrant for 1964.[93] Thirty-three girls were ultimately selected from photographs to contest the Moomba Queen final. Each girl had a chance of winning a Ford Falcon deluxe and 250 pounds in cash from The Sun News-Pictorial. The finalists were judged while wearing street clothes and evening wear on February 25th 1964.

Tricia Barrett recalls Yvonne being asked to launch the contest so as 'to get people interested in' the event. Yvonne accepted the fact that she couldn't win the contest because her

---

91 Tricia says her marriage 'was doomed from the start. I put in 24 years, and got two beautiful daughters out of it, so it wasn't all bad.'

92 Jack Edwards played Australian Rules football for North Melbourne in the Victorian Football League during the 1950s. After retiring from playing football, he coached for a period of time. He then became a football commentator on Melbourne's Channel 7.

93 'She's Set For Big Moomba', The Sun News-Pictorial, February 4th 1964.

theatre commitments in the soon-to-open *Stop The World I Want To Get Off* production would restrict her ability to promote the contest. Yvonne was told however that she would be a finalist in the contest. She was ultimately chosen as runner up to Ria Luyben who was some five years Yvonne's senior.[94]

Yvonne told a Melbourne western suburb press reporter that she hoped to play the lead part in a musical show in the near future. The reporter noted in his article that Yvonne was unaffected by her rise. 'Mrs Barrett told me she was very proud and pleased that Yvonne's success had not affected her in any way.' The reporter went on to say that he was impressed when Yvonne paid tribute to her mother and her dancing teachers.[95]

Yvonne didn't win a lead part in a musical show. She was however given a private audition in front of John Brome, the producer of the Melbourne production of Anthony Newley's and Leslie Bricusse's hit musical *Stop The World I Want To Get Off*. Brome was very impressed with Yvonne, and she was immediately given a part as a chorus girl in the musical. Yvonne was subsequently hard at work at rehearsals every day for three weeks before *Stop The World I Want To Get Off* opened.

The musical had been a hit in London and was due to open soon on Broadway. A Tivoli Circuit, Aztec Services & Bernard Delfont presentation, the musical premiered at Melbourne's Tivoli Theatre on February 7th 1964.[96] Set against the backdrop of a circus, the musical, which starred American actor, singer, comedian and dancer Jackie Warner as the main character

---

94   Luyben had previously been runner up in the contest.

95   'A Great Future,' Footscray Advertiser, February 12th 1964:

96   The Melbourne season closed on May 9th 1964.

"Littlechap"[97] told the story of the seven seasons in a man's life. The musical also starred Evelyn Page, one of America's most experienced musical actors.

On his arrival in Melbourne, Jackie Warner hadn't hesitated to admit to waiting journalists that he was perfect for the part of Littlechap. 'Like the main character in the play, I love myself,' said Jackie. Then he explained, 'To be a success as a performer, one has to have a big ego.' Warner refused to reveal his age when asked by one reporter. Instead he replied 'I am ageless, if not numerically, then in spirit.'

Warner then went on to say that the role of Littlechap was the most demanding role any male actor had ever had in a musical comedy. 'The lead is off the stage for only six minutes during the show. He has to mime, sing and be a comedian as well as an actor. The actor part is the most important, of course, because the character goes through seven stages, from a new born baby to an old man. The theme could be summed up as a man's inability to communicate with his fellow man. The play has a lot to say on contemporary events, and I think it will have a big influence on future theatre.'[98]

Much to his delight, eleven-year-old Frank Howson was one of the performers chosen to play the role of Littlechap in the early stages of that character's life. Frank recalls being 'pretty well much entrenched in the theatre' by that time. His love of the theatre was fostered by his mother taking him to several theatre productions and enrolling him in dancing lessons when he turned seven. He'd also gained valuable experience

---

97 Anthony Newley had starred in the show as "Littlechap" for two years in London's West End. He didn't come to Australia because he was busy preparing to do the show on Broadway.

98 'I'm the Man for the Job,' says Stage Star. The Age, January 14th 1964.

from his appearance in J.C. Williamson's production *Noddy In Toyland*.

Frank had previously seen Yvonne appear in theatre productions and he'd watched her on *Swallows Juniors*. He was impressed with Yvonne as a performer, but above all as a person. 'Yvonne should be remembered! I liked her a lot. When you're young a lot of older people in show business tend to not take you seriously or not talk to you. I always found Yvonne to be lovely and very caring. She was very down to earth, very kind, and she would engage you in conversations. She was not snooty in any way. Even though a lot of people talk about how flamboyant she was, I found her to be quite shy.'

Frank also has fond memories of Yvonne's fellow chorus girls Joan Stuart and Sue Menlove[99]. 'They were lovely girls too.' As was the case with Yvonne, Frank appreciated Joan and Sue also spending time with him.[100] Frank turned twelve some five weeks into the show's Melbourne season. The entire cast duly signed his *Stop The World I Want To Get Off* record album to mark his birthday. Yvonne wrote "To one of my favourite little chaps, hope you have a very happy 12th birthday. Love Yvonne Barrett."

Frank opines that Jackie Warner wasn't great in the role of Littlechap in the Melbourne production. 'He certainly wasn't Anthony Newley!' Moreover, Frank wasn't overly impressed with Warner as a person, in particular because he believes

---

99   Sue became known as Sue Donovan following her marriage to actor Terence Donovan. That marriage ended in divorce. She is now known as Sue McIntosh having married John McIntosh.

100 As a result Frank spends most of his spare time today trying to help people. 'When I was starting out, I had so many people who didn't help me. I think the least you can do is try to help people who are trying to create something.'

that Warner took advantage of Yvonne. 'I know they had an affair despite him being quite a bit older than Yvonne.'

Warner and Yvonne both appeared in the musical's Sydney season which ran from May 13th to June 18th 1964. Warner immediately returned to America when the musical ended in Sydney. Frank recalls that Yvonne was devastated when this happened. 'I remember tears in the dressing room at times. She thought it was serious, but he was just making the best of a wonderful opportunity with Yvonne!'

In February 1993, Jackie Warner returned to Melbourne to direct the musical *Ain't Misbehavin'*. He told reporters that he had 'a whole bagful of memories, some good, some not' from his time in Australia in 1964 starring in *Stop The World I Want To Get Off*. One reporter noted that Warner proclaimed that 'his darkest memory belonged to a girl from the chorus line. Jackie fell in love with her and wanted to get married, but the doorman at the Tivoli, an old friend (supposedly) told him to go back home and think about it. The girl was Yvonne Barrett.'[101] Tricia Barrett attests to the fact that Warner proposed to Yvonne. 'She just said to me, "He asked me to get married, just like he was asking me for coffee!" That's all she ever said about that!'

Yvonne quickly got over Warner by auditioning for the role of the junior female lead, and as one of six dancing girls, in the Sydney production of *A Funny Thing Happened On The Way To The Forum*[102]. The musical told the bawdy story of a slave named Pseudolus and his attempts to win his freedom by helping his young master Hero woo the beautiful girl next door. Yvonne was ultimately chosen to be the understudy to Geraldene

---

101 'Reprise for old hoofers,' Herald-Sun, February 18th 1993.

102 Also known as "Forum"

Morrow, the junior female lead, and to the six dancing girls. Yvonne only had three weeks to learn Morrow's role as well as the dancing roles in case she ever had to replace one of the performers in the production.

Having learnt the roles, Yvonne managed to return to Melbourne for a few days to see her family before the Sydney opening of *A Funny Thing Happened On The Way To The Forum*. Tricia Barrett recalls that Yvonne returned to Melbourne from Sydney by train. 'I remember her getting off the train and swearing about never doing the train ride again. She didn't like the ride at all.'

Jan Field recalls that she and her twin sister Lyn first met Yvonne in Sydney at the *A Funny Thing Happened On The Way To The Forum* rehearsals. Jan says they 'soon became very good friends with Yvonne.' Born on December 5th 1945, the Field twins were raised on a Gippsland dairy farm. They began their singing careers when they moved to Melbourne to begin a hairdressing course. 'We brought the house down when we auditioned as singers at the weekly dance at the Springvale Town Hall,' recalls Lyn. 'So we got a permanent position there singing pop songs like "Then He Kissed Me."'

The duo decided to have publicity photos taken to help their singing careers. It was a smart move as it led to the twins landing 'plum dancing roles' in *A Funny Thing Happened On The Way To The Forum*. Jan Field remembers photographer Athol Smith telling them that he'd heard twins were needed to play a part in the musical comedy. 'So he suggested we send our photo to the theatre.' The twins had no previous acting experience at this time, nor had they ever had a dancing lesson. Nevertheless, they auditioned for the roles and won the parts, over some 200 sets of twins from around Australia. 'Before we did anything at all for the production, we had to dye our dark hair blonde,' the twins said.[103] 'Then they gave us dancing lessons.'[104]

Shortly before the premiere of A Funny Thing Happened On The Way To The Forum, Yvonne mentioned to a show business reporter that she loved 'everything about the theatre. It has become my life. We work odd hours, but it doesn't worry me. I've never known a nine to five job and it's wonderful to be able to sleep in in the mornings.' Yvonne noted that "There's No Business Like Show Business" was one of the songs in her repertoire, and 'it might well be my personal theme song.' She added that she hoped to go to New York eventually to work in musicals there, and to meet her favourite entertainer, Sammy Davis Jnr. She thought his characterisations were brilliant. 'These coupled with his terrific audience appeal make him a complete star.' Yvonne went on to mention that she wanted to be a top musical comedy star, and she'd also love to play the role of Gypsy in the show based on the life of Gypsy Rose Lee, an American burlesque entertainer and vedette[105] famous for her striptease act.[106]

A Funny Thing Happened On The Way To The Forum premiered at Sydney's Theatre Royal on July 18th 1964. The musical, presented by J.C. Williamson Theatres Ltd, starred Jack Collins, Clifford Mollison, Richard Walker, Jack Gardner, Bob Hornery, Will Mahoney, Don McManus, Geraldene Morrow, Pauline Garrick and the Field twins.

---

103 'We've been blondes ever since!', says Lyn.

104 "A Double Role — for two," The Sun, November 18th 1964.

105 A vedette is the main female artist of a show derived from cabaret and its genres.

106 'Broadway's Her Goal', The Australian Women's Weekly, July 22nd 1964.

The Field twins played the divinely assembled twin courtesans Geminea in the house of Lycus in ancient Roman days. Lycus, the owner of a brothel, was a snaky, slimy, lecherous procurer of courtesans. The twins didn't have speaking roles or singing roles in the show. 'We just came on stage and did a couple of movements,' says Lyn Field.

Lyn and Jan Field stayed with Yvonne in Paddington during the production's Sydney season.[107] 'We lived together for some five months,' says Lyn. 'Yvonne was in one room and we were in another. We were very quiet and she was out there. She would wake up every morning and start singing "We're happy little Vegemites, as bright as bright can be." She helped us and we were good for her too.'

Notwithstanding her aforementioned 'loving everything about the theatre' comments, Yvonne grew frustrated at times having to wait for her opportunity to appear in *Forum*. 'I have to be at the theatre for every performance of the show and sometimes it's very boring just sitting around waiting. I've waited through more than sixty-eight performances for an opportunity to go on stage, but so far it hasn't been necessary.'[108]

Jan Field recalls Yvonne bungling her stage entrance the night she finally appeared in in the production as a replacement for one of the musical's six dancers. 'We all had to come on stage a certain way. Not having done it before, Yvonne came on stage and went the opposite way. We all got the giggles, so did she! But she got away with her mistake by making fun of what she'd done.'

As much as Yvonne enjoyed her close friendship with Jan

---

107 The season ended on November 13, 1964.

108 'Young World Spotlight', The Sun-Herald, September 20th 1964.

and Lyn, she missed not being able to see her family as often as she would have liked. She told a reporter at the time that she didn't know many people outside the theatre. She said by the time the show finished at night, 'it's too late to go anywhere and I'm too tired. You've got to be very enthusiastic and prepared to work hard and give up a lot to be a success in this career.'[109]

Towards the end of the musical's Sydney season, Yvonne and the twins decided to go out one night after the show had finished. Lyn Field recalls that she and Yvonne 'got all dressed up' for the occasion, whereas Jan decided not to wear any makeup. 'We went to a gig in Coogee Bay and who should be there but Colin Cook![110] We had met him before and we thought he was a bit of alright! He was a heart throb at the time,' says Jan. 'And who finished up with the popular Melbourne singer? Me with no make-up on!' asserts Jan.

Yvonne's spirits lifted when *A Funny Thing Happened On The Way To The Forum* commenced its Melbourne season at Her Majesty's Theatre on November 18th 1964.[111] She was now able to see more of her family. Tricia Barrett recalls seeing the show five times. 'Anything Yvonne was in, I saw it at the time.'

In an interview with *People* magazine, Yvonne mentioned that her job as an understudy in 'the Forum show' could be rather hard on the figure. 'A normally hard working dancer who suddenly does nothing much but wait around, must begin to put on weight.' She added that this was the fate which constantly threatened her as understudy to the six dancing

---

109 Ibid.

110 Melbourne rocker Colin Cook was carving out a very successful recording and performing career. By this time, he'd had big hits with "It's Up To You" (#9 in 1963) and "Heart" (#8 in 1964).

111 The Melbourne season ended on March 27th 1965.

girls and the leading lady of the production. 'I put in as much time as I can surfing, but even then, that's not enough to keep me trim. When I'm not dancing, I have to choose between taking up exercise and giving up eating. I love food too much even to consider giving up eating, so there's nothing for it, but to exercise.' Yvonne added that she spent 'a good deal of time' at a health studio, working away on such figure-trimmers as a rotating belt-massager and a pedalling machine.

Yvonne also recalled that she had only ever wavered once in her ambition for a stage career since she was taken, at the age of two-and-a-half, by her mother to dancing classes held by Edna Hardy of Footscray. That was during a brief infatuation with the Big Top. In a 'childhood dream of glory' she said she saw herself as the daring young girl on the flying trapeze. 'But as soon as I came back to earth, and ever since, I have been undeviating in my pursuit of stage success.'

Yvonne opined that the peak of her theatre career at that point had been her multiple-understudy roles in *Forum*. She added that even if she never took over any one of the roles in the production, she felt understudying all of them was an excellent preparation for the assault on English theatre which she planned for the near future.[112]

During an interview with *Everybody's* magazine, Yvonne expressed the view that playing so many parts in a musical, such as *Forum*, could be confusing. She added that 'in [her] complicated world, schizophrenia was not a state of mind, but a way of life!' She noted that being an understudy for six characters in the bawdy musical farce meant that she could

---

112 'Forum Girl Keeps Her Form', People, December 2nd 1964. Yvonne appeared on the cover of the magazine wearing a patterned bikini. She didn't however ultimately appear in an English Theatre production.

be any one of six people during her working day. 'Before I get to work each day, I seldom know what part I'll be playing.'

Yvonne went on to discuss the six characters in the musical. She described Panacea 'as a robust beauty who wears little and shows much. The Gemini twins could only be purchased as a set. Philia was the virgin. Vibrata was a coloured girl in a costume so brief that she would never be allowed to linger on Bondi Beach. Tintinabula is an Indian girl who wears belly bells on her fingers and toes, but who really dazzles all eyes with the ruby in her navel.'

According to Yvonne, the most confusing day of all was Friday. That was the day she had to rehearse all her parts. 'I do one and then rush off to change and do the next,' she said. The annoying part for Yvonne as an understudy, however, was having 'to wait many boring weeks', before she could actually play the part of any one of the six characters.[113]

By the age of eighteen, Yvonne had appeared in *Sound of Music, Carnival, Wildcat, Stop The World I Want To Get Off* and *A Funny Thing Happened On The Way To The Forum*. As much as she had enjoyed these stage shows, she was now considering a career change.

---

113 'Six Little Maids Is She', Everybody's, December 2nd 1964.

5. 'I WOULDN'T HAVE MISSED THE TRIP FOR ANYTHING!'

Yvonne was kept very busy during 1965. She had appeared in *A Funny Thing Happened On The Way To The Forum*. She was a regular performer on the *GO!! Show*. She had climbed to the top of Melbourne's Exhibition Building and she had cut her first record. Little did she know that by year's end, she would be in Vietnam.

Australia's involvement in the Vietnam War has long been a controversial issue. Many Australians believed it was not our war to fight. The controversy was primarily caused by the re-introduction of 'a form of conscription' by Prime Minister Robert Menzies in 1964. Menzies brought in legislation and renamed it 'national service'.[114] Any Australian male turning twenty could now have his birth date drawn out in a ballot system. Unless ruled as medically unfit, those males were committed to two years full-time service in the Australian Regular Army.

The National Service Act of 1964 was considered to be unjust by numerous protest groups. Some believed that no one had the right to order another person to join the army or to take up arms. Others argued that it was morally wrong to send

---

114   Peter Luck, This Fabulous Century, Lansdowne Press, Sydney, 1980, p. 128.

drafted soldiers to fight in Vietnam. Moreover, the penalty of two years jail for refusing to register for national service was considered severe.

The police force was given 'great powers to break up demonstrations and arrest demonstrators. New Acts of Parliament and council by-laws were quickly introduced thereby giving authorities the power to declare demonstrations illegal. A strong law and order campaign was mounted against the protest movement.'[115] Nevertheless protesters continued carrying placards, shouting slogans, distributing pamphlets, and impeding traffic in public places and outside US consulates and businesses.

There was little doubt that Australia's motivating reason for joining the war was primarily to maintain good relations with its ally America. In mid-1965, the Australian Government sent troops, including conscripts, to join the Americans in Vietnam. As a result, Australian conscripts served outside Australia for the first time.[116]

The last thing the Australian Government wanted was bad publicity coming out of Vietnam. Like every other aspect of Australia's involvement there, entertainers had to fit into a structure already established by the Americans. Prominent American entertainers were not paid for entertaining their country's troops. Instead, they received a daily living allowance of $16. The same rules were applied to Australian entertainers. They were not paid, but they received a meagre living allowance that equated to $10 a day.

---

115 Garry Disher, 'Australia Then & Now', Oxford University Press, 1987, p. 174.

116 Federal and state Labor politicians were highly critical of Australia's involvement in the Vietnam War and the sending of conscripts to Vietnam, but they were reluctant to take an active role until the latter part of the war.

Actors Equity was invited by the Government to participate in its sponsored entertainment scheme when it was being set up in November 1965. In line with the Australian Council of Trade Unions and the Trades and Labor Councils throughout Australia, Actors Equity was implacably opposed to the war. It refused therefore to support any scheme which selected performers to entertain troops taking part in an 'undeclared war' in Vietnam.[117]

In early November 1965, approval was given for a system of live entertainment for troops serving in operational areas overseas. This provided for sponsored and unsponsored tours and outlined the conditions for each. The Army was named as the coordinating service.

A set of principles for control of officially sponsored entertainment in South Vietnam was established.[118] The principles stipulated that entertainers of high repute should only be sponsored and those entertainers were required to provide their services free.[119] Accommodation within South Vietnam was to be provided at public expense.[120] Entertainers had to be willing to accept field accommodation if hotel

---

117 In doing so, Actors Equity could not negotiate with the Government on pay and conditions. Had the organisation worked with the Government, its involvement could probably have made much easier the Australian army's later struggle with Treasury to have more equitable allowances paid to entertainers.

118 A condition of granting official sponsorship stipulated that entertainers would not be permitted to accept private engagements whilst on tour in South East Asia. The U.S. entertainment agency imposed this condition on sponsored entertainment visits to American forces overseas.

119 Air transport from Australia to South Vietnam and return was to be provided at public expense. Service air or surface transport would be provided without charge within South Vietnam.

120 Accommodation within South Vietnam was to be provided at public expense. Entertainers had to be willing to accept field accommodation if hotel facilities were not available.

facilities were not available.[121]

Lt. Col. E.D. Hirst, from the Australian Forces Overseas Fund, Army Headquarters, Canberra, had been instructed to look into the feasibility of arranging a concert party for Vietnam by Christmas 1965. By mid-November, it was reported that the first sponsored show was to leave for Vietnam before Christmas. Hirst noted in his Concert Party No. 1 Report that 'because of the lack of time, the method of selection was to seek the advice of Mr. Horrie Dargie[122] of DYT Services, Melbourne. The requirement was discussed with Dargie and it was agreed that the concert party had to be led by a well-known personality. It was further agreed that all members of the party had to be of good character. They also had to be capable of withstanding a very rigorous tour which would involve a great deal of travel. Moreover, they had to have the capacity to perform two self-contained shows daily which were to appeal to the 19 to 25 years age group.

In late November 1965, the Australian Government announced that TV personality Tommy Hanlon Jnr.[123] had been chosen to lead the first Government-sponsored entertainment team to Vietnam.

A TV Times reporter subsequently asked Horrie Dargie

---

121 A daily allowance for meals and incidental expenses at rates equivalent to public service rates were to be paid. Indemnities to the Commonwealth against damages for loss or injuries suffered were to be obtained from all entertainers. Vaccinations, inoculations and prescribed examinations were to be provided at public expense. Essential medical treatment in Vietnam was also to be provided at public expense.

122 Lt. Col Hirst told TV Times magazine that Dargie's was the first application 'months ago' from the many people who wanted to organize entertainment for the troops. 'We are more than happy with Mr. Dargie's selections,' said Hirst.

123 Hanlon, American born actor and comedian, emigrated to Australia in 1959. He became a major TV personality in the early 1960s. He ultimately won a Gold Logie award as host of the top rating TV show "It Could Be You".

how he selected Tommy Hanlon Jnr. to lead the tour. 'Tommy Hanlon is an all-rounder,' said Dargie. 'He's a mature entertainer who's young at heart. We want to give these boys, most of who are young, a show which they'll dig.' Dargie opined that Ian Turpie was another all-rounder, 'although not in quite the same way as Tommy. He sings, plays the guitar, and he can do most things.'

At this time Ian Turpie was one of the most promising all-round talents on Australian television. Selection on the tour meant a great deal to him as it afforded him the opportunity to work with Tommy Hanlon Jnr. This had been an opportunity previously denied him because of television network ties.

Tommy Hanlon told TV Times that during the twenty years he'd been entertaining troops he'd formulated some ideas on what the boys wanted. He pointed out that 'comedy and pretty girls are the most important things.'

Tommy was a good choice to lead the group. Entertaining the forces was nothing new to him. He had previously worked for the U.S. Government in Iceland, Germany, England, Japan, Africa and Newfoundland. He had also entertained American servicemen in the Pacific during World War II and during the Korean War.

In addition to being M.C. of the shows and appearing in it for an hour or two, Tommy was to perform a comedy act, and be responsible for technical advice on how the shows should be produced. 'It's not easy. Microphones break down, lights go out, and all sorts of things can happen on these tours.'[124] Tommy was very pleased to be going on the tour, but he said he wasn't 'as excited as the kids in the team. After all, I've

---

124 'TV Stars' Vietnam Journey', TV Times, undated press clipping.

done something like three years of entertaining troops in all sorts of situations.'

Joining Tommy on tour would be Ian Turpie, Yvonne Barrett and Pat Carroll. Ian Turpie was well known in Melbourne as compere of the *Go!! Show*. He was chosen as a vocalist, guitarist and as a reserve compere for Hanlon. In those days the touring groups had to be self-contained. "Turps"[125] was a very accomplished muso so he would back all artists on stage throughout the tour.

Ian Turpie was thrilled and excited to be making the trip, albeit he initially didn't know he had been nominated for the tour. 'The first I knew about being chosen for the trip was a couple of days before it was announced. Somewhere in the back of my mind I have a shrewd suspicion my mother put my name down to get me out of her hair over Christmas. With nine children in the family, it wouldn't surprise me if she did.'[126]

Yvonne and Pat Carroll were well-known Melbourne singers. They were selected to tour Vietnam on the basis of having made records and having made numerous appearances on TV shows such as the *Go!! Show*.

It was reported in the press that 'the Hanlon troupe's visit would be followed by others at regular intervals. The government would establish a small committee of people well respected in the entertainment and theatrical field to consider applications for future visits to troops overseas.'[127]

Ron and Lesley Fletcher were responsible for organising all the Vietnam shows that came out of Melbourne. Ron recalls that while his wife Lesley worked very closely with Lt. Col.

---

125 Ian Turpie's nickname.

126 'They're Off To Entertain Our Troops', Listener In-TV, December 4th — 10th 1965.

127 'Hanlon to visit troops', The Canberra Times, Monday November 22nd 1965.

Hirst, he was 'running around doing other stuff.' Lt. Col. Hirst and Capt. L.R. Summers were chosen to escort the concert party to and from Vietnam.

Before leaving for Vietnam, Lt. Col. Hirst reported that 'the tour was organised in a hurry, and it is therefore more than coincidence that all artists come from Victoria. Owing to the short space of time available, it will facilitate passports and injections if they can all be arranged in the one spot. I'll just ask you to stress that we, the Army, take complete responsibility for the artists' safety. The plan at the moment is for them to visit eight to ten bases and do three or four shows a day. However, should there be any danger involved at any one of these war zones, they just won't go there.'[128] Hirst added that he favoured the choice of young artists to accompany Tommy Hanlon Jnr. 'because most of the Australian soldiers in Vietnam were between 19 and 25.'[129]

Hirst praised Ron and Lesley Fletcher's organisational efforts. 'With the assistance of the DYT management, we feel we have chosen the best possible team to blaze the entertainment trail to the troops.' He noted that the small size of the entertainment team was dictated by the difficulties involved in moving them about the rugged Vietnam countryside.[130]

Lt. Col. Hirst opined that the selected party appeared to meet most requirements. He believed those selected would be compatible with each other. He expressed the belief that 'the right mental approach by the artists to the tour, and to the other artists, was essential because there could be stresses and hardships on tour which cannot be met by anyone who

---

128 'TV Stars' Vietnam Journey', TV Times, undated press clipping.

129 'Tommy's Off To Vietnam To Entertain', Undated Women's Weekly article.

130 'They're Off To Entertain Our Troops', Listener In-TV, December 4th — 10th 1965.

is temperamentally unstable, no matter how skilful their act.' Hirst noted that he had hoped to include singer Buddy England in the party, 'but Defence would not agree to the party being enlarged. England has been told that he will be considered for a future show.' A reporter noted that 'the most disappointed person in Melbourne at the time had to be England, who was dropped at the last minute to keep the group down to a manageable size.'[131]

Inoculations and vaccinations to meet international requirements were given to all members of the party prior to departure.[132] Additional injections to meet military requirements were also offered and accepted by all members of the party. Malaria suppressives were started on December 15th and a supply was carried to give each artist two per week for the trip and for a period on return. Enteric medication was also carried as a precaution against stomach disorders.

Yvonne saw the tour as being a career highlight, but she confessed that she was 'scared stiff' about making the tour. 'It wasn't about the tour itself. But one look at the 6ft 4in.[133] tall Lt. Col. Hirst calmed any fears I might have had in that direction.'

Yvonne did however have one real concern. 'I was just terrified of all those injections they said we would have to have.'[134] Nevertheless Yvonne underwent the ordeal with a brave, but strained smile, a stifled gasp, and set her chin in a determined way as Sister P. Foote (RAAF) administered the needles under the supervision of Dr. D.E. Gowenloch. It

---

131 Ibid.

132 Each member of the party received a smallpox vaccination and cholera and typhoid injections.

133 193 centimetres.

134 'They're Off To Entertain Our Troops', Listener In-TV, December 4th — 10th 1965.

was reported in the press that Yvonne 'hit a high note as she received her injections.'[135]

In an effort to have a bit of fun, Ian Turpie was 'dragged' by Yvonne and Pat Carroll into the medical centre at Melbourne's Victoria Barracks to get his medical jabs, namely the smallpox vaccination, and cholera and typhoid injections. After having their injections, the performers were shown a map of the areas they would visit. They were then issued Army clothing.

Yvonne and Pat were each issued with the field working dress of Army nursing sisters. That consisted of olive green slacks and olive green tailored jackets. Yvonne topped her uniform off with a slouch hat. Pat chose a baseball cap. Neither was at all happy about the Army's sense of fashion. They were aghast when they first tried on their new jungle fatigues. But they knew they'd have to get used to them because they'd be wearing them while travelling on tour. Ian Turpie and Tommy Hanlon Jnr. weren't overly bothered when issued with jungle greens.

Prior to leaving on the tour, Yvonne mentioned to a newspaper reporter that she would wear something 'a little more sophisticated' for the Diggers in Vietnam than the Mod slacks suit she was wearing when interviewed by him. 'I might take some cocktail dresses, but I don't think I'll be doing a Marlene Dietrich act.' While admitting to being 'a little bit frightened of all the shooting' she'd hear, Yvonne stated she was looking forward to the trip. When asked if the thought of a large audience of vocal Diggers unnerve her, Yvonne replied 'I'll love every minute of it. I think they'll be appreciative.'[136]

---

135 'She said Wow', Army magazine, December 9th 1965.
136 "Style...For The Boys", The Sun, December 1965.

Pat Carroll subsequently told a reporter that she was 'under strict orders from Yvonne's boyfriend John Farrar to make sure she doesn't get into any danger, and Olivia Newton John has asked me to keep an eye on Ian while we are away.'[137] Pat envisaged that the upcoming tour meant that she would be performing to an all-male and appreciative audience after battling on an Australian pop scene dominated by male singers and their teenage female fans.

Prior to leaving for Vietnam, Yvonne admitted that she would miss being with her family for Christmas for the first time. She was thrilled, however, at being given the opportunity to help brighten Christmas for the Australian soldiers. She was also 'excited at the prospect of travelling overseas for the first time and gaining valuable experience.'[138] Discussing her act, Yvonne said she would sing, do a few dance steps of the "mod" and "shake" variety, and appear in comedy sketches with Hanlon and Turpie.[139]

Sheila Barrett wasn't initially in favour of Yvonne making the trip. That view changed when she was assured that the army would look after Yvonne and take care of everything.[140]

Lt. Col. Hirst told the press that the largest audience would be at Bien Hoa[141] and would include 1,000 Australian soldiers, 200 New Zealanders and any available American servicemen. He went on to say that 'the trend will be for intimate entertainment in messes, halls, on wayside stops,

---

137 'She said Wow', Army magazine, December 9th 1965.

138 "Yvonne To Sing For Diggers in Vietnam", The Mail, November 25th 1965.

139 xxii "Envoy of Christmas Cheer", Melbourne Truth, November 27th 1965.

140 'Christmas Gifts For The Troops', Melbourne Truth, November 25th 1965.

141 Biên Hòa is a city in Đồng Nai Province, Vietnam, some 30 kilometres east of Hồ Chí Minh City (formerly Saigon).

and on the backs of trucks. We have chosen the best possible team to blaze the entertainment trail to the troops.' Hirst also noted that Tommy, Ian, Yvonne and Pat had been accredited as "war entertainers", the first appointed by the Australian Army since World War II. [142]

Prior to departure from Essendon airport on December 22nd 1965, Ian Turpie told reporters that each entertainer had lists of personal messages to pass on to the Australian soldiers in Vietnam. The concert party was farewelled at the airport by some 30 relatives, friends and show business personalities before flying out to Sydney later that same day. Lt. Col Hirst travelled with them as their escort and liaison officer. He was accompanied by Capt. L.R. Summers. Hirst was also tasked with gauging troop reaction to the concert party's visit and reporting on any improvements which could be included in future tours. The troupe's shows were to be conducted in conjunction with the American amenities' organisers, the United Services Organisation.

The party landed in Saigon on December 23rd 1965 after an overnight stay in Manila. Despite being hit with hot and muggy weather on their arrival, they were all delighted with the welcome reception they received.

All travel from this point on, to places whose names had developed a legendary aura since the Australian troops entered the Vietnam War, was by courtesy of the U.S. Air Force. They also saw to the safety of the performers, by placing bulletproof vests under the seats whilst travelling by helicopter, and by seeing that they wore them most of the time spent in the air between bases.

---

142 'Popping Up In Vietnam', Everybody's, December 22nd 1965.

On Christmas Eve, the group did their first show at Bien Hoa. It attracted some 290 attendees.[143] Pat Carroll noted in the diary she kept of the trip that soldiers from the 1st American Ranger Bn 1 division were so happy to see them. 'They cheered, whistled, yelled and sang with us. It was well worth putting up with the heat and conditions[144] to see a welcome like this.'[145] That night the group performed at the 3Fd hospital in Saigon. Once again, they received a great reception, this time from some 350 soldiers.

On Christmas Day the group was driven under the protection of armed guards to the 1 RAR Australian base in Bien Hoa, which was near the centre of South Vietnam. Pat Carroll opined that their show went off in true Australian style. 'The reception was really wild. They were tremendously happy to see us. The Aussies are wild in camp. At the concert they lounged in the front chairs with their shirts off and cans of beer in their hands, and they didn't stop whistling and cheering during the whole show.'[146]

A press report noted that 'the highlight of Christmas for Australian troops was not coffee and rum in bed, turkey dinner served by their officers, or even the beer, but two attractive young girls from home.' Yvonne and Pat were 'an

---

143 Lt. Col. Hirst noted in his final tour report that concert party attendance figures quoted in his report were confined to Australians, New Zealanders and Americans present at the start of the show. In most cases however there were many late arrivals and always a lot of Army of the Republic of Vietnam (ARVN) soldiers. At one location some VC prisoners and their guards attended.'

144 The soldiers were subjected to these conditions on a daily basis.

145 'A Girl In Vietnam', TV Times, January 19th 1966.

146 ibid.

unqualified success before they had sung a single song. The 570 troops called the girls back time and again for encores.'[147]

After the Christmas Day concert, the party divided into two groups and visited two company messes each for dinner at 1 RAR. The general pattern after each show was for the artists to be photographed and pose with the soldiers and then visit the messes of soldiers, sergeants and officers. This was appreciated by the troops and accepted willingly by the artists who were good mixers on these informal occasions.

Yvonne and Ian Turpie went to lunch with one company of soldiers, and Tommy Hanlon and Pat Carroll lunched with another. The menu consisted of crème of tomato soup with sippets[148], roast seasoned turkey, roast leg of pork, sliced leg of ham, veloute sauce and cranberry sauce, baked potato, buttered French beans, baton carrots, Christmas pudding, and brandy sauce, mixed nuts, assorted sweets, and chilled beer.

Yvonne and Ian first met in 1961 when Yvonne auditioned unsuccessfully for a role in the *Bye Bye Birdie* musical at Her Majesty's Theatre in Melbourne. They met again four years later on the *Go!! Show*. Ian loved Yvonne as a friend. 'She was a good dancer, good singer and a beautiful chick. When we started doing the American bases, which were like palaces, the Yanks couldn't hear the girl who'd been in show business most of her life. They'd call out to Yvonne, "Hey babe, what's your day job? What do ya really do?" She'd get the shits[149]

---

147 'Christmas was 2 Girls From Home', Brisbane Courier Mail, December 28th 1965.

148 Sippets are small pieces of dried toast or fried bread.

149 Yvonne had every right to 'get the shits' (a slang term for getting annoyed, angry or pissed off) with some of the Yanks. She was performing to the best of her ability in the heat and dusty conditions. It wasn't her fault that she couldn't be heard. That responsibility lay with the sound system operators.

and say, "I flog the rags in Coles."[150] They'd just go (in their American accent) "Ah right!"[151]

Ian Turpie didn't have any trepidation about going to Vietnam. 'When we got there, the first shows were outdoors, whether we liked it or not. I'd had suits made before we left but I didn't wear any of them. I ended up wearing shorts and a T shirt because it was so hot. It was 38°C[152] every day and 100% humidity. How our guys, who had just arrived there, fought and retained their sanity over there is beyond me. They were just unbelievable!'[153]

Ian was on stage throughout each concert. 'I played guitar backing each performer on stage. I was the band! The girls opened each show and did about 40 minutes on stage together. They'd sing a duet. Yvonne would then do three or so songs. Pat would do the same and then they'd do another duet. I'd then sing a few rock'n'roll songs before I'd introduce Tommy to do his magic act. He was a joy to work with. After our shows, we'd all have drinks. We'd begin at the Officer's Mess, and then go to the sergeants' and the enlisted men's clubs. Tommy and I would be standing there talking to each other, while ten or twenty blokes would be standing around the girls. We hardly got spoken to.'[154]

Lt. Col. Hirst noted in his official tour reports that the requirement to perform two shows per day on most occasions made the tour more arduous because of movement problems.

---

150 Yvonne was more than capable of handling insults from ignorant audiences. She knew that the Yanks wouldn't be familiar with Coles stores in Australia, so she thought she'd retaliate and return like for like.

151 Ian Turpie interview with Jodie Newell, January 2011.

152 Equivalent to 100 degrees F.

153 Ian Turpie interview with Jodie Newell, January 2011.ibid.

154 ibid.

He went on to say that 'the program was a free-flowing succession of acts for an hour and a quarter. Tommy Hanlon Jnr. commenced with a short introduction followed by a line of humorous patter similar to Bob Hope's style. Then Yvonne Barrett sang three songs during which she danced, then Tommy Hanlon did an act in which he read a newspaper. Pat Carroll sang and danced and Hanlon did an act of cutting a soldier's head off with a guillotine. Ian Turpie then sang numbers from The Beatles, Tommy Steele and a song written by Jack Davey. Turpie and the girls then sang numbers together. Turpie played the guitar for the whole show either as background music, accompanying the singers or adding to Hanlon's patter.'

The adequacy of one guitar was doubted initially by Hirst, but he noted in a tour report that 'Turpie proved skilful enough to provide all music successfully. In fact, in my opinion, the singers were able to show their own talent without a noisy band.'

Hirst further noted that 'no act was in bad taste. The jokes were appropriate for a service audience. Hanlon changed jokes or phrases to suit either an Australian or American audience. On one occasion he learnt when he went on stage that most of the audience had attended the previous show. He was able, without any trouble however, to run with a completely different line of jokes.'[155]

On December 26th the party was flown from the Tan Son Nhut airbase[156] by helicopter to Vinh Long[157] for another show. This time they entertained some 460 soldiers at Vinh

---

155 That was the sign of a true performer.
156 Located near the city of Saigon.
157 Vĩnh Long is a city and the capital of Vĩnh Long Province in Vietnam's Mekong Delta.

Long's Hel Bn. Soldiers with machine guns sat near the helicopter's doors all the time with guns trained on the jungle below. After lunch and their performance, the touring party attended a party in the officer's club. Pat Carroll recalls that a siren suddenly sounded and panic and confusion set in. 'Men and women were running in all directions. An American officer grabbed Yvonne and me and we drove off in a jeep. I was hugging Yvonne. We expected to die any minute. We both prayed. I'd never had such a fright before.'[158]

The group was told later by the aforementioned officer that it was just a practice, but Pat Carroll didn't believe that. She thought he said that to console her and Yvonne. In any event, some fifteen minutes later, order was restored.

December 27th saw the party travel to the small American Advisers Compound in Bac Lieu.[159] A group of twelve Viet Cong prisoners attended the party's concert there. 'They ranged from teenagers to old men and they seemed to be thoroughly enjoying the show,' said Tommy Hanlon. He went on to say that 'after every show, we had American soldiers asking us about Australia and many of them wanted to spend their leave in Australia, instead of going to Hong Kong or Bangkok. Some even wanted to live in Australia.'[160] Performances on December 27th attracted some 130 soldiers to the Advisers Compound concert and some 540 were entertained at Hel Bn, SOC Trang.[161]

By day five (December 28th 1965), several of the group were

---

158 'A Girl In Vietnam', TV Times, January 19th 1966.

159 Bạc Liêu Province is a coastal province of Vietnam situated in the Mekong Delta region of the southern part of the country.

160 'Viet Reds Enjoyed Hanlon', Sunday Telegraph, January 9th 1966.

161 Soc Trang is a province in the Mekong Delta of southern Vietnam.

beginning to tire of the heat, travelling, rushing meals and having to sleep in hard army beds. Nevertheless, the party entertained some 120 personnel that day at the Kon Tum[162] Advisers Compound and approximately 360 personnel at the Combat Support Group, USAF, Pleiku.[163] Approximately 160 attended the performance at the Advisers Compound, Tuy Hoa[164] on December 29th. The party was forced to stay there that night due to poor weather. Another dreary day on December 30th 1965 resulted in the late departure of their plane flight to Da Nang. The tired group ultimately landed at 8pm.

Because of USAF transport failure, scheduled shows were missed at Vung Tau[165] (on December 26th), Ban Me Thout[166] (December 29th), and Marine Brigade, Da Nang (December 30th). Notwithstanding the aforementioned attendance figures, it was conceivable that overall attendance figures for all the performances combined could have been somewhere between four to five thousand, with the inclusion of late arrivals and countless Army of the Republic of Vietnam (ARVN) soldiers.

On December 31st 1965, the group visited Quang-Tri[167] which was only eight miles from the North Vietnam border.

---

162 Kon Tum is the capital town of Kon Tum Province in Vietnam. It is located inland in the Central Highlands region of Vietnam, near the borders with Laos and Cambodia.

163 Pleiku is a city in central Vietnam, located in that nation's central highland region. It is the capital of the Gia Lai Province.

164 Tuy Hoa is the capital city of Phú Yên Province in south-central Vietnam.

165 Vung Tau is the largest city and former capital of Ba Ria — Vung Tau Province in Vietnam.

166 Ban Me Thout is the capital city of Darlac Province and the largest urban concentration in the Central Highlands of Vietnam.

167 Quang Trị is a city in Quang Trị Province in the North Central Coast region of Vietnam.

The group was driven to the concert venue at the Quang Tri Advisers Compound, under the protection of armed guards who were looking out for snipers. Some 83 soldiers attended that mid-afternoon performance. The party then took a short flight to Da Nang[168] in a helicopter because it was even more dangerous than earlier in the day. That night 210 soldiers were entertained by the party at the Da Nang Officers' Club.

Pat Carroll said at the time that New Year's Eve 1965 was the saddest New Year's Eve she had ever spent. 'We did two shows which were fun, but as soon as they were over I began to feel depressed again. There was a party at the officer's club but I couldn't stay there. I missed my family and friends at a time like this. It had just turned midnight and I just wanted to go to bed.' Pat wished Yvonne a Happy New Year and then went off to bed.

Yvonne agreed that she and Pat were both homesick on New Year's Eve. They missed their parents and boyfriends and did not wish to hear "Auld Lang Syne" being sung. But at about five minutes into the New Year they were awakened by some eight American soldiers outside their windows singing "Waltzing Matilda." They then broke into "Auld Lang Syne" and "Tie Me Kangaroo Down Sport." 'American soldiers have a passion for "Waltzing Matilda"', said Yvonne. 'We were frequently asked to write out the words of the song.'

The weary party returned to Saigon by helicopter on New Year's Day because of the need for increased security. This was due to the Caribou aircraft being hit by five bullets during the party's long trip from Da Nang to Quang-Tri the day before.

The party gave one performance on a boiling hot New Year's

---

168 Da Nang is the fourth largest city in Vietnam. It is located on the coast of the South China Sea at the mouth of the Han River.

Day 1966 in Bien Hoa for an appreciative audience of 120 Australian soldiers from the 1 LSG battalion, Royal Australian Regiment. Later that night three American soldiers took Ian Turpie, Yvonne and Pat Carroll to the Caruso nightclub in Saigon. Pat noted in her diary that the club wasn't much different from clubs back home.

Lt. Col. Hirst noted in his tour report that audiences were enthusiastic and appreciative of all performances given by the concert party. He observed that 'American audiences were slightly more demonstrative than Australians.' He noted that comments were most flattering and placed the Hanlon show ahead of the Eddie Fisher show, and in some aspects better than the Bob Hope show.

Hirst went on to say that 'it was very noticeable that the audience reaction was affected by the environment existing at the time of the shows. For example, an audience standing in the hot sun and preparing for an operation the next day demonstrated their appreciation less than an audience who had come in from an operation and were in a comfortable recreation hall and preparing for the New Year holiday. The RAAF at Ubon declared a holiday when we were there, and this led to a relaxed and appreciative audience.' Hirst concluded by noting that 'artists withstood most rigorous conditions cheerfully and maintained faultless performances.'

Ian Turpie recalls learning, after the event, that Yvonne was placed in a compromising situation on one occasion during the tour. 'I knew she was in the Officer's Mess, but I didn't see her for a few minutes till she came back. I didn't see this happen. The story is that a quite good looking little guy, who was obviously older than Yvonne, invited her back to his unit, which was pretty plush by Australian war standards. He'd probably been there a couple of years and there wasn't much fighting there. Apparently, he had a couch, that when he pulled a button or a lever, the couch went back into a sofa bed. He took Yvonne back to his unit and tried to put the word on her. I think she slapped his face.'[169]

Ian opined having the 'best time' of the tour at Bien Hoa. 'They were fun days. We played Aussie rules football and cricket there. It was bloody marvellous until we ran out of Aussies to play with. They were pretty hairy times, and they were in the thick of things as Bien Hoa was only three or four miles away from the fighting.'[170]

During the tour the group witnessed a Bob Hope show being recorded in front of some 10,000 soldiers. Ian Turpie recalls that it took ten hours to record a one-hour show. 'He had a twenty-piece band and special guests.[171] The poor guys were exhausted watching because Hope kept saying "Cut". They'd go "Oops wrong! Let's do it this way." It was so boring!'[172]

On the eve of their departure from Vietnam, all performers received a letter, dated January 1st 1966, from the Commander of the 1st Australian Task Force, Brigadier Oliver David Jackson OBE, thanking them for going to Vietnam to entertain Australian troops. He wrote: 'Arriving, as you did shortly after the return of 1 RAR from a long operation and performing for them on Christmas Day, proved a great boost to morale. Your tour round Vietnam must have been extremely exhausting but I can assure you that your performances have been greatly

---

169 Ian Turpie interview with Jodie Newell January 2011.

170 ibid.

171 Such as singers Eddie Fisher and Jackie de Shannon.

172 Ian Turpie interview with Jodie Newell January 2011.

appreciated. I am told that you have given up your holidays to do this tour. This is a most generous gesture and one which will be long remembered by the members of the Australian Army Force in Vietnam. With all best wishes for the New Year. Yours sincerely O.D. Jackson OBE, CBrigadier Commander, Australian Army Force, Vietnam.'

On January 2nd 1966, the concert party departed Vietnam for Thailand after an exhausting tour of operational units during which time they gave twelve performances to Australian and American troops. Although tired, the performers were all happy that they had been able to brighten the soldiers Christmas.[173] A war veteran himself, Tommy Hanlon Jr. described the tour of embattled Vietnam as a rough one. 'At one time we gave four performances in four towns in one day.' He went on to describe the Vietnam War as a strange one. 'Crossbows and poisoned arrows are used and ten-year-old boys take part by throwing grenades.' He formed the opinion that there was 'respect in Vietnam for the Australian as a fighting man and his morale was high.' According to Hanlon, 'the presence of Australian servicemen in Vietnam had created a lot of interest in Australia among the United States soldiers and many have expressed the desire to settle there.'[174]

Hanlon described as 'marvellous' the welcome given them by Australian servicemen in South Vietnam and Thailand. He told an Australian Associated Press reporter that he believed more tours would be arranged in the future because of the success of this first tour. He added that on several occasions

---

173 'Soldiers' Welcome To Group', unsourced press clipping.
174 'Hanlon's Show Success', unsourced press clipping.

an alert was sounded during their shows and performers had to jump off the stage and barricade themselves.[175]

After flying into Bangkok, the group took what Pat Carroll described as being a 'funny old tram' to Ubon Royal Thai Air Force Base where they performed two shows on January 3rd 1966. The first show attracted an audience of 150, and the second 140. The audiences were made up of RAAF personnel and American troops. The last performance staged on January 4th 1966 at the EMs Club, USAF, Ubon attracted some 260 personnel. The performers then took time out to do some shopping in Ubon.[176]

The group had performed a total of fifteen concerts at twelve bases in Vietnam and Thailand for Australian, American and South Vietnamese servicemen. So before flying home to Melbourne on January 8th 1966, the party enjoyed a well-deserved brief stopover in Singapore. The provision for two days rest at the Cathay Hotel was most appreciated by the artists and served to help them forget the previous inconveniences of the tour.

Yvonne and Pat Carroll were wearing colourful Asian costumes on their arrival back in Melbourne. They told a newspaper reporter that the tour 'was a great experience and we hope to go back again some day to sing for the boys.'[177] Ian Turpie commented that 'the work was not hard, but the constant travelling made us all very tired.'[178]

---

175 'Viet Men Loved The Show', Australian Associated Press clipping.

176 Ubon Ratchathani is one of the four major cities of Isan. The city is on the Mun River in the south-east of the Isan region of Thailand. It is known as Ubon for short and is located 615 kms from Bangkok.

177 'Home Again', The Sun, January 8th 1966.

178 Ibid.

Lt. Col. Hirst estimated in his tour report that the party had travelled 13,460 miles[179] on the tour. He went on to say that 'travel was by airliner, C123, C130, Caribou, Helicopter HUE and H34, train and truck. Transport in the war theatre was scheduled on USAF C123. Civil transport in and out of theatre was satisfactory, although it seldom ran on schedule.'

Hirst reported that USAF transport frequently failed and as a result 'the concert party had to hitchhike on helicopters, a C130 and a RAAF Caribou. This was an arduous program and it was made harder not only by transport failure, but by irregular or missed meals and noisy sleeping conditions. Moreover, no laundry, dry cleaning or pressing facilities were available to the party. The tour was rigorous and frustrating because of chaotic USAF transport facilities for artists, particularly for the girls. Personal discomfort was accepted reasonably well and had no effect on their shows.

'The party all proved to be good travellers. There was no incidence of sickness or injury. Care was taken not to eat out of service establishments and not to drink untreated water. Malaria suppressives were taken and future doses issued.'

Hirst went on to note that 'strict attention was paid to standard security procedures and no dangerous incidents occurred. Movement in Saigon was by vehicle and loitering in streets was kept to a minimum. Movement to Bien Hoa was in daylight by fast vehicle. Artists were not armed, but their escort always was.

'Military clothing was not used by the girls because they appreciated the desirability of presenting a female appearance to the soldiers at all time. Although they toured

---

179 Approximately 21,670 kilometres.

with one suitcase between them, they didn't wear the same dress twice. The men only wore military clothing when they ran out of clean clothes. It is to the credit of the party that they accepted the conditions without complaint, and it was little wonder that they arrived home totally exhausted!'

A few days after her return to Melbourne, Yvonne relaxed with a cup of tea while being interviewed by a newspaper reporter. Yvonne leant back and sighed as she took a sip of her 'cuppa'. This was her first in sixteen days. 'Ah!' she said approvingly, 'there's nothing like a good cup of tea, especially after the rotten coffee we had to endure in Vietnam. We would have given anything for this during the past fortnight, but I wouldn't have missed the trip for anything.'

When asked to describe how the soldiers had reacted to their visit, Yvonne replied 'They loved us. After every show, they shouted, "Come back, come back!"' Ian Turpie summed up the thoughts of the group when he stated that 'the Australian soldiers gave us a tremendous welcome. They were a marvellous audience.' Yvonne, Pat Carroll and Ian Turpie all said they would return to South Vietnam to entertain Australian troops again, but only after a lengthy rest.[180]

Pat Carroll said the morale of the Australian troops was 'fantastically high. They all seemed so happy and so fit'. She went on to say that they were never allowed to forget the war in Vietnam. 'Even when we were having Christmas dinner with the troops at Bien Hoa during the so-called truce, we could hear gunfire in the near distance.'[181]

Yvonne subsequently spoke about the tour to Rex Davis, a

---

180 "Come Back, Diggers Said", "The Sun", January 10th 1966.
181 'The Vietnam Singers Come Home', The Herald, January 8th 1966.

local Melbourne western suburbs newspaper reporter. She began the discussion by showing Davis several souvenirs that she had picked up while on tour in Vietnam. Among them was a Viet Cong flag[182] given to her by an American soldier after much persuasion from Yvonne. The soldier had captured a Viet Cong guerrilla and he'd taken him and the flag to the compound at Vinh Long where the group was entertaining troops.

During her interview with Rex Davis, Yvonne recalled that Australian soldiers gave the concert party 'a fantastic reception' at each of the Vinh Long concerts. 'The Australians went right off.' When the group finished the shows at Vinh Long, the entertainers were invited to the officers' mess. The group was to appear elsewhere that same day, but never got there. The soldiers didn't want the group to leave and for some inexplicable reason the transport was delayed, forcing the group to stay overnight.

Yvonne had been given a RAF map of South Vietnam during the tour. Rex Davis noted in his article that the map when fully unfolded 'covered about 30 square feet[183] of the Barrett's lounge room floor.' Yvonne used that map to show Davis where the concert party had performed. Davis was amazed with Yvonne's ability to recall 'such fascinating names' as Bac Lieu, Soc Trang, Vinh Long, Bien Hoa, and Tuy Hoa, let alone her ability to pronounce them.

During the tour Yvonne had been given a serviette by an

---

182   The Rayon Viet Cong pennant is divided horizontally red over blue. An inset five-pointed yellow star is hand-stitched across both sections. There is a casing on the hoist to allow the flag to be suspended from a length of dowelling or a stick. The water stained and fading pennant is now housed at the Australian War Memorial (AWM) in Canberra. A collection of unit badges and patches, collar badges, rank badges, and a pair of sterling silver US Army pilot wings badge were given to Yvonne by US servicemen. These are also housed at the AWM.

183   Equal to 2.787 metres.

Australian soldier. On the serviette the soldier had written a message to his wife in Sydney. She had recently given birth to a baby which her husband had yet to see. The soldier had sent letters to his wife, but he believed that she had not received them. Yvonne promised the soldier that she would send the serviette to his wife.

Yvonne mentioned to Davis that the tour was not always fun. She said she didn't always like the food; nor would she drink the water which she claimed 'tasted like bath water! Water there is loaded with chlorine which can even be tasted in the ice in cool drinks.'

Yvonne commented that the South Vietnamese looked the same as the Viet Cong 'so you didn't know who was who.' In Saigon, Yvonne rode in a taxi and was glad when the ride was over because she feared the driver might have been a Viet Cong and may have stopped the taxi and knifed her.

In reply to a question on transport from Rex Davis, Yvonne noted that the group often had to wait hours for transport to arrive. 'It was mainly helicopters or jeeps. And then there were the 123s. These were the worst planes ever made! They were bullet ridden and we had to have life jackets under the seats to protect us if shot at from below.'

When asked if there was any set route for the tour, Yvonne replied: 'No! There was no pattern of places to visit. We went where there were no bombs falling! At one place, however, the airstrip was bombed only twenty minutes after we left.' Yvonne then spoke briefly about the sad, human tragedy of the Vietnam War being poignantly illustrated by twelve Viet Cong captives, who she estimated to be about fourteen years old, being allowed to watch one of the concerts. Yvonne concluded the interview by stating that she would like to participate in another tour, not only for the experience gained from it, but also for the pleasure it would give her for boosting the troops' morale.[184]

Several months after her return to Australia, Yvonne told a reporter she 'felt playing to all male audiences in Vietnam was a refreshing change after the predominantly female attended teen shows in Australia.'[185]

Shortly after Yvonne returned home from Vietnam, she learnt from her mother that her twenty-year-old cousin Liz Dennis had been placed in the Dandenong psychiatric hospital. She gave birth to her second child Patrick in October 1965 and she subsequently developed severe post-natal depression. She was in hospital for a long time, during which she had electric shock treatment. When she began to recover, Liz phoned Yvonne and asked her to visit the hospital and sing for the patients on a party night. They were held once a week or fortnight. 'Yvonne didn't hesitate. She brought Denise Drysdale with her to the hospital. Denise was a dancer at that stage.'

Liz recalls Yvonne being very upset seeing her so sick. 'I remember her getting quite emotional while holding me. It was a long way for her to come from Braybrook that night, but she did it for me! A resident in the hospital backed Yvonne on guitar while she sang. Everybody at the hospital was so pleased; I was so happy that Yvonne did that. After all this was Yvonne Barrett. She was a star! I recovered several months later and I haven't looked back since. It was a very gracious and lovely thing for Yvonne to do because she had just come back from Vietnam and she was very busy at the time!'

---

184 'Singer Would Like To Return To Vietnam', Sunshine Advocate, January 13th 1966.
185 'Aiming For A Big Name — That's Yvonne Barrett', The Herald, September 12th 1966.

6. THE *GO!! SHOW* YEARS

I t wasn't until Yvonne appeared in the *Wildcat* musical that she began thinking of singing as a serious alternative to dancing. 'I wanted to be a dancer, but the more I thought about it, the more I realised there was no big future for dancers in Australia. All the money was in singing.'[186] Yvonne had also sung in stage show chorus lines, but she had never thought she was good enough to be a singer until she began taking singing lessons from Jack White.[187] Those lessons led to her spending some two hours daily practising as often as she could.

While Yvonne was in Sydney performing in *A Funny Thing Happened On The Way To The Forum*, the *GO!! Show* teenage television show, produced jointly by Melbourne's TV channel ATVO and DYT Productions' Julian Jover and Dennis Smith, debuted on August 2nd 1964. The first edition of the show, compered by British entertainer Alan Field[188], starred

---

186 "Introduction to The Trap" document, December 1967.

187 Jack White was the singing teacher for numerous Melbourne singers including Normie Rowe and Grantley Dee.

188 Field compered the highly successful Beatles tour of Australia and New Zealand in June 1964. Field initially signed a six months contract to compere the "GO!!Show". Provision was made for his contract to be extended if the show proved to be a success.

nineteen-year-old singer & guitarist Ian Turpie[189], sixteen-year-old singer April Byron,[190] and singer and musician Colin Cook.[191]

Dennis Smith said at the time that while these established singers would appear at regular intervals on the *GO!! Show*, 'the main purpose of the show was to provide a vehicle for young singers with no television experience, who had become very popular with teenagers through singing at dances. There is no doubt that there's an abundance of this kind of talent in Melbourne.'[192]

The *GO!! Show* was an instant success, so much so that ATVO and the *TV Week* magazine were 'swamped with applications for tickets to the show, and with letters congratulating the station for giving local performers the same television opportunities teenage artists had in other Australian states.'[193]

Modelled on British music shows such as *Ready Steady Go!*, *Thank Your Lucky Stars* and *Oh Boy!*, the *Go!! Show* proved to be arguably the most important Australian TV pop show of the 1960s. It confirmed that Australians could produce a local

189 Ian Turpie's entertainment career began at the age of ten when he was accepted at the prestigious Hector Crawford Drama School, where he gained recognition as a juvenile actor working in radio and theatre. He starred in several radio programmes alongside Sir Robert Helpmann and June Bronhill and featured in the top rating radio series D24. He subsequently discovered a passion for music and focused on playing guitar, songwriting and singing. Turpie went on to tour Australia in such hit shows as "Peter Pan", "Auntie Mame"and "Bye Bye Birdie". Television appearances in "Consider Your Verdict" and "Homicide" soon followed. Source: https://en.wikipedia.org/wiki/Ian_Turpie.

190 April's first recording on Festival's Leedon Label, 'Make the World Go Away', won her 3UZ's Golden Sound Award 1963–64 for best-produced song in Australia. April was also awarded the 5KA (Adelaide) Best Female Artist Award 1964–65.

191 Colin had Top 10 hits on the Melbourne charts with "It's Up To You" (1963) and "Heart" (1964).

192 'Beatles Compere To Handle ATV Teenage Show', undated TV Week article.

193 'Teenagers Welcome Their Own Show', TV Week, August 1st 1964.

pop show, featuring local talent, who were at least equal, if not superior, to overseas artists. The *Go!! Show* was originally only screened in Victoria, but in due course it was shown by interstate affiliates as new television stations came on line in other cities.

Yvonne was aware of the *Go!! Show*'s success, but she was committed to perform in the Melbourne season of *A Funny Thing Happened On The Way To The Forum* from November 18th 1964 to March 27th 1965. By now she was going out with John Farrar, having been initially introduced to him by Pat Carroll and Fred Weiland from The Strangers.

John Farrar was born on November 8th 1945. As a youngster he appeared on such children's television shows as the *Happy Show* and the *Tarax Show*. He took up playing the guitar at the age of twelve. In 1961, he began playing guitar in The Jaguars group. He then joined The Mustangs for a brief period before replacing founding guitarist Laurie Arthur in The Strangers in January 1964.

Once Yvonne had completed her *Forum* commitments, with encouragement from John Farrar, she plucked up the courage to attend an audition with the *GO!! Show*'s producer Julian Jover. He was acting on behalf of DYT Productions, a company founded and run by legendary musician Horrie Dargie with partners Arthur Young (the musical director for GTV Channel 9) and John Tillbrook (the assistant sales manager for GTV9). Marcie Jones states that Dargie, Young and Tillbrook were 'an integral part of the television industry' at the time. She remembers 'these very talented men going around dances looking for the cream of young singers' to be on the *GO!! Show*.[194]

---

194 Marcie Jones, 'Marcie Jones: Runs In The Blood', Network Creative Services Pty Ltd, Melbourne, 2008, p.93.

Yvonne said at the time, 'John Farrar played for me and helped me to prepare for the audition. John has been a tremendous help to me and I consult with him about most songs I use. He has written several songs for me and I hope to record them some day.'[195]

Yvonne impressed Julian Jover at her audition, so much so that she made her first appearance on the *GO!! Show* on April 19th 1965. Marcie Jones, Pat Carroll, Buddy England, Stan & Lee Conway, Terry Dean, The Easybeats and The Strangers appeared in the same episode. By now Ian Turpie had replaced Alan Field as compere. Shortly thereafter, having decided to pursue a full time singing career, Yvonne was signed to a management and recording contract with DYT Productions. The pretty, slim girl with the sparkling eyes and pixie face was on her way!

The Strangers were the resident band for the *GO!! Show*. 'They backed everybody,' recalls Pat Carroll. 'They were all really good musicians. When we did shows on weekends at pubs and elsewhere, all us singers used to keep our fingers crossed that we'd have The Strangers backing us, because they were the best. The group also backed Yvonne and other *GO!! Show* artists on record in those days at Bill Armstrong's Studios.'

Yvonne and Marcie Jones met for the first time when Yvonne debuted on the *Go!! Show* on April 19th 1965. Marcie was born in the Melbourne suburb of Coburg on June 26th 1945. After leaving school, she started an apprenticeship as a hairdresser, but her ambition was to be a singer. One Saturday night she went to a dance at the Canterbury Ballroom. Malcolm Arthur was singing that night with the backing of The Thunderbirds

---

195 'From Stage To Song', The Sun, October 1st 1965.

band. It just so happened that Malcolm was looking for a new female singer. Marcie auditioned for the position and she got the job.

Ivan Dayman owned a chain of dances in Melbourne, including the Canterbury Ballroom, Preston Circle, Glen Iris Rock, and the Marianna Hall in Sunshine. Dayman also owned dances interstate. Marcie worked with The Thunderbirds on the Melbourne circuit for some eighteen months. After singing with them for four years, Marcie was approached by DYT Productions to join the *GO!! Show*. Marcie didn't hesitate to accept the offer.[196]

Marcie really got to know Yvonne when they started to appear on the *Go!! Show* together. Marcie remembers that they soon became really good friends. 'We were both Cancerians, so we both led with our heart. I did to my detriment and Yvonne did to hers too. She was very kind and such a big softie. She was a really lovely girl with a really beautiful heart. I would go over to her place in Braybrook and we'd sunbake in her backyard covered in cooking oil or something like that. She could stand it longer than me. She was always brown and loved having an all year suntan.

'Yvonne's mum was lovely, like all our mums. She was very supportive of Yvonne, but she wasn't a stage mother. I only ever saw her at Yvonne's home. I never saw her at shows. My mum wasn't a stage mother either, nor was Pat Carroll's mum.

'Yvonne was a really nice girl. I loved her. She didn't have a big ego. I never did either, but a few did. I was, what you see is what you get. Yvonne was the same. She was very approachable. Yvonne and I were easy going and easy to work with. There

---

196 Marcie Jones, 'Marcie Jones: Runs In The Blood', Network Creative Services Pty Ltd, Melbourne, 2008.

were no tanties.[197] We just did our thing.

'We all got on really well when we'd catch up. We were kids and we all just fell into performing. We were all having fun. All the kids who would come to the shows were so excited to meet us. We didn't think for one minute that we were big stars. That didn't occur to me and I don't think it occurred to Yvonne either. We were just having a good time singing on stage.' Tricia Barrett recalls that Yvonne often said to her that Marcie Jones had the best voice of all the female singers![198]

Marcie recalls that all the *Go!! Show* music was pre-recorded at ATV Channel O. By doing so, each performer was afforded the opportunity to listen to their vocals before the show went to air. That enabled each performer and each group to make sure they were happy with their vocals. 'We would record our songs a week before the show and then tape during the week with a live audience. We mimed the songs on the show most of the time, but occasionally we'd do a live performance.'

Marcie maintains that the *GO!! Show* was the perfect springboard for a career in music. 'It gave all artists the most amazing start to their careers, and the rest, of course, was up to us. The audience consisted of mainly young teenage girls and they were loud and fantastic. They made these funny stuffed toys called 'gonks' and they would put their favourite singer's name on them and throw them at us while we sang. I collected quite a few, but of course the boys collected the most. It was exciting for the kids and for us.'[199]

---

197 Tantrums.

198 Tricia remembers seeing Marcie perform at shows after Yvonne's death. 'She used to show a clip of Yvonne singing. That was really lovely of her.'

199 Marcie Jones, 'Marcie Jones: Runs In The Blood', Network Creative Services Pty Ltd, Melbourne, 2008, p.95.

Yvonne made her second appearance on the show on May 10th 1965. Normie Rowe, Buddy England, Billy Adams, Pat Carroll, Diane Gilbert, and The Strangers also appeared on the show.

On Sunday May 16th 1965 Yvonne took part in a fashion parade at St Kilda which was organised for "The Sun Miss Teenage Quest". The Quest was aimed at raising money for Melbourne's Royal Women's Hospital. A photo of Yvonne wearing the latest in wool slacks and sweater appeared on the front page of The Sun News-Pictorial newspaper the following day.

Yvonne's career rose to great heights in July 1965 when organisers of the sixth annual Melbourne Boat Show dropped formal speech making from the opening ceremony. The press reported that instead of speeches, 'attractive eighteen-year-old blonde Yvonne Barrett will climb to the top of the Exhibition Building's dome on Thursday July 22nd to hoist the Blue Peter.[200] Several girls were given a trial, but Yvonne, a singer and dancer when she is not climbing towers, was the only one who lasted the distance. She expects to take three quarters of an hour to reach the top. In case you think that's a pleasant way of spending the morning, the forecast for Thursday is windy and cloudy with possibly a few showers.'[201]

Come Thursday July 22nd 1965, Yvonne, dressed in black tights and a yellow yachting jacket, began the 67.06 metres[202] climb to the top of the dome at 11am. Her climb, without a harness,

---

200 The Blue Peter flag features a white square on a blue background. It is flown from the foremast of ships in harbor to signify that a ship is ready to sail.

201 'Dizzy', The Age, July 20th 1965.

202 220 feet.

entailed scaling a 21.34 metres[203] ladder outside the building on the face of the tower. She then climbed another 24.38 metres[204] up three steep ladders inside the dome, before stepping out of a window to climb another 21.34 metres ladder on to a narrow window ledge above the dome. Once there, Yvonne ran up the 3.66 metres[205] long Blue Peter flag on the Exhibition Building's main flag pole. Yvonne then waved from the top of the dome to the large crowd below. The sixth National Boat Show was now officially opened. Having completed the climb, Yvonne told a reporter that 'it was pretty creepy inside the dome and very dirty, but I wasn't frightened. Heights don't scare me.'[206]

Tricia Barrett agrees that Yvonne wasn't fazed by the climb. 'She wasn't tied on to anything when she did the climb. She was very brave and up for anything that day. It was just another job for her. She wouldn't be allowed to make that climb now.'

Lesley (Zimmermann) Kirk remembers first meeting Yvonne in 1965 when her cousin John Farrar[207] took Yvonne to meet her in hospital. Lesley remembers that 'John and Yvonne had been going together for a few months when I met her. I had seen Yvonne on TV on the *GO!! Show*. I thought she had a lovely voice and I was very excited to meet her. I liked her straight off. She was absolutely beautiful and so friendly!'

At the time Lesley was living in Frankston with her parents Harry and Wyn Zimmermann, while John lived with his parents Eric and Gladys in Niddrie. Lesley recalls John driving to Frankston 'quite a bit for holidays' whenever he got a break.

---

203 70 feet.

204 xviv 80 feet.

205 12 feet.

206 'Singer at the top,' The Age, July 23rd 1965.

207 John's father Eric and Lesley's mother Wyn were brother and sister.

'When the *Go!! Show* started he didn't get so many holidays, but when he had a few days off, he'd come down to see us. He would always bring Yvonne if she had time off work.'

Lesley remembers Yvonne being very down to earth. 'She had a great personality and she fitted in and related so well with all our relatives. In October 1965 Yvonne and John stayed with us for about a week. My parents allowed me to have a couple of days off school to spend with them at the beaches in Frankston and Dromana. We also went shopping in Frankston. That was exciting for me as quite a few people pulled them up for autographs and a chat. They always obliged.

'John and Yvonne seemed perfect together. They were both so easy going and they seemed to have the same temperament and personality. They wouldn't hesitate to join in with things. A couple of times when they were staying with us, Yvonne, John and my Mum did yoga in our lounge room.'

Lesley has never forgotten a particular occasion when she was staying with John's parents in Niddrie. 'We were sitting in the lounge room one Sunday when the phone rang. Yvonne was there at the time. She said, "That'll be my Mum." Yvonne didn't like going to church, so she told my Aunt Glad to say, "Sorry she's gone to church." My aunt did that, then said with a sigh, "Oh Yvonne, did I really do that!"'

Lesley recalls another occasion when Yvonne stayed at her home. 'We only had a two bedroom house, so much to my delight Yvonne slept in my room and I slept in the sunroom. Mum took her into my room to put her stuff away while John, Dad and I were in the lounge room. When I heard Yvonne call out, "John come and have a look", I knew Yvonne had seen the heaps of photos I had of her and John inside my walk-in wardrobe. They both came out of the room laughing, then Yvonne said, "That's gorgeous and so nice!" I was so embarrassed, but at the same time I was so proud.'

On October 1st 1965 Yvonne cut her first record "Little People"[208]/You're The One" to be released on the Go!! Records label.[209] "Little People" was chosen for Yvonne by Astor Records and DYT Services. Yvonne, who preferred ballads at the time, picked the flip side "You're The One" which had been previously recorded by Petula Clark.[210]

Braybrook's Di Senn recalls Yvonne being invited to promote her "Little People"/ "You're The One" record on one of Melbourne's radio stations. 'Listeners were asked in advance to send in questions for Yvonne to answer. I remember Yvonne being totally convinced that no one was going to send in questions for her to answer. So, I took it upon myself to write as many letters as I could. Although it was unnecessary, she really appreciated that and 40 gave me a copy of the record.'

"Little People" subsequently entered Melbourne radio station 3DB's National Top 40 at No. 39 on November 26th 1965. It rose to No. 32 on December 3rd 1965, and to No. 28 on December 10th 1965. It then dropped the following week to No. 36. A week later it dropped out of the Top 40. "Little People" ultimately reached No. 58 on the national charts and No. 3 on the Sydney charts.

Yvonne's record release saw her kept busy singing at dances in Melbourne and in country towns. She had also been booked

---

208 Chloee Harris was a 16-year-old student in West Nashville when she recorded the original version of "Little People" in 1964 on the Nashville based Hickory label.

209 The label, also owned by DYT Productions, afforded the opportunity to a new generation of pop performers to record. Those performers subsequently promoted their records on the *"Go!! Show"*. The releases were manufactured and distributed by Melbourne based recording company Astor.

210 'From Stage To Song,' The Sun, October 1st 1965.

for a weekend singing engagement in Devonport, Tasmania. She said at the time that as she was making a success of her singing, she had no desire to return to dancing. She noted however that she believed that ballet helped her singing. 'It helps a song if you can combine singing and dancing. There is more future in singing than dancing. It is very difficult to rise higher than a chorus girl in live shows, and while you're popular, singing is more secure!'[211]

Yvonne went on to say that she was striving to be an individual with a style all her own. 'Nothing can be gained by being a carbon copy of someone else. You have to live up to the original and you are always compared with them. Audiences want somebody fresh and bright, and I try to keep away from other singers' styles, although I do admire Barbra Streisand and Shirley Bassey very much.'[212]

The year 1965 had been a good one for Yvonne. It got off to a great start when she was selected as the Sunshine Council's "Miss Australia Day" on Australia Day 1965.[213] She appeared on the *Go!! Show* on twelve occasions that year. She also made a number of live appearances throughout the year. She was particularly pleased to be chosen that year, along with a number of other entertainers, to perform during an hour-long show for prisoners at Melbourne's Pentridge Prison. One of the songs she sang was appropriately entitled "Run For Your Life." 'They listened attentively and were most appreciative,' she said later.[214]

---

211 Ibid.

212 Ibid.

213 On Australia Day 1966 Yvonne was a member of the three-person judging panel for the Sunshine Council's "Miss Australia Day" 1966.

214 'They Liked Her Advice', unsourced 1965 press article.

It is thought that Yvonne first met Ronnie Burns on November 1st 1965, on what was Yvonne's tenth appearance on the *Go!! Show*. Ronald "Ronnie" Leslie Burns AM was born on September 8th 1946. He was the lead singer of the Melbourne band The Flies in the early 1960s, before leaving the group in the mid-1960s to pursue a solo career. It was a smart move on his part as he subsequently became one of Australia's most popular pop singers.[215]

Ronnie recalls finding Yvonne to be charming, very attractive and very feminine from the outset. 'Although I didn't spend a lot of time with her, we became friends and I really enjoyed her company. Yvonne wasn't shy. She was quite funny and she was a practical joker. She was vivacious, but she wasn't a person that was in your face. She could be quiet at times. At the same time, she was a bit of a jester.'

Ronnie's wife, dancer Maggie Stewart,[216] also became friends with Yvonne. She recalls that Yvonne was a bit of a prankster and loved telling jokes. Ronnie agrees. 'Yvonne had a lovely sense of humour. She was always out for a good joke and having a laugh. She'd say something like "Isn't it terrible when you go to the toilet and your finger goes through the toilet paper?" It's a common situation, but it's not talked about. But we were young in those days and not long out of school. This was our first job or something like that and we were

---

215 Ronnie's first single "Very Last Day" was released in June 1966 and it peaked at No. 12 on Melbourne's Top 40 singles chart. His second single, "True True Lovin" reached No. 15. His next single "Coalman", released in January 1967, peaked at No. 6. He had another Top 20 single with "Exit, Stage Right". Ronnie's biggest hit "Smiley", written by Johnny Young, reached number two on the Go-Set National Top 40 in February 1970.

216 Maggie Stewart was a regular cast member on *"Kommotion"* which was a fast-paced Top 40 pop show originally hosted by 3UZ disc jockey Ken Sparkes. It was co-produced by ATV-0 and Willard King Productions at the ATV-0 Studios in Nunawading. It ran from December 1965 to late 1967. Maggie also danced on the Don Lane Show and other major television shows.

happy. We were not larrikins. We were just enjoying our lives.'

Maggie Stewart recalls an amusing event involving Yvonne that took place in the make-up room at the ATVO studios. 'I was in the make-up room along with two make-up artists, dancer Megan Hicks, and several singers. Yvonne subsequently entered the room and we were chatting about our day. Yvonne said she had been sun baking the day before in a crochet bikini that she had either made or had it made. Consequently, she unwittingly gained a 'bikini impression' which had left an impressive pattern on her bottom! With that, Yvonne pulled down her mini-skirt, to reveal a beautifully designed tattooed bum! It was firmly imprinted as per the swim suit pattern. It wasn't as though she dropped the bikini bottom, but more that she folded it down discreetly so as to not create too much attention.'

Maggie thought it was hilarious. 'It had everyone in stitches! Yvonne reacted to the fun and surprise at how the tattoo had eventuated. We all thought it very funny and to this day it still makes me smile. It was all spontaneous and, in the moment, a light hearted moment. As there were no mobile phones in those days, no saucy snaps were taken to capture the moment. However, I would not have been surprised if a few more crocheted bikinis were sold in the following week.

'As you can imagine, everyone was in on the fun. It was very reflective of our professional relationship and the fun of these encounters with a group of lovely girls. But I must say, Yvonne was lucky that none of the boys were in on the fun, otherwise she may have been asked to reveal all on camera!'

Maggie recalls that things were very simple, free and easy, and spontaneous in those days. 'Yvonne was such a dear soul and very much enjoyed being outgoing and playful with the girls. We were all of twenty years old and enjoyed the innocence and the laughter. Not to mention, that the following week Yvonne took off for the beach with a g-string!' Ronnie Burns comments that Yvonne was that type of a person. 'I can identify with that because I've always been a practical joker!'

Maggie remembers Yvonne being so dedicated to her craft. 'She had all these sets of beautiful outfits and she was very conscious of how she looked. She paid a lot of attention to her hair, her make-up, and how she was presenting and where she was going. She was certainly going somewhere!'

Ronnie Burns adds that Yvonne wasn't alone in that respect. 'We were all doing that same thing. Some people like Ian Turpie had the gift of the gab, whereas someone like Yvonne, and even myself, would look at him and wonder if we could ever do it the way he did. Ian could talk his way out of a paper bag, but that wasn't in our make-up. So, we drew from our own scene.'

A strong camaraderie developed among the regular *Go!! Show* artists, given that most had started performing around the same time and they were all feeling their way in the early days of the show. Ronnie remembers that 'we probably weren't really conscious that we were doing that, but that's what actually helped us to build an industry of good-hearted people. It was a different time back then and the world was very different. Things were very simple and there was a very simple approach to each other.

'We didn't look at singing as our job or as our profession in those early days. We were doing what we loved to do, that was to sing, entertain, have fun and have freedom. That's all we wanted to do. It was almost like if we don't make it, it doesn't matter because we're singing and liking it, so off we go. A string of young performers began hitting their straps. The *Go!! Show* put Yvonne, Marcie Jones, Pat Carroll, Olivia Newton John and The Field Twins on the map, as it did Normie Rowe, myself, and Johnny Young. We all knew we had this incredible opportunity. The network and the producers of the shows could see we were reliable and that there was talent there. So, they gave us every opportunity to develop that talent.'

With Yvonne and Ronnie both coming from working-class backgrounds, it wasn't surprising that they, and others in similar situations, set their sights on achieving success in music and television. 'We had a dream that we wanted to attain,' recalls Ronnie. 'I feel Yvonne's theatrical background helped her a lot. That dream in Yvonne's case was initially her dancing. Then she probably thought maybe I can do some singing. I was also trying to work out where do I fit into this. What do I want to do and how can I be a little different? We were all going with the flow. We were cutting our teeth in an industry which was changing. Coming from a working-class background I think was fantastic for all of us because we had to work our way out of a corner. Success didn't come on a silver platter!'

Ronnie contends that he and the likes of Yvonne appreciated every opportunity they had to sing, to do an interview for a magazine, or every time they did a radio interview or a teen television show. 'These opportunities increased our ability. It was always there, but what got transferred to television was paramount I think.'

Singers and groups were honing their craft in the early days of the *GO!! Show*. They were looking up to, and being inspired by, singers and groups in England and America.

Ronnie comments that it was difficult to do that in Australia 'because there were divisions between the Melbourne and Sydney television artists. In Sydney you had the likes of Lucky Starr, Digger Revell, Johnny O'Keefe and Little Pattie doing it differently on shows like *Bandstand* and Johnny O'Keefe's *Where The Action Is.*'

Ronnie recalls that 'Yvonne, Marcie Jones and all of us were constantly looking for songs that we could sing. Elvis had started a trend of doing your own thing and changing the music genre and the structure of songs so that they would appeal to a bigger mass new audience. That's what we were part of. We got swept up in that wave because we wanted to be.

'When Melbourne started to make television pop shows like *Uptight, Happening 70, Kommotion* and others, we had an incredible base. The shows didn't just go for one hour. They went for four hours on a Saturday morning. Every time I had a birthday, Ross D. Wyllie would bring out a cake on *Uptight* and everyone would sing to me or whoever was having a birthday. It was like a family sitting around a loungeroom all taking the piss out of one another and having a lot of fun. We were all having so much fun that I had to pinch myself.

'The boys got into bands and solo careers like the girls, but there were fewer of them. There was Joy Lemmon, Pat Carroll, Marcie Jones, Yvonne, Lynn Randell and others, but there were less girls than the number of boys. The girls evened up the balance eventually. There was a wonderful group of people. I can't speak more highly about it. I think it was because of the goodness of all those parts coming together and forming a solid industry.'

Ronnie remembers Yvonne being a vital part of it. 'Her

personality was goodness and a lovely clean image. Everything was transferred through on television. She wasn't forward like a go-getter who was going to do this and knock other people out of the way. That wasn't in her nature. You can call that being humble, but the working-class background that was coming through was a mighty thing!' By the end of 1965 Yvonne was a regular performer on the *GO!! Show* and her first record had made the Top 40 charts.

Come February 1966, Yvonne was as busy as she could be. On February 5th she appeared at the Cohuna Town Hall. She followed this up on February 7th with an appearance at 431 with The Changing Times, Roland Storm, Billy Adams, Tony Cole, and The Sonamatics. Later that night that same party of entertainers performed at the Ballarat Civic Centre in what was the first of four performances on The Mod Spectacular tour. Over the next three nights the group appeared at Horsham's Town Hall, Swan Hill's Town Hall, and the Shepparton Civic Centre.[217]

Yvonne was now managed by Ron Fletcher. Ron started his music career as a solo singer in 1958. He subsequently became the lead singer of The Checkmates group, before turning to

---

217 The search for two Shepparton teenagers began late on the night of February 10th when they failed to return to "The Mod Spectacular" concert at the Shepparton Civic Hall after leaving to go for a drive. The bodies of Garry Heywood and Abina Madill were ultimately found 20 miles from Shepparton in a paddock at East Murchison. Heywood had been shot through the head and Madill had been raped and then bludgeoned to death. Detectives found two fingerprints on the top of Heywood's FJ Holden car. As these murders were committed before the development of computerised processing, fingerprint matching had to be done manually. The fingerprint evidence was deliberately kept quiet so as to not panic the perpetrator of this heinous crime, let alone help him become more adept at hiding his prints. In March 1985, Raymond Edmunds (dubbed "Mr. Stinky" by a newspaper because of his offensive body odour) was arrested on unrelated charges of indecent exposure in Albury, New South Wales. He was fingerprinted and the prints were a match with those found at the Shepparton crime scene. He is now serving two life sentences with no minimum term for the murders and a total of thirty years for five rape convictions.

managing performers. 'As I'd been a performer, I had a feel for what they needed,' says Ron. 'I'd had a manager when I first started, but all he wanted to do was get a free ride. That taught me a valuable lesson.'

Ron recalls first meeting Yvonne during the early days of the *GO!! Show*. 'At that stage I was managing Billy Adams and The Strangers. It was through that association that I met Yvonne. During that period of time, I became the talent manager for DYT Productions. As a result, I got associated with most of the artists on the show and I managed some of them.

'I met Yvonne a number of times in the early stages because of my being in the recording studio with The Strangers when she was getting backed by them on records. Yvonne would also do backing vocals on a frequent basis for various people like Pat Carroll, Billy Adams, and The Strangers. Peter Robinson and Johnny Farrar would do the arrangements. They nearly always got Pat and Yvonne for backing vocals. When Olivia Newton John was living locally she did a bit too. The female voices backing a lot of people who recorded during that *GO!! Show* era were mostly Pat, Olivia, Yvonne and funnily enough Johnny Farrar. He had a remarkable falsetto voice!'

Ron doesn't recall the exact conversation he had with Yvonne at the time, but he remembers saying he'd start looking after her affairs for her. It wasn't long before he became Yvonne's manager. 'Once we agreed on that, I took care of her bookings on television and personal appearances. I negotiated her fees and made sure she got paid and all those sorts of things. I didn't handle her financial affairs. She had independent people handling her accounting stuff.

'In those days if you got booked for a gig, you normally

rehearsed with the bands who played at the venue. You would be told the name of the group who'd be backing you and you'd contact them and do your rehearsal with them. You would also take a record for the band to hear. These days you go along with your charts. Back then Yvonne would drive to these rehearsals and have a quick run through with the bands getting the keys and the timing right. The artists chose the songs they wanted to sing. Most of them were cover songs and most of the bands knew them all anyway. The artists usually sang anything up to eight songs in their 30 to 40 minutes spot on stage.'

Ron remembers there being a strong camaraderie at the time between the performers. 'There was very little jealousy. Everyone shared their experiences and had a lot of fun and a lot of parties. Bear in mind we're talking about pioneers in the industry here. Everybody was looking to kick off their careers, so there was no point of reference as to what was good and what was bad in terms of achievements at that stage.

'The GO!! Show was our first opportunity to break into national exposure from a Melbourne point of view. As a result of that it was a pretty tight little community. Julian Jover was an incessant producer and I was the talent manager. There was a small niche of girls which included Yvonne, Marcie Jones, Pat Carroll, Olivia Newton John, April Byron, and The Field Twins. The guys included Buddy England, Billy Adams, Terry Dean, Normie Rowe, Ronnie Burns, Bobby Bright and Laurie Allen. Then there were the various bands.

'Once everyone started to record, their pecking order started to fall into place based on record sales. Yvonne was never a big record seller, but she was a very popular and sexy looking girl.

She was one of the best female vocal presenters on television and on stage that I've seen. She was a total extrovert on stage. She was bright and full of vitality. She used her body as an entertainment feature in terms of the way she moved on stage. She moved the most out of all the other female performers. Yvonne was somewhere between a singer and a go-go dancer! She had a classic voice and she was a bloody good singer, as too were Marcie Jones and Pat Carroll.'

Ron recalls that all his time with Yvonne revolved around show business. 'Like all of us, Yvonne couldn't get enough of it. We all had big dreams. She had great respect for her audiences. She knew her job was to entertain people. It wasn't an ego trip. She wanted to make sure that people enjoyed her performance. Yvonne was pretty diligent from that point of view. Every time she would ask me "How did I go?" If it was good, bad or indifferent, I'd tell her.'

Ron didn't attend every one of Yvonne's gigs. Yvonne was independent from that point of view, but if Ron was at one of her gigs Yvonne would always seek his opinion as to how he thought she had performed. She would also ask him had he received good feedback from anybody in the audience that night or had anyone subsequently rung him to make a complaint.

Ron remembers that Yvonne was always concerned that people were satisfied. 'That was a hell of a quality for people to have back in that era. A lot of that was borne out of Yvonne's early days on stage as a child where she was taught to present. The theatre was a lot different to rock'n'roll dances. You've got to project both your voice and your image because it's a visual thing. I think she carried that through. She was very determined and very keen to give people value for their money by way of satisfying her audiences.'

Off stage Ron Fletcher found Yvonne to be quite introverted. 'She wasn't shy, but she was a little quiet. Once she got going though and had a few beers or drinks at a party, like everybody else, she'd loosen up a little bit. But generally, she was pretty down to earth. She came from a fairly basic background. Her dad was usually pissed every time he came home. There are a lot of funny stories about that. He'd bring home a couple of bottles of beer every night and plant them in the garden so his missus wouldn't know he'd bought any booze home. He'd go to work next day and Yvonne's mother would retrieve the two bottles of beer he'd planted in the garden. The lady next door would come in and they'd have a drink during the day.

'Yvonne told me a funny story about watching her father cook his own tea one time. In those days you used to get canned food. You'd stick the can into a saucepan of boiling water and heat it up. Then you'd open it up and eat the contents. Yvonne sat and watched him do all that with a can of Tuckerbox dog food. On toast mind you! He didn't have a clue because he was pissed. That was the kind of family environment Yvonne came from. But they were lovely down to earth people.'

Yvonne's nickname was "Gracie" and Pat Carroll was "Pearl." Ron recalls them being hilarious together as "Gracie and Pearl". 'They used to take the piss out of each other. It was very funny to listen to them. It was just like girls nagging at the back fence. Those names stuck. Yvonne would answer to Gracie as quick as she would Yvonne. My nickname was "Basil". I was just as responsive to Basil as I was to Ron.'

Ron Fletcher recalls that he and Yvonne were fairly close

in terms of their working relationship. 'Yvonne finished up being Godmother to our eldest daughter Kylie Jane. Billy Adams was her Godfather so it was a dynamic duo. Kylie was born in August 1966. She was christened some six or eight weeks later. Kylie was enamoured with Yvonne being her godmother!'

Yvonne's singing career began to gather real momentum in 1966. She continued to make monthly appearances on the *Go!!Show* and thanks to Ron Fletcher she was appearing at numerous venues around Melbourne such as the Caribbean Gardens, Penthouse (Ormond RSL), and Opus (Ormond Hall, South Yarra). In early March Yvonne appeared on stage at Bendigo's Pacific Ballroom along with Ian Turpie, Buddy England, and Tony Henry as part of Bendigo's *Go Month*.

Yvonne appeared in the Moomba edition of the *GO!! Show* recorded at Melbourne's Myer Music Bowl on Saturday March 12th 1966, for replay on ATVO two days later. Johnny O'Keefe was the special guest on the show. Others appearing were Bobby Bright and Laurie Allen, The Rondells, The Easybeats, MPD Ltd, Merv Benton & The Tamalas, Buddy England, Billy Adams, Terry Dean, Tony Shepp, Lynne Randell, Pat Carroll, and The Strangers.

Tony Healey reported in *Go-Set*[218] that 85,000 screaming fans filled the Myer Music Bowl to see one of the most successful *GO!! Shows* ever produced. 'In teeming rain, the audience danced and screamed through each particular act. Soon after the start the stage was littered with streamers and trinkets that were thrown to the singers. Police lined the

---

218 *"Go-Set"* was Australia's first pop music newspaper, published weekly from February 2nd 1966 to August 24th 1974. It was founded in Melbourne by Phillip Frazer, Peter Raphael and Tony Schauble.

front of the stage to stop girls from rushing the artists during each set. This gave the appearance of what could have been another Beatles' tour. Overall the crowd was very orderly'.[219] After filming of that *GO!! Show* episode was completed, Yvonne appeared at Opus along with Ronnie Burns, The City Stompers and The Spinning Wheels.

Radio 3AK held their national awards for Australian artists at the Myer Music Bowl during those same Moomba celebrations. The artists appearing on the show arrived in two chartered buses and it took them twenty minutes to get into the Bowl as screaming teenagers milled around the stage doors preventing them from getting in. 'Police were kept busy controlling the huge crowd in attendance throughout the three hour long show. All performers who appeared at the award night had made at least one record during the last year. These included Normie Rowe, Billy Thorpe and The Aztecs, Tony Worsley, The Easybeats, Bobby and Laurie, MPD Ltd, Merv Benton, Buddy England, Yvonne Barrett, Marcie Jones, Pat Carroll, Little Pattie, and The Strangers. Near hysterical fans were waiting for the entertainers outside the Bowl after the show and it took police almost an hour to clear the road so the buses could proceed.' [220]

Yvonne was kept very busy with singing engagements throughout March, April and May 1966. On Easter Sunday night, April 10th 1966, she appeared on the *Easter Parade* show with Terry Dean, Tony Shepp, The Lonely Ones and Peter and the Silhouettes[221] at the Plaza Theatre in Bendigo. All proceeds from the show aided local charities.

---

219 *Go-Set*, Vol. 1 No. 8 — March 23rd 1966.

220 "The Scene at 3AK Sound Awards". "Go — Set", Vol. 1 No. 8 dated March 23rd 1966.

221 Led by the very talented singer, musician and songwriter Peter Rechter.

Music reporter Colin James opined in *Go Set*[222] that the *Easter Parade* concert was a 'beauty, spectacle wise. Tony Shepp made a most successful debut in Bendigo. Terry Dean went over really good, while Yvonne Barrett killed 'em (the boys that is). Backing for these three *Go* artists was supplied by northern Victoria's most polished group without a doubt, The Lonely Ones. These boys just don't know how to play badly.'[223] Yvonne appeared in Cohuna with The Lonely Ones on Easter Monday April 11th 1966 before returning to Melbourne.[224]

In late April 1966 Yvonne attended a Bon Voyage party for Pat Carroll at Pat's home in Brunswick prior to her departure for England. Other attendees included Tony Worsley, The Strangers, Joy Lemmon, Ronnie Burns, Patti McGrath, Bert Newton, Buddy England, Mike Furber, and Ken Sparkes.

In an effort to raise funds for the Sporting Globe-3DB Royal Children's Hospital Appeal, 3DB disc jockey Bruce Stewart had staged a dance concert at Melbourne's Festival Hall one Sunday afternoon in May 1962. Much to Bruce's surprise, the first show was so successful that Festival Hall's owner Dick Lean suggested to Bruce that he should stage another concert. 'So I did the following month,' says Bruce 'and that went just as well.' Lean then suggested Bruce should stage a show every week, so Bruce took up the challenge. The concerts ultimately caught on, so much so that they ran weekly through to the end of August 1962.

Buoyed by the 1962 success, Bruce restarted the Sunday concerts in May 1963. Bruce recalls that he 'would normally contact the artists and groups and they were always willing

---

222 "Go-Set", Vol. 1 No. 12 dated April 20th 1966.

223 The author concurs having seen them perform numerous times during that period.

224 Yvonne ultimately appeared four times at Cohuna's Town Hall.

to appear if they were available. Generally, they gave their time for free on the first show each year. After that they were paid a nominal amount for appearing on additional shows.'

A number of future *GO!! Show* performers gained invaluable stage experience by appearing in these concerts. Bruce remembers Yvonne, Lynne Randell, Joy Lemmon and Normie Rowe being quite young when they first appeared in these shows. 'Yvonne came with her mum the first couple of times, as too did Joy Lemmon. Lynne Randell was always accompanied by her manager Carol West.'

Yvonne ultimately made a number of appearances in the concerts. Bruce observed that 'Yvonne was very friendly. She was also a terrific performer on stage! I would have had her appear every week, but obviously I couldn't do that, as I had to give everybody, including new artists, a go. A lot of young artists came early to Festival Hall to do a spot on the show as a type of audition before the bulk of the crowd got there. Even Normie Rowe did that!'

The Sunday concerts started at 2:30pm and finished at 5pm. Bruce compered the shows, which normally featured four bands and eight to ten singers. If The Saxons, The Phantoms or another group were backing artists, they would initially perform two of their own songs. Then Bruce would announce the next performer. They would sing four songs, then the band would do one to finish off before the next act came on stage. Bruce remembers that he usually allowed four minutes for each song. 'Generally, the shows went pretty well and ran spot on time. At about ten to five, we'd get all the artists, who were still hanging around, to form a line on stage. They'd then do a song that everybody knew like "What'd I Say" while passing the microphone from one to the other.'

Festival Hall was the iconic venue for music in Melbourne at the time. Bruce recalls that the artists all got a big buzz while performing on the same stage as had legends such as Frank Sinatra, Bill Haley & his Comets, Buddy Holly, and The Beatles.

Bruce Stewart ran the Royal Children's Hospital Appeal concerts from 1962 to 1968. He was in admiration of the talent in Melbourne through those years. For example, he cited the talent in the May 1st 1966 line up which included Bobby and Laurie, MPD Ltd, Billy Adams, Johnny Chester, Lynne Randell, Yvonne Barrett, The Strangers, The Field Twins, Ronnie Burns, and Terry Dean.

Yvonne made further appearances at Fireball (Brighton Town Hall) on May 6th 1966 along with The Deakins, Johnny Cooper, and the Bay City Band. On May 18th 1966, she appeared twice at the Myer Chadstone record department. Other *GO!! Show* artists, namely The Field Twins, Billy Adams, Peter Briggs, and The Cherokees, made similar appearances that same week. Yvonne then appeared at Claxton on May 21st 1966 along with Ronnie Burns, 5 Fingers, and The Castaways. She next appeared at the Boardwalk (Masonic Hall, Brighton) along with Grantley Dee, The Sonamatics, and The Blackouts.

Yvonne subsequently appeared on the *GO!! Show* on May 23rd 1966 along with Ian Turpie, Ray Brown & The Whispers, Buddy England, The Field Twins, Mike Furber, Ja-Ar[225], Glen Chapman, and The Strangers. Yvonne then appeared at Opus (Ormond Hall, South Yarra) on Saturday May 28th 1966

---

225 Now known as John Rowles.

along with The Cherokees, The Dymonds, Ronnie Burns, The Dougden Quintet, and The Twilights.

On June 13th 1966, Yvonne appeared again on the *GO!! Show* along with Ian Turpie, Normie Rowe, Tony Worsley, Donna Gaye, Steve Juhari, Joy Lemmon, The Five, The Twilights, The Mystrys, and The Strangers. In late June 1966 Yvonne attended Marcie Jones's twenty-first birthday party held at Marcie's home. Other guests included Normie Rowe, Stan Rofe, Toni McCann and Royce Nicholls (bass player of The Blue Jays).

In July 1966, Yvonne's second single "Send Her Away"[226] / "Won't Someone Say"[227] was released on the Go!! Label. On July 11st 1966 Yvonne gave a superb performance of the Carole Bayer Sager and Toni Wine composition "Off & Running" on the *GO!! Show*. Graeme Thompson, Peter Robinson & John Farrar from The Strangers[228] provided the vocal backing on the track. Unfortunately, Yvonne's version of the song was never released on record. On that same episode Yvonne sang a splendid version of Verdelle Smith's classic song "Tar and Cement".[229]

Yvonne performed "Send Her Away" on episode 100 of the *GO!! Show* on August 1st 1966. This episode was the second birthday edition of the show and the final appearance by compere Ian Turpie. As ATV0 had altered its recording schedules earlier in the year, Ian was forced to choose between

---

226 English singer and songwriter Jackie Trent (coincidentally born Yvonne Burgess) recorded the original version of Tony Hatch's composition "Send Her Away".

227 "Won't Someone Say" was written by John Farrar.

228 Performers were typically backed by the "*GO!! Show*" house band The Strangers.

229 Sadly, there is very little footage left of Yvonne's performance of the song. The author strongly believes that Yvonne's version should have been released on record.

remaining compere of the *GO!! Show* or staying on the panel of HSV7's *Time For Terry* variety show, hosted by English comedian and jazz musician Terry O'Neill. Ian Turpie turned his back on the pop scene to concentrate on his developing role as number two to O'Neill.[230] Julian Jover subsequently chose Johnny Young[231] to compere the *GO!!Show* from August 8th 1966 onwards.

Yvonne and fellow *GO!! Show* regular Billy Adams made several appearances on HSV7's *Time for Terry* during the latter part of 1966. Billy was the lead singer of Melbourne rock'n'roll band The Checkmates from 1961 to 1963. He then went solo and became popular on the local dance and disco scene in the mid-1960s. As a consequence, this led to Billy signing a recording contract with the Go!! label. He had five singles released on the label, but his only hit was a cover of Eddie Quinteros's 1960 hit "Slow Down Sandy". His four subsequent singles failed to chart and he eventually quit the music scene.

In the meantime, Yvonne was promoting her "Send Her Away" single at every opportunity. She performed the song on ABV2's teenage show *Dig We Must*, hosted by Bobby Bright and Laurie Allen, on September 23rd 1966, and on Brian Henderson's *Bandstand* on October 22nd 1966. Despite her fine performances on those very popular shows, the single failed to take off. It debuted at number 35 on Melbourne's 3KZ Sound

---

230 "Norman Spencer grooms Ian Turpie for top TV job" — The Age TV/Radio Guide December 8th 1966.

231 Born Johnny Benjamin de Jong in the Netherlands on March 12th 1947, Johnny Young's family migrated to Perth, Western Australia in the early 1950s. Young had a number one hit with the double-A-side, "Step Back" and "Cara-lyn" in 1966. He subsequently penned number one hits, "The Real Thing" and "The Girl That I Love" for Russell Morris, "The Star" for Ross D. Wyllie and "I Thank You" for Lionel Rose. He also wrote Ronnie Burns's hit "Smiley".https://en.wikipedia.org/wiki/Johnny_Young.

Survey Top 40 chart on September 20th 1966. Sadly, it dropped out of that chart the following week.

Yvonne's follow up single "Don't Bother Callin'"/ "I'm Taking Him Back" (Go!! G-5040) was released in October 1966. Despite both songs being written by John Farrar, Yvonne's third single failed to chart.

One newspaper article summed up the situation for Australian female singers at the time. 'One of the peculiarities of the local pop music business is that our girl singers, with the exception of Lynne Randell[232], don't sell enough records, whereas international female stars like Petula Clark, Cilla Black, Nancy Sinatra, Connie Francis, Dusty Springfield, Verdelle Smith, Dionne Warwick, Brenda Lee and others sell a lot of discs here. Our local lads fare well against overseas opposition.[233] But for some mysterious reason, our girls are having a rough time. Right now, it's hard to find a record by an Australian girl among the first 40 records on any of the radio station's charts in Melbourne.

'The record companies are producing the goods. Over the past few weeks, single play discs have been cut by Joy Lemmon, Lynne Randell, Judy Stone, Little Pattie, Yvonne Barrett, Donna Gaye, Margie Bayes, Betty McQuade, Lynne Fletcher and Judy Jacques. It's too early just yet to see how most of them will go, but if they're true to form, the prospects aren't bright. People close to the business say the reason is that girls, who buy most pop records, are reluctant to buy

---

232 Randell's "Going Out Of My Head" spent eight weeks in the latter half of 1966 on 3DB's National Top 40 charts peaking at Number 14.

233 The likes of Normie Rowe, Johnny Young, Grantley Dee, Ronnie Burns, Bobby & Laurie, and groups such as The Loved Ones, The Group, The Easybeats, and The Twilights were having great success at the time.

records made by girls. But this doesn't explain away the popularity of overseas female artists. Are our girls good enough? The experts have listened closely and say beyond doubt that our girls should be getting a bigger share of the market. If anyone has the answer, there are a lot of local artists, managers, record and music publishing companies who would like to know.' [234]

Another article took an alternate view as to why Australian female singers were having a very lean run on the record charts. 'The success of any disc is dependent to a large extent on air play. Are records by Australian girls given equal air play, or are overseas artists getting more because of their big reputations? The position has become so serious for local girls that record companies are reluctant to contract girls for records. Yvonne Barrett, Little Pattie, Annette Steele, Lynne Fletcher, Joy Lemmon and others have all contributed fine releases with almost disastrous results.'[235]

Marcie Jones agrees that record labels of the era were reluctant to take a chance on female artists. She recalls that her records got a certain amount of air play at the time, but she didn't get that elusive hit. 'Girls were harder to push in those days because most of the kids that went to concerts and bought records were young girls. They just wanted to hear the boys. The girl fans mainly bought the records and of course the boys were number one.'

Marcie comments that female artists in Australia at this time 'were an afterthought. We had to work harder and we had to be tougher to get anywhere.' She asserts that she would

234 'Hard for girl pop singers,' undated & unsourced press article.
235 'Are Our Girls getting a fair go on the air?,' undated & unsourced press article.

have given up, but for her 'warped sense of humour and a tough attitude.'[236]

Ronnie Burns suggests that 'it had to be a special relationship or a fan relationship for a girl to go out and buy the record of a girl, unless it was a song about her boyfriend in some way and they were identifying with the song. Fan based buyers of our records were girls. Yvonne, Pat, Olivia and Marcie just weren't as popular in those days. I don't say that in a derogatory sense. It didn't discredit them, but the girls just had to work harder to get over it. They did very well to survive in the industry at that time. When we would appear at shopping centres or showrooms in Sydney, or wherever we were, there were guys there, but it was predominantly lots of girls and a few guys. The Beatles concert was indicative of that.'

Sandy Glenny grew up in Edithvale and would travel to the ATVO studios in Nunawading by train and bus nearly every week to see the *Go!! Show* recorded. Sandy met Yvonne for the first time while waiting outside the studios to meet 'Garth' Thompson from The Strangers. 'I liked the way he drummed,' says Sandy. 'I saw Yvonne talking to Pat Carroll that day and I heard Yvonne say "Oh shit!". I thought "God, Yvonne's human!" So I asked her if I could join her fan club. She said, "I've got one, but the girl doesn't do anything." I said, "Can I take the club over?" She said, "Yeah. Here's my address and my phone number."'

Sandy was eighteen when she began running Yvonne's fan club. Not surprisingly, most of the members were males. The fan club's membership card No. 1, however, was bestowed by Sandy on a female, Yvonne's mother Sheila, on February 25th 1967. Sandy worked for a printing business at the time. 'It

---

236 Marcie Jones, 'Marcie Jones: Runs In The Blood', Network Creative Services Pty Ltd, Melbourne, 2008, p.103.

was perfect for printing the fan club's membership cards and everything else I needed. I initially spoke to Yvonne over the phone about her interests[237] and what I was supposed to write in the newsletters. She'd tell me what she was doing and I included that in the newsletters that I produced once a month. After a while Yvonne and I started ringing each other. I also went to Yvonne's home quite a bit. My stepmother would drive me out there and we'd have a chat.'

Club newsletters were always cleared by Yvonne. Sandy would also tell Yvonne about promotional material she planned to send to such magazines as *TV Week*, *TV Times*, and *Everybody's*. She also sent material promoting Yvonne's fan club to various Melbourne radio stations such as 3UZ and 3KZ. Each week, Sandy would prepare banners for herself and other fan club members to hold up during the recording of the *GO!! Show*. 'Lyndon Johnson was the U.S. President at the time, so we'd hold up signs saying things like "All the way with Yvonne Barrett!"[238] The banners would appear on tele.'

Sandy would go to as many of Yvonne's live shows as she possibly could. She recalls that 'Yvonne was really down to earth and she loved her fans. When Yvonne got work at a hotel, I'd take a whole group of friends with me to see her performance. I'd have a stack of pamphlets about the fan club with me and I'd hand them out to everyone in the audience.'

Towards the end of 1966, voting opened for *Go!! Show* viewers

237 In an interview with a show business reporter, Yvonne mentioned that she didn't get much time for hobbies, 'but she enjoyed reading travel and mystery books and collecting records.' 'Yvonne's A Straw Hat Girl', Listener-In TV — September 1966.

238 Sandy's sign was inspired by the "All the way with LBJ" slogan associated with U.S president Lyndon Baines Johnson.

to vote for the annual Go!! Awards for that year. All artists who had appeared on the show during the year were eligible for votes as Most Popular Artist, Best Female Artist, Best Male Artist, or Best Group (vocal or instrumental). Lynne Randell had been the previous year's Best Female Artist winner and was expected to win again despite strong opposition from Yvonne and Dinah Lee.[239]

Much to her great surprise, Yvonne beat the highly favoured Lynne Randell for the Best Female Singer award. Normie Rowe was accorded the Most Popular Australian Artist title. Johnny Young was acclaimed the Best Male Singer. The Best Group award went to The Strangers. 'The popularity poll carried no prize other than the specially designed trophies, the honour and glory, and the assurance of many bookings in the following year's *Go!! Show*.'[240] Yvonne's trophy was engraved "Best Female Singer 1966 *Go!! Show* Award. To Yvonne Barrett for Best Female singer presented by DYT Services producers of the *Go!! Show*".

Fifty years later, Sandy Glenny revealed how Yvonne had won the award. 'You had to send your name and address with your nomination. I didn't know enough people, so I got the phone book out and asked the twelve people I worked with to pretend they were the people whose names appeared in the phone book. I had an agreement with the Normie Rowe and The Strangers fan clubs that we'd nominate them if they'd nominate Yvonne. We prepared hundreds of forms nominating Yvonne, Normie and The Strangers. It cost me a whole week's pay in stamps. Yvonne was blown away when

---

239 'It's 'GO' For Pop Awards,' Listener — In TV, undated article.
240 'They're Tops On 'Go!', Listener — In TV, late January 1967.

she won the award and received it on the *Go!! Show*. I never told her what I'd done as I didn't want to put her down.'

Denise Drysdale recalls seeing Yvonne for the first time when she started taking dancing lessons at the age of three-and-a-half at the May Downs School of Dancing. Denise was two years and five months younger than Yvonne. The pair never met each other at that time. Denise recalls first meeting Yvonne around 1965. 'I thought she had a beautiful face, beautiful figure and pixie haircut, and the most fantastic clothes. She always looked gorgeous and she sang so well. We attended quite a few fantastic parties where everyone would get around a piano and sing during the *Go!! Show* years. Yvonne loved the sun and loved sunbaking. In summer she always had a beautiful golden tan. She always looked like something you'd aspire to be. I've always struggled with weight whereas she was just perfect to me!'

The *GO!! Show* took on a new format in 1967. Instead of a one hour presentation on Mondays, it was seen in half hour editions at 6pm on Mondays, Wednesdays, and Fridays. Yvonne made some fourteen appearances on the *GO!! Show* that year.

In February 1967, Terry Walker replaced Fred Weiland in The Strangers. Weiland left to join The Mixtures. Terry Walker had previously been with Ray Hoff and The Off Beats and he had just left Glen Ingram and The Hi Five. Terry recalls meeting Yvonne for the first time when The Strangers backed her on the *GO!! Show* on March 27th 1967. He remembers Yvonne being easy to work with. 'I got to know Yvonne pretty well as we all did. I had a great affection for her. She was a lovely, friendly, happy, bouncy, attractive and delightful person. I knew her Mum quite well too.

'Yvonne was a very good singer. She was very professional and her stage presence was excellent. We always did the backings for people like Yvonne, Ross D. Wyllie, and Ronnie Burns. We played on most of the records where the artist didn't have a band. Most of them were recorded at Bill Armstrong's studio in Albert Road.'

On September 17th 1967, a special 55-minutes long final episode of the *GO!! Show* aired on ATV0. Yvonne appeared in that episode together with Ronnie Burns (Host), Patricia Amphlett, Bobby Bright, The Cherokees, Peter Doyle, Denise Drysdale, Buddy England, The Groop, Marcie Jones, Normie Rowe, The Strangers, and The Twilights. The Go!! record label folded soon after that.

On Saturday December 2nd 1967, identical singing twins Jan and Lyn Field[241] from Nambrok in Gippsland married in identical gowns[242] in different churches in Sale. Jan married Terry Dillon[243] at 3pm in St. Mary's Catholic Cathedral. Lyn attended Jan's wedding. Not yet dressed in her bridal gown, but wearing a plain street dress, Lyn hid from view in the organ loft. Looking down into the cathedral she could see all that went on. When Jan's ceremony was almost over, Lyn hurried away to dress for her wedding to Neil Glendenning which was timed for 4.30pm.

Moments before Lyn and Neil made their vows in St. Columba's Presbyterian Church, newlyweds Jan and Terry

---

241 The twins celebrated their 22nd birthdays the following day.

242 liii The twins wore slim fitting gowns of ice white chiffon over satin, edged with lace. Their long mantilla trains fell over a cluster of tiny flowers. A short tulle veil fell across their faces and they each carried a small bouquet of off white carnations tied with white ribbon.

243 Terry Dillon sang with The Tridents at the Springvale Town Hall every Saturday night for thirteen years. 'That's where I met him,' says Jan.

Dillon entered the church and sat in the chapel. The 240 guests, which included Sheila Barrett, packed St. Mary's Hall for the double wedding reception.

Busiest of all on the day was Yvonne as she was chief bridesmaid for both twins. As soon as Jan's wedding was over, Yvonne had to dash back to the Field home with Lyn to help her dress. Yvonne and her fellow bridesmaids (in both weddings) wore junior navy blue chiffon over white satin empire line dresses, featuring three bands of white satin ribbon under the empire line and around the sleeves and hem. Three white covered buttons trimmed the sleeve. They carried posies of off-white carnations and wore a cluster of small white flowers in their hair.[244]

The Field Twins retired from show business immediately after their weddings. Jan was pregnant with her son Jamie within two months. Lyn was pregnant two months after that.[245] Jan recalls that she and Lyn used to go over to Yvonne's home quite frequently. 'When Jamie was about two[246] we'd have lunch. The three of us loved the sun, so we'd have coffee and we'd sunbake with Yvonne. Yvonne's mother was lovely. She adored Yvonne. Yvonne's dad was a character. We met him, but we didn't see a lot of him as he was always working.'

Lyn recalls a prank that her husband Neil and Yvonne played on staff in a hamburger shop at the St Kilda Junction. 'Neil and Yvonne got on really well together. Yvonne was a real character, whereas Jan and I were quiet and reserved. Neil

---

244 lv Details of the weddings were obtained from newspaper reports 'Singing Twins Wed Today,' The Herald, December 2nd 1967, 'Weddings Separate Singing Twins,' Gippsland Times, December 4th 1967, and from interviewing Jan & Lyn Field.

245 lvi Jan ultimately gave birth to three boys and a girl. Lyn had two boys and two girls.

246 He was born on November 26th 1968.

was, and still is, an outgoing sort of person. Yvonne would get dressed in a mini skirt and Neil would dress like a hobo. Then they'd walk into the hamburger shop and act it out. Yvonne would have a chunk of chewie in her mouth and with the lisp going, she'd say to Neil "What'da ya want luv?" and that sort of stuff. Neil would reply "I'll have a hamburger with the lot luv." You had to be there to see it. They'd make you laugh.'

Lyn Field recalls that Yvonne was going out with John Farrar when she and Jan were still singing. 'They were in a strong relationship. We had a flat in Windsor and Yvonne would stay at our place with John. We saw quite a bit of John and he got to know us quite well.'

Opinions vary as to the impact the breakup with John Farrar had on Yvonne. Lesley Kirk remembers Yvonne and John's mother, her Aunty Gladys, being very close. 'John's parents were devastated when John broke up with Yvonne in early 1968 as they just adored Yvonne. John's Mum told us that Yvonne was devastated. I was devastated and Mrs Barrett was furious.'

Lesley remembers that Yvonne definitely still loved John. 'He was the love of her life. We thought she was the love of his, because they were just perfect together. I and the rest of the family definitely expected John and Yvonne to marry. I didn't discuss the break up with John, so I don't really know how he felt. Yvonne never discussed the break up with us because we didn't see her for some time afterwards. She then began visiting us again. She would drive down to Frankston in her very pale green Datsun 120y to see us. She brought my Aunt Gladys with her. I was very close to Aunt Gladys. She was my favourite aunt. Yvonne liked my parents. She called them

Aunty Win and Uncle Harry. Yvonne and I stayed in touch for a while.'

Lesley married in 1971. Yvonne attended her wedding and sat with all the family. Lesley recalls that Yvonne visited John's mother not long after that. 'She told my aunt that she would have to break ties with the family as it brought back too many memories, and she was finding it hard to move on with her life. She asked my aunt to tell us as she didn't have the heart to tell us herself. We understood that. I caught up with Yvonne a couple of times at music shows after that. I saw her at the Waltzing Matilda hotel in Springvale and in Frankston at the Nepean Room, Pier Hotel on the Nepean Highway. The last show I saw was at the Sandown Park Hotel. Yvonne came and sat with us after her show as she always did.'

Marcie Jones contends that Yvonne was very much in love with John Farrar. 'He was the love of her life. Yvonne was shattered. She never got over John. I think when you really love somebody, there's that little place in your heart that just doesn't go away. Yvonne and Pat Carroll were good friends. John is lovely, but he was a naughty boy! When they broke off he was taking out Pat behind Yvonne's back. That broke her heart. She was a sucker. I'd take so much, then I'd say "Go to buggery!" But she was softer than me.'

Margie Bayes agrees that the breakup broke Yvonne's heart. She also agrees that John was the love of Yvonne's life. 'I think she thought this is the man I'm going to spend the rest of my life with.' Yvonne's fan club president Sandy Glenny maintains that Yvonne deeply loved John. 'Yvonne was devastated when John cheated on her. I can still hear her on the phone crying her eyes out.' Yvonne's cousin Liz Dennis recalls Yvonne telling her that she really didn't mind about the breakup with John, 'but I think it hit her deep down.'

On the other hand, Tricia Barrett has a different opinion. 'I just think it was one of those things. John was her first love and you probably don't forget your first love. I don't know that there was any great talk about them breaking up. They were pretty young. I'd had lots of boyfriends who I'd broken up with. So I think my mother was used to breakups. I don't think it was such a big deal back then with Yvonne!'

Pat Carroll says that she 'never really saw very much of Yvonne after she left for England in 1966. I came back to Australia in 1968 and that's when I started dating John Farrar. We were married at the Christ Church, South Yarra on January 6th 1970.' Lesley Kirk remembers being surprised that Yvonne and Sam Anglesey were among 'the 150 or so guests invited to the wedding. We didn't know Yvonne and Sam had been invited until we were in the church and I looked around and saw them.'

Yvonne wore a full-length dress of pale blue Thai silk which featured cut-out sides and a deep plunging back and she had her hair back in a ponytail. The press reported that Yvonne wore 'the most daring dress at the wedding. You've gotta hand it to Yvonne. She stole the limelight by wearing that revealing backless dress.'[247]

Ronnie Burns strongly believes that Yvonne's greatest attribute was her singing. 'She had a lovely body, a lovely style, and she moved in a very feminine way. That was part of her look and part of her appeal. It was very easy to put her in those situations, but she didn't go to the levels where other girls went.'

---

[247] TV Week, January 1970.

To this day, Ronnie remains disappointed, that while starting her career with the likes of Olivia Newton John, Pat Carroll and Marcie Jones, Yvonne didn't reach the level of fame they did. 'She could have carried it, but maybe doubt crept in. I don't know because I wasn't in her head, but I never saw doubt in Yvonne.'

Marcie has a different view. She attests to the fact that Yvonne really doubted her ability. She tried to encourage Yvonne, but she didn't have a lot of success. Ronnie acknowledges that Marcie would have been closer than him in Yvonne's circle, given that they were singers on the same show, and they would have been hanging around in dressing rooms and going out for lunch. Had Ronnie known that Yvonne had doubts about herself, he says 'I probably would have gotten inside her head and told her to work it out, as people have helped me over the years. You don't leave someone with that lovely nature, and who is dedicated to her craft, when they are trying to work it out and they are not getting anywhere. We were very supportive with that camaraderie.'

Ronnie recalls that his career started to really take off after the early television shows. 'I was singing all over Australia and I eventually started singing in clubs in Sydney. I went over to England and spent a couple of weeks with Barry Gibb, but I wasn't interested in going to America.' Ronnie didn't want to follow John Farnham, Johnny Young, The Bee Gees or The Seekers overseas. 'I didn't want to do it, so I didn't go. I was a big fish in a small pond here. My career was going well and I was doing this and that. But I wanted to do other things with my life. I realise now, looking back in hindsight, that I wanted to keep my life pretty simple. Perhaps Yvonne did too!'

Some years later Ronnie had a need to go to Ballarat. 'My manager Jeff Joseph asked me to call into Yvonne's place in Braybrook to pick up something or to do something. I thought "where in the bloody hell is Braybrook?" I found out that it was out on the highway going to Ballarat. As I was driving, I was thinking "I'm going to meet Yvonne's Mum and I'll get to go into her house". Time had moved on, but it was lovely to see Yvonne again. We had changed and we weren't as close, but we were still friends. I really enjoyed that opportunity to catch up with Yvonne.

'As someone who has worked with Yvonne, I can honour her as the wonderful person that she was. She represented her family well. She did her thing and she did it gracefully and that's probably why she was called "Gracie".[248] She did it with finesse and she did it with talent and she never made ripples or waves to upset other people. I can never remember anything like that happening. She was very respectful of other people. It's an honour now to go back and remember some things and talk about her with love and joy. The effect that Yvonne had on my wife and me is memorable and it's cherished!'

---

248 Ronnie didn't call her by that name.

7. 'GRACIE, THE BEAUTIFUL TALENTED GIRL FROM THE PARIS END OF BRAYBROOK!'

John Vallins recalls meeting Yvonne in late 1965. John was fifteen at the time. He grew up in the Melbourne suburb of Kew. His early life was surrounded by an eclectic mix of musical influences. From bebop to the classics and the hit parade of the day, the Vallins family home was always filled with music and musicians. In his early teens John met guitarist Steve Groves at high school. Heavily influenced by the music coming out of the UK at the time, The Kinetics band was formed with John on guitar, drums and clarinet, Steve on vocals, guitar and harmonica, and friends Ken Leroy on bass guitar and Ian Manzie on drums, piano and banjo.[249]

Ken Leroy and Ian Manzie met while students at the Deepdene State School. Ian went on to gain his intermediate certificate at the Swinburne Technical College, before leaving school to join The Kinetics. Ken started his secondary education at Trinity Grammar School and he too left school to join The Kinetics. The group's average age at the time was fifteen.

John remembers each member of the group being 'quite

---

249 http://www.johnvallinsmusic.lpexproductions.com/John_Vallins_Music/About.
html.

excited' about being chosen to back Yvonne on stage. The Kinetics had just started working a regular Friday night gig at the Nepean Mod, which was staged at the Mechanics Hall in Frankston. It was, as far as John recalls, one of the first regular gigs the group did as a band. The promoter who ran the dance booked stars from the 'Go!! Show to appear every week at the Nepean Mod as he knew they would attract a big crowd. The Kinetics backed the guest stars each week.

John also recalls each group member being 'a little in awe at meeting Yvonne' at the rehearsal at Ian Manzie's home. 'She was, after all, one of the best known faces on Melbourne TV at the time. At the rehearsal we ran through all the songs that Yvonne was going to sing. She chose her set well as they were mostly straight up 12 bar things like "Hallelujah, I Love Him So." The songs were simple to do even for a young inexperienced group like us. Yvonne was so nice to us at the rehearsal that day. She was easy to work with, and genuinely funny. Oh, and gorgeous of course! I think we all fell a little in love with her that day.'

Friday December 17th 1965 was a busy day for Yvonne. She initially appeared at the Havana Promotions presentation of Victoria's First Open Air MOD Spectacular at the Dandenong Showgrounds. Others on the bill included Bryan Davies, Johnny Chester and The Chessmen, Colin Cook, Buddy England, Grantley Dee, and Marty Kristian. Later that night Yvonne appeared at the Nepean Mod in Frankston along with The Kinetics, Billy Adams, and Silver Strings.

The Kinetics' workload increased in 1966 when the group signed a recording contract with the international label CBS. The four members of The Kinetics were approaching sixteen years of age when their first single "Excuses"/ "I Know Where You're Hiding" was released. The group all left school to go on tour when "Excuses" hit the Top 20 music charts. As live performers, the group forged an impressive reputation among critics and other musicians over the next two years.

"Excuses" ultimately reached Number 19 on the Melbourne music charts. The group's second single "Gone to Work It Out"/ "Feduping Day" charted, but their third single "Tomorrow Today"/ "You're So Good To Me" didn't.

John Vallins recalls that the group was working flat out in those days. 'Sometimes we'd do three gigs a day. Yvonne would have been doing a hell of a lot more than that though. Sooner or later we'd end up on the same bill as Yvonne. We backed her a few times over the next year or two.

'Having worked together before, we'd talk through the songs and then just do the show. She was good to work with because she understood the paradigm of the gigs. I mean you couldn't, as a singer, work three or four gigs on a Saturday night, and do songs like "Alfie" or "Anyone Who Had A Heart" because you would need to rehearse them properly with the band. She understood that. She knew if you were going from gig to gig, the songs had to be things she could make work for her, and yet be not too much of a stretch for the band.'

John remembers Yvonne being very popular with audiences. 'She always looked great. She sang and danced well, but more importantly she had a sort of girl-next-door friendliness that people liked. After all, underneath the makeup and the usually quite revealing wardrobe, she was really quite down to earth, incredibly charming, and she could be amazingly self-deprecating.' Yvonne would refer to herself as being

"Gracie from Braybrook, but at least I'm from the bloody Paris end of Braybrook!"

By the end of 1967, The Kinetics was a three-piece group. 'It was just Ian, Ken and me,' remembers John. 'We'd lost Steve Groves through some silly argument. We were now doing gigs booked through promoter Eddie Floyd. Eddie had recently gone into partnership with Col Jones, and together they had launched a new venue named The Winston Charles which was on the site of the old Playboy club in Toorak Road, South Yarra.'

Eddie Floyd called the group into his office one day and asked them what they thought about forming a new band with Phil Blackmore[250] on keyboards and Edgell James[251] and Yvonne on vocals. John recalls that 'we were a little sceptical at first as we didn't know Phil or Edgell, but of course we knew Yvonne! Whatever doubts we had must have been put aside however, because the next thing I remember was the six of us sitting around a table at Winston Charles toasting the new band, which was to be called The Trap. Eddie Floyd and Col Jones had come up with that name. We all loathed it, but there was no changing it as they had already started doing press releases.'

The Trap consisted of Yvonne Barrett and Edgell James (on vocals), John Vallins (guitarist/vocals), Phil Blackmore (keyboards), Ian Manzie (drums), and Ken Leroy (bass). The group rehearsed every day for some time, getting the feel of the band together.

After leaving Glenroy High School, Edgell James joined a series of groups, but they never stayed together long enough to get really settled and hit the big time. Edgell was quoted

---

250 Blackmore had previously been with The Playboys.
251 His real name was Allan James Walker.

as saying 'someone always seemed to make it big from those groups. They'd leave and do well. I must have been stiff. It was never me.'[252] Edgell subsequently joined The Beachcombers group which in turn changed its name to The Changing Times.

Up to this point in time, Edgell had been better known as a bass guitarist than as a singer. That impression changed by the time the newly renamed group recorded Ronnie Hawkins's hit song "Mary Lou" on the RCA label. Edgell's lead vocals on the recording were outstanding, so much so that the "Mary Lou" single subsequently reached number four in Melbourne and number ten nationally. Edgell also sang superb lead vocals on the group's cover of the Johnny Mathis song "Wonderful Wonderful".

Edgell stayed with The Changing Times for almost three years. He then joined The Mixtures just in time for the group's participation in Crispian St. Peters's 1966 Australian tour.[253] Touring with Crispian St. Peters proved to be a real fillip for Edgell. 'I learnt more working with Crispian than I have all the rest of the time I've been in the pop business. He was tremendous, not just as a singer, but as an all-round entertainer. Everything had to be done perfectly or he wasn't happy.'[254]

Edgell ultimately decided that his time with The Mixtures had convinced him that he wanted to be a singer pure and simple. He was quoted as saying 'I could never concentrate when I was playing and singing at the same time. When I

---

252 'An Introduction to The Trap' document, December 1967.

253 Crispian St. Peters was an English pop singer-songwriter, best known for his 1966 hits "The Pied Piper" and "You Were on My Mind".

254 'An Introduction to The Trap' document, December 1967.

gave up playing, I realised I could still do a lot more with my singing.'[255]

The combination of the old Kinetics and the talented Phillip Blackmore on organ[256] gave Edgell James the type of backing that he had wanted all along. The addition of Yvonne for duos and harmony produced the sound he loved. Generally, Yvonne and Edgell agreed on the type of music they liked and wanted to sing.[257] There was one exception however. Edgell liked the popular Irish singing group The Bachelors, but Yvonne thought the group sang 'rotten harmonies!'[258] Despite Yvonne's opinion, The Bachelors had worldwide hits with such songs as "I Believe", "Ramona" and "I Wouldn't Trade You For The World".

After leaving school, Phil Blackmore played the organ for two years on 3DB's *Hillbilly Time with Dick Cranbourne* program, while also playing with The Roulettes group. He subsequently joined Normie Rowe and The Playboys. His ultimate aim now was for The Trap 'to be kings of the world, so that manager Eddie Floyd won't bash me up.'[259]

A reporter from The Sun newspaper wrote a brief article on The Trap a day before the group made its first public performance. 'A brainchild of promoter Eddie Floyd, The Trap will stage its first public performance on Tuesday December 12th 1967. If the group's members live up to their reputation, it should do very well indeed. With their line-up, it's hard to see

---

255 Ibid.

256 Besides playing organ, Phil Blackmore was also responsible for doing the group's musical arrangements.

257 'An Introduction to The Trap' document, December 1967.

258 Ibid.

259 Ibid.

how they can fail, and having had a couple of sneak previews of their work, it's even harder to see.'[260] The group had been practising constantly for the previous couple of weeks behind closed doors at the Winston Charles. Eddie Floyd opined at the time 'as the manager of this new group, I am confident that they will make an impact on the scene.'[261]

John Vallins recalls that Edgell James and Yvonne swapped lead vocals back and forth, and they also threw in a duet or two on debut night, December 12th 1967. 'I remember them doing "The Two of Us" which was a big hit for Tony Hatch and Jackie Trent at the time. It was a featured song the night we launched at Winston Charles in front of what you could only call a captive audience, namely a lot of press. The event was very well organised by Col Jones and Eddie Floyd. We must have gone down quite well that night, or maybe the assembled journos had enjoyed the free beer, because the reviews in the papers the next day were quite complimentary.'

Yvonne was quoted at the time as saying that she was thrilled at the thought of singing with The Trap. It was the first group she could claim as her own, and if she had her way, The Trap would be playing a fair percentage of ballads.[262] The group's confidence grew upon reading a review in *Go-Set* which expressed the view that 'this is a good solid group, with brilliant vocals and harmonies.'[263]

Not all reviews were complimentary however. One reporter

---

260 'Young Sun,' The Sun, December 11th 1967.

261 Eddie Floyd's invitation (dated December 5th 1967) to attend the launch of The Trap on the Australian Pop Scene. He noted that 'the usual three course meal will be provided together with liquid refreshments with my compliments.'

262 'An Introduction to The Trap' document, December 1967.

263 'Yvonne Barrett In New Group,' Go — Set, December 27th 1967.

commented that The Trap 'failed to snap at their first public performance at the Winston Charles. The choice of numbers for their floor show was unfortunate — mainly slow, mainly old, not the sort of stuff to send anyone into fits of ecstasy. Basically, they should be good. The main trouble appeared to be nerves and the choice of songs.'[264] Another reporter noted that 'The Trap hardly set the world on fire when it gave its first public performance.'[265] Yet another critic wrote 'although there's a wealth of experience in the group, things won't go too easy. Melbourne has its established names and it's becoming increasingly difficult for new outfits to crack the scene.'[266]

Nevertheless, the group's momentum began to build in late December 1967 following performances over three successive nights[267] at the Cambridge Dance in Frankston. The Vibrants, The Dream, and The Mixtures were also on the bill. On December 26th 1967, The Trap performed at the Q Club along with The Dave McCallum Powerset, Adele Smith Blues Band, and The Gingerbreadmen. The Trap returned to the Cambridge Dance for another three performances[268] in Frankston together with The Vibrants, The Dream, and The Mixtures. The four groups rotated each night between the 10th Avenue, The Cambridge, and the Winston Charles venues.

Following those appearances, Ian (Molly) Meldrum expressed a more positive view of the group in *Go-Set* by noting that The Trap was 'gaining a lot of ground after a shaky start.

---

264 'Young Sun,' *The Sun*, December 18th 1967.

265 'Break-Down on the Break — Ups,' *The Sun*, January 24th 1968.

266 *Everybody's*, December 20th 1967.

267 December 22 — 24th 1967.

268 December 29 — 31st 1967.

It just goes to prove that one shouldn't jump to conclusions.'[269] A follow up article in *Go-Set* noted that while The Trap was a new group of familiar faces, 'they have a promising future in the pop world. But as they are so new, *Go-Set* assures you that you watch out for them.'[270]

The Trap's workload began to increase in the early months of 1968. The group performed at the Victoria & Albert venue with Procession, Impulse with Peter Doyle and The Dream, and the Prince Albert George Sebastian 11 with Jeff St. John and Yama.

On February 10th 1968, The Trap performed at the Tom Foolery psychedelic disco (St. Johns Hall, Camberwell Junction), together with the Party Machine. The Trap subsequently performed at Opus (Ormond Hall, South Yarra) on February 17th 1968, together with Somebody's Image, The Vibrants, Grantley Dee, The Soul Searchers, and The Iguana. On March 2nd 1968, the group appeared at Swinger (Coburg City Hall) along with The Dream, Carmel Chayne, and Noddys Banned. Shortly thereafter The Trap performed at Menzies Hotel (509 Bourke Street), and at Glu Pot (Whitehorse Road, Box Hill).

Yvonne had met Edgell James for the first time when she appeared on the same episode of the *GO!! Show* along with The Changing Times on June 7th 1965. The pair met again when Yvonne undertook a brief country tour with The Changing Times, Roland Storm, Billy Adams, Tony Cole and The Sonamatics in February 1966.

At some point during the early days of The Trap, Yvonne and Edgell became an 'item'. But as John Vallins recalls 'we started

---

269 'Ian Meldrum Looks Thru Keyholes,' GO-Set, January 10th 1968.
270 'The Trap- New Group Old faces,' GO — SET, January 17th 1968.

doing regular gigs, which always included working out of town in places like Shepparton, Warrnambool or wherever. It soon became obvious however that the relationship was fading. Yvonne was looking unhappy, and I remember our roadie Peter Carr [271] shaking his head and saying something like "This is not good mate!"

'It all came to a head late one night at the "Winston Charles" when we were packing up after the show. Suddenly I could hear loud voices from the street. We all tumbled outside just in time to see Yvonne pitch the ring Edgell had given her a week before on to the roof of the Cafe de Paris across the road from the Winston Charles. Apparently, he was still up there trying to find it hours after we'd all gone home. It may have been an engagement ring. That would partly explain why Edgell spent such a long time looking for it I guess!'

In late January 1968 *The Sun* newspaper announced that Edgell James had decided to quit The Trap. No definite departure date was given at that time. The newspaper article went on to note that 'the group has been lucky enough to get a really sensational replacement, Peter Doyle. Peter may be just the tonic The Trap needs to really kick off. Peter's recent work has been first class, and on records like "Plastic Dreams and Toy Balloons" he has been showing new-found maturity, excellent range and a very easy-to-listen-to style.'[272]

The Herald newspaper subsequently reported that Peter Doyle had 'decided to shelve 50% of his single status as an artist and throw in his lot with The Trap. The Trap, notable so far only for their open welcome to musical refugees, should

---

271 He'd been The Kinetics roadie previously.
272 'Break-Down on the Break — Ups,' The Sun, January 24th 1968.

now look forward to a great deal of success. Peter can only enhance any group he joins. This doesn't mean that Peter is throwing his solo work down the drain completely. It means he is taking the wise step of appreciating how little work there is for a soloist and how little remuneration there can be unless you are regularly employed. Peter will continue to record under his own name for Astor Records. There is no finer young vocalist in Australia today than Peter Doyle. Watch him prove it both as a soloist and group member for The Trap.'[273]

Melbourne's leading disc jockey Stan Rofe reported a short time later that Peter Doyle didn't feel that his joining The Trap should have been made public until negotiations were finalised. Stan went on to say that 'Peter has had second thoughts on joining The Trap, or any group for that matter, due to the sudden influx of highly paid work, plus some rather needy and helpful advice passed on to him by his booking agent in Melbourne, Miss Carol West.' Stan then expressed the view that he didn't believe a few appearances with The Trap would have done Peter much harm. He noted however that Carol West 'argued many good points against Peter aligning himself with any group.'[274]

Peter Doyle subsequently rang The Trap's manager Eddie Floyd and told him that he would not be joining the group. This left The Trap without a lead male singer from early in February 1968, when Edgell James was due to leave the group. Eddie began frantically looking for a replacement. He was confident he would have a good replacement late in February when another group split.[275]

John Vallins had initially read in the press that Peter Doyle

---

273 The Herald, mid-January 1968 article.

274 'Stan Rofe's Tonic', GO-SET, January 31st 1968.

275 The Sun, January 29th 1968.

was going to join the group. 'I thought how fantastic that would be because he was such a great singer. But that was the last I heard of that! There was some talk then of new singers joining the band, but nothing ever came of it. With Edgell[276] gone, I stepped in to do some of the male lead vocals, along with Kenny and Phil. Yvonne was back to her old self, and really enjoying being out front, and the general feeling in the band was "Let's just keep working and see where it goes."'

Not long after that, the group landed a summer gig at the Ocean Grove Surf Club. John Vallins recalls that some friends of Ian Manzie's family lent the band the biggest caravan he'd ever seen. 'We were all piled in together. Yvonne had one of the bedrooms. The other was taken by Phil Blackmore and his wife, and Ken, Ian and I all slept in the annex.'

The group was at Ocean Grove for five weeks. Yvonne absolutely loved the fact that their caravan was across the road from the beach. She tanned naturally, and she spent a great deal of her spare time sunbathing or swimming in the surf.

John remembers the group being billed as Yvonne Barrett and The Trap at the time, as though they were two different acts. 'It happened quite a lot because that way the promoter could use Yvonne's name to boost attendances, because nobody really knew anything about The Trap. At night we'd play at the Surf Club dance, and then drift back to the caravan for some drinks and laughs. I started to get to know Yvonne a little better while we were down there. We shared a slightly odd sense of humour, and we made each other laugh out loud a lot. She was always happiest when she felt she was just one of the band!

---

276 Edgell James passed away from a brain tumour in 1990.

'But the reality was that she could never be "just one of the band" because she was Yvonne Barrett, and like it or not, she was constantly approached by people wanting autographs, or just wanting to talk to her. She was never rude or impatient when this happened. She always seemed to have plenty of time to talk, or have a picture taken, or whatever. She never made anyone feel in any way inferior or uncomfortable. She just didn't think that way. I admired her immensely for that. By the time we got back to Melbourne, we were all wondering what was going to happen to The Trap. But Eddie and Col still had gigs for us to do, and so we played on.

'Somewhere around this time Yvonne and I started being more than fellow band members. I don't remember how it happened, but I know at the time I really couldn't believe that it did. I wasn't the only one who couldn't believe it, because no one bloody could! Everyone loved Yvonne. We all called her Gracie. She had been given that nickname by her old friends from the theatre days I believe. So, when all of a sudden we were together, there were more than a few eyebrows raised. Not in the band itself, but definitely outside of it.'

When they were not working, Yvonne and John spent their days wandering through the city, taking in a movie or eating in restaurants, sometimes with friends, sometimes just the two of them. At times Yvonne would show a level of sophistication that would take John by surprise.

John remembers Yvonne having impeccable manners and being comfortable in any company. 'She and Pat Carroll were old friends, and I remember Pat coming to lunch with us occasionally, and just generally being part of the group of her friends, who included Ian Turpie, Patti McGrath, Olivia

Newton John, John Farrar, who was seeing Pat even back then, and the other guys from The Strangers. They had all known each other for years!'

John recalls he and Yvonne having a drink one day at the Southern Cross Hotel. 'I had just gone off to the loo for a few minutes, and when I came back Yvonne was sitting there surrounded by a group of Americans who were in Australia for some scientific conference. They were all smiling from ear to ear and buying her champagne. I was introduced, slapped on the back a lot, and given a glass. They turned out to be excellent company. We had a very funny day trying to understand what it was they did exactly, because the more champagne they drank the more difficult the explanations became.'

This type of thing happened all the time when John was with Yvonne. She would take it all in her stride, and always with a smile or a wink at John. He recalls the time he and Yvonne were with his family at a friend's house for a barbecue one Sunday. 'The entire local football team turned up. It wasn't long before Gracie was again surrounded by admirers. Someone asked me how I felt about all the attention she was getting. I remember saying that she'd let me know when she'd had enough. She would never be rude, not even in those circumstances. She managed to hold court for quite a while, but eventually with a smile, she stood up, walked over to me, took my arm and said "Take me home Johnny, I've had enough forward passes for one day!"

'I met her parents Sheila and Ted. Sheila kept almost every newspaper clipping and photograph of Yvonne since she was a kid. She was very much the proud mum in that sense.'

John recalls that The Trap was still working a number of

gigs, so a lot of time was spent on the road. 'Ian Manzie, Ken Leroy and I had already spent many hours being driven all over Victoria and NSW in a dear old blue VW van. Peter Carr did all the driving. He was a professional driver and drove trucks during the day. He had been with us for quite a while. He drove us to all our gigs, all the parties, and sometimes to the drive-in when we had a night off. We would have been lost without him because we were all too young to drive. He was a great bloke, good-hearted and strong as an ox!

'I have some nice memories of travelling to various country towns in the van, eating hamburgers from our favourite place on Dandenong Rd in the early morning, and all of us laughing like drains at some story Gracie would tell about someone or something that had happened to her.'

Eventually The Trap dissolved. John estimates that the group had been together for approximately a year. 'I can't remember exactly what happened, but one day it was over and that was that! Gracie and I stayed together after the band split, but things were beginning to change for both of us. My old friend Steve Groves had come back from working in Sydney with Steve Kipner[277] and we got together to do some TV and

---

277 Steve Kipner's first band, Steve & the Board achieved chart success in Australia with the song "Giggle Eyed Goo". Steve sang backing vocals on some songs on the Bee Gees album Spicks and Specks which was produced by Steve's father Nat Kipner. Steve & The Board broke up in early 1967. Kipner then formed a duo with Steve Groves and relocated to England in 1968, where they recorded an unsuccessful LP. Kipner ran into Barry Gibb in 1969. That meeting resulted in Kipner and Groves being signed to Robert Stigwood with Maurice Gibb as their producer. Under the name Tin Tin, the group scored an international hit with "Toast and Marmalade for Tea". The song reached the Top 20 in the US in 1971. The next year Tin Tin, with additional member John Vallins, supported the Bee Gees on their American tour. John and Nat Kipner made record history in 1978 when their song "Too Much, Too Little, Too Late" hit the No.1 spot on the U.S. Billboard Hot 100 pop chart, Adult Contemporary chart, and R&B chart for Johnny Mathis and Deniece Williams.

some gigs. This was actually a forerunner of Tin Tin which I was to join in London sometime later.

'Meanwhile Gracie was doing more and more session work. She had always done sessions, singing on a lot of commercials for Bruce Clarke. I remember her doing sessions at other studios too for as long as I'd known her. But it seemed suddenly the demand was getting higher. We used to take taxi's everywhere, but she ended up buying herself a Morris Minor car so she could get around to all the gigs on time. She loved it. She took me for a drive the day she got it. I thought I was going to die laughing the way she kept talking to herself and to the car. She'd say things like "Oh shit, where did you put second gear?" She'd also talk about other drivers.

'One of my favourite memories of her is of the day we were just lazing about at home with some friends. We needed to go to the pub for some supplies. Gracie had been messing around in one of my mum's wardrobes, and she came out dressed in an old dress and hat with her face made up like an old lady's. She said to us "Let's go." We all followed her into a bottle shop pretending we didn't know her. We waited until she was served. She started talking very loudly, and with the most incredible lisp, she asked for a bottle of "That nishe ssherry ssherved sssometimes on SShundays."

'We all fell about laughing, but the chap who was serving her got very annoyed at us laughing at her, and he told us to get out. A little while later she appeared at the car with a bottle of sherry in tow. She laughed and said, "He was so nice to me. I just had to buy it!"'

John maintains that the lessons he 'learnt from Gracie were more "life lessons" than anything else. She had an uncanny knack of knowing how to talk to people, and how to make them feel comfortable in conversation, so that they would open up about themselves. This made almost everyone who met her immediately feel comfortable in her company. It was fascinating to watch. She really did like people. It wasn't an act or a ploy with her. We used to eat in flash restaurants a lot at that time. She taught me the rules about dining in expensive or posh restaurants and how to handle head waiters and sommeliers without being ignored.'

Yvonne and John had shared a love of the movies. They spent many a day in cinemas watching a lot of movies. John remembers Yvonne being invited to the premiere of *Bonnie and Clyde* when it opened in Melbourne in April 1968. 'She wasn't going to go because the invitation was just for her. I thought it was crazy for her to miss it. So she went along and came home saying we had to go see it together, which we did the next day.'

John recalls them going to see the French movie *A Man and a Woman* and then going to Allans Music to buy the soundtrack album. 'We shared a great love of music of course. What we liked was incredibly diverse, ranging from Stan Getz to Petula Clark, and from The Beatles to Henry Mancini. Yvonne had an album of American Songbook standards played by Andre Previn that she loved. We would often sit around at home with a glass of wine. She'd sing and I would play guitar, things like "I Wish You Love" and "The Shadow of Your Smile." She could really sing those tunes. She had a lovely sound when she sang softly, which she just did naturally when doing those types of songs. I don't know whether anyone else ever heard her sing like that.

'One night at home in Kew, my mum, Gracie and I were watching a TV show recorded in Sydney called something like *Shirley Bassey live at Chequers*. It was terrific to see Bassey doing her show. She was amazing, sexy, funny, and charismatic. Man did she work hard! Gracie was completely blown away by her. Very excitedly she asked me what I thought about her doing something like that. It was obvious to me that she could do it, so I said "Of course you can!"

'Suddenly it seemed like I wasn't seeing her as often as usual. One day she came over to our house in Kew and told me of her plans to go back to doing solo work. She had an idea about a whole new act she wanted to try, with different sorts of material and costumes. I thought it sounded great and I told her so. She then grabbed her keys and said she had to go to a rehearsal at Channel 9. On her way out, she turned and kissed me on the cheek, and although she didn't say anything, I knew then, just by the way she looked at me, that it was over for us.'

John ran into Yvonne on a few occasions in the following couple of years. They were always pleased to see each other. John remembers getting a letter from Yvonne while he was touring the USA with Tin Tin two or three years later. John recalls Yvonne describing a gig, in her letter, that she had just done somewhere in Tasmania. 'That made me laugh so hard my chest hurt for days!'

John considers himself very lucky to have known Yvonne Barrett. 'She was an important part of my life, in so many ways. As I was just seventeen when we started seeing each other, she taught me a great deal about a great many things. But more than anything else, she was enormous fun.'

Sometime after Yvonne and John Vallins had broken up,

John was working with a new line up of The Kinetics. Yvonne rang John and asked if she could book the band for a gig. It turned out that Yvonne had a forty minute spot to do at a rather ritzy gig at the Exhibition Building. 'We were happy to oblige of course and arranged for a rehearsal. I wasn't surprised at the change in her act. She was doing a much more cabaret type of show and the songs supported that. I remember she closed with "Big Spender." She was great that night and went down a storm! I think that this was sometime after she had done the shows at the Lido, but I can't be sure.

'It had been a while since we had broken up, but every time I picked up a paper or turned on the television, there she was. Even after that amount of time, it still hurt a little, but I was very happy for her renewed success. To me she'll always be "Gracie", the beautiful, talented girl from "the Paris end of Braybrook", who took me by the hand when I was seventeen years old and showed me a side of life I never knew existed. I'll never forget her for that!'

Sheila Mary Smith & Albert Edward (Ted) Barrett – Wedding Day 23 April 1936

Yvonne's parents on their wedding day

Peter, Tricia & Yvonne

The Barrett siblings

Yvonne and Patti McGrath at a dancing competition held in Ballarat.

Yvonne and Pat Carroll in matching costumes on the Swallows Juniors.

Photographs courtesy of Ballarat Courier

156

Promotional photo of Yvonne

The last known photo of Yvonne

Gravestones of Yvonne and her parents

8. "WOW, WHAT A BABE!"

Sam Anglesey was born in Perth in 1944. He applied for a radio gig in Perth when he was nineteen. He recalls that 'radio was king back in those days! I was given stuff to read, but I missed out on the job. That didn't surprise me because there must have been a hundred guys applying for the job. I got a telegram a couple of days later asking if I wanted to work at their sister station 6KG in Kalgoorlie. I said, "Yeah, no worries!"'

Sam recalls that being the only job he ever applied for. 'It snowballed from there. People just rang me and made me offers after that. I was working at 7HO in Hobart when I got a call from 3UZ's program director John McMahon. He offered me a job at 3UZ. I wanted to hit the big time, so I accepted the position at 3UZ and I moved to Melbourne in 1968.'

Before moving to Melbourne, Sam had seen Yvonne on television. 'I guess like a lot of guys, I thought, "wow, what a babe!" She had that real physical attraction.' Soon after his arrival in Melbourne, Sam was out on a date at a St. Kilda restaurant. Coincidentally, Yvonne happened to be sitting at a table with her date at the same restaurant. Sam recalls that he and Yvonne 'caught eyes across the room as I passed her on the way to the toilet and we smiled at each other. I was thinking "wow she's even more attractive in real life" particularly with the pretty daring clothing she wore at the time. That was the first time I'd seen her in the flesh, so to speak.'

Attending promotions and functions was part of Sam's job at 3UZ. Shortly after seeing Yvonne at the St Kilda restaurant, Yvonne happened to be at the same function as Sam. He remembers they got chatting and left together after the function. 'Going down to the carpark we jumped in the dumbwaiter. It was a bit of a lark. I was showing off and trying to impress her.

'We started going out after that first meeting. We were pretty much besotted with one another after that. We really clicked and you couldn't tear us apart. She had a great sense of humour, so we laughed a lot. Yvonne wasn't that shy when we were together. She might have been when she was on her own somewhere. I think she enjoyed having a fellah. She liked to turn up to things with somebody's arm to hang on to. I think she wanted to be loved.'

Sam ultimately met Yvonne's family. He describes them as being 'a typical working class family. Yvonne's mother really doted on her. She was her mum's life. I didn't see a lot of her father Ted. He was a bit of a character in the area and he was well known at the local pub. When he knocked off work, he'd go to the pub, then he'd go home. His dinner would be in the oven or on the stove. He'd eat his dinner then go to bed. He'd get up the next morning and go to work and do it all over again. Yvonne's sister Patricia was lovely. There was lots of love there between her and Yvonne and between Yvonne and Peter, who I only met a few times.'

It wasn't long before Sam and Yvonne moved into a flat in

Rathdowne Street, North Carlton. Tricia Barrett recalls that 'this was the first time Yvonne had set up house.' The flat wasn't far from the 3UZ studios which were located at 45 Bourke Street. Sam remembers living in Carlton was great for both of them. 'It was nice and central and so vibrant in those days. It was great living close to theatres, restaurants, and all the alternative culture in the area.' Yvonne and Sam ultimately planned to form a company for managing entertainers, but nothing ever eventuated.

Sam remembers Yvonne working almost every night of the week at the time. 'Yvonne used to work late into the evenings and I used to work in the early evenings. I'd finish my radio gig and I'd often pick her up after her gigs.' Sam recalls that Yvonne didn't have a manager in their early days together. 'She did her own bookings. It was so easy for her because she was in such demand. So why have a manager! All she needed was a phone and promoters would ring her. She'd just quote her fee and that was it. Take it or leave it!'

Yvonne and Sam loved dining out and socialising,. 'We didn't talk much about our work. I'd just say, "How was it?" She'd say "Good" and I'd say "Okay, let's go out". We dined out most nights of the week after work, and we'd have a bottle of wine. Being in the middle of Melbourne, there were so many good places to eat and they were open till midnight. We'd go out for lunch too. I introduced Yvonne to every type of food I could, including Hawaiian and Jamaican.

'We got invited to every new movie premiere. We both loved the movies, so much so that sometimes we'd see two or three movies in the one day. Films came of age in the 1970s. We saw films like *Easy Rider, Zabriskie Point,* and *2001: A Space Odyssey* and all the other Stanley Kubrick films. We also loved the theatre, restaurants, and the finer things of life that perhaps she didn't grow up with. There was a fairly vibrant sort of neighbour culture in Carlton in those times. I was always into art, so we'd go to every little art exhibition that was on in Carlton.'[278]

Sam had two nicknames for Yvonne, namely "Yve" and "Yvie". Yvonne's nickname for Sam was "Woolly". That was a reference to his thick hair. Sam isn't aware how Yvonne got the often used nickname "Gracie", but it's one that he still likes. He believes Ian Turpie might have given her that name. Sam recalls Yvonne and Ian being close friends. 'Turps was a great guy! I had a lotta good times with Turpie. He was your typical knockabout Aussie. He liked a beer and a game of pool.'

Sam describes Yvonne as being a typical knockabout Aussie too. 'She was really down to earth and totally natural. She never hid her working class background and she was never up herself! That's what I loved about her. If people are up themselves, forget it! I don't like pretence. She was totally the opposite to that. You never got the impression, "Look at me, I'm Yvonne Barrett!". She was pretty humble. To me that was part of her charm.'

Yvonne and Sam shared a similar sense of humour. 'In some ways our humour together was almost like Barry Humphries's humour for Yve and I with the things we laughed at. We laughed at stuff like the mundaneness and the funniness of it all. We also laughed at our careers. Neither of us took them too seriously. That was something nice we shared together.'

Yvonne and Sam agreed early in their relationship that

---

278 Sam recalls they didn't go out as much after he started doing 10pm shifts towards the end of his time at 3UZ.

they would keep their careers completely separate from each other. Nevertheless, Yvonne told a reporter that she wouldn't hesitate to ask Sam for advice if she thought it was necessary. 'Sam hasn't influenced me at all. If I need advice, I'll ask him. But we never criticise each other's work or offer suggestions unless asked. That's probably why we've been friends for three years.'[279]

Sam recalls only ever giving Yvonne 'a few career suggestions.' Recording "Lu", a song written by Laura Nyro, was one such suggestion. 'I said to Yve, "If you're going to have a hit record, it all gets down to you finding a decent bit of material."'

As a disc jockey, Sam knew that for Yvonne or any singer to have a hit record, it all boiled down to the material. He knew the type of material that would suit Yvonne's voice. 'I was a fan of Laura Nyro's song writing. No one had heard of Laura out here as she wasn't known as a performer. She was a songwriter. So I suggested Yvonne should look at some of the songs that Nyro was writing and pick one out that hadn't been done here. "Lu" hadn't been recorded here, so I suggested that Yvonne record Nyro's composition "Lu".' Yvonne recorded "Lu", much to Sam's delight! He was very happy with Yvonne's version of the song. 'Yve's recording sounded good. I think it made the 3UZ charts.'

Yvonne previewed "Lu" on Bert Newton's *In Melbourne Tonight* TV show on February 4th 1970, ATVO's *Uptight* on February 7th 1970, on the *Musical Cashbox* TV program on February 13th 1970, and on ATVO's *Breakfast A-Go-Go* on

---

279 'Yvonne Goes For Cover' (You Won't Be Seeing Much Of Me in Future'), Listener In — TV, May 6th to 12th 1972.

February 26th 1970. The "Lu" single[280] was released on the Columbia /EMI label in March 1970.

One music critic agreed with Sam's comments on Yvonne's first recordings in four years. "Lu" was described as a 'ripper' by that critic who went on to say that 'the swinging catchy ballad is superbly sung with the good arrangement making it a class production!'[281] Another described Yvonne's version as featuring 'her big voice with a brassy jazz-rock, Blood Sweat & Tears style arrangement.'[282]

Sam made numerous trips with Yvonne. 'She liked me going with her. I went with her to Darwin, Adelaide, Tasmania and to heaps of gigs all over Victoria. We also went to King Island for a gig. They flew us there and back in a little aircraft and gave us a good time.

'Yvonne was a great performer. She really worked the crowd well. She took all the pop music charts with a grain of salt. It's all very well to have a hit record, but you don't get much money out of it. The money was really in live performances. She was in big demand for them. She wasn't terribly ambitious. If she had been a lot more ambitious and got top management, she could have gone anywhere. She could have done anything she wanted to, but she just rolled with the flow. She always had work rolling in. I went on lots of gigs with her particularly on the weekends when I wasn't working. I never saw her blow a gig. Even though she might have had shitty backing at times, she always pulled it off.'

Sam recalls that Yvonne appreciated the purists and the really good singers like Mel Torme. 'I played Mel to her and

---

280 "Picture Me Gone" was on the flipside of "Lu".

281 'Aussies Top The Pops,' The Herald, March 3rd 1970.

282 https://en.wikipedia.org/wiki/Yvonne_Barrett.

she said, "Yeah I like that. He is so good!" She more or less liked songs rather than the artists. Because that was her craft, she listened to the craft rather than the name of the singer. I don't think it was any big deal for her appearing with big name artists. She would have picked up a lot from Eartha Kitt, Frances Faye and all the different people she performed with over the years, but she took stuff like that in her stride. She just said, "Yeah they were good." She never got carried away with herself. I think she'd been used to that from a young age. It was a case of that's just what she did.'

On March 21st 1970, Yvonne and Sam departed Melbourne on a working holiday cruise of the Pacific on the Achille Lauro. The cruise included stopovers in Sydney, Tonga, Fiji, Noumea, and Sydney again, before returning to Melbourne on April 9th 1970. Sam remembers that the cruise 'was a good gig' because the entertainers only worked the nights at sea. 'We didn't work when we were in port. We had a great time cruising for a few weeks. When you're touring around all the islands, you are hardly at sea much anyway. It was just like having silver service all the way. We had the best food and wine and everything was carte blanche.'

The ship's entertainment in first class each night consisted of Yvonne, the Ron Moss Trio, a fifteen piece orchestra, Chris & Penny[283] (a duo from Melbourne), and a light opera singer. Sam was the MC/producer of the entertainment.

Yvonne was backed on stage by the Ron Moss Trio.[284] The Trio's pianist Barry Hirst recalls Yvonne being very easy to work with. 'Yvonne's most notable song on the cruise was "Hey

---

283 Penny Dyer later joined Brian Cadd's "Bootleg Family Band."

284 The Trio consisted of Ron Moss on drums, Barry Hirst on piano, and Peter Thornton on vocals and bass.

Big Spender." She sang it Shirley Bassey style and she moved her scantily clad body rather well. She was a very impressive performer. She worked the tables very well. She sat on guy's laps whilst singing love songs such as "Can't Take My Eyes Off You". She certainly knew what the audience wanted.'

Barry remembers Yvonne claiming to be the inventor of the first push up bra. 'She said she stuffed panty hose in them for a "lift up". She also said that she made her own costumes. Nobody else would have made them that brief! She wore practically nothing underneath. She had lace covering vital places, except from behind. That really startled me.'[285]

Kaye Johnston was a passenger on the Achille Lauro cruise with Judy, a friend from Adelaide. She remembers boarding the ship in Melbourne, 'but the cruise didn't start till we got to Sydney. It was still full of people migrating from Europe and the UK. As soon as we got to Sydney we got off the ship. When we got back on, all the decorations had gone up and the staff were dressed differently. So it turned into a party ship from Sydney onwards.'

Kaye and Judy were in tourist class on the cruise. Kaye recalls meeting John Kelly, a first-class passenger, on board. 'John won his cruise. He was a car salesman with Kevin Dennis Motors, which was situated right at the end of the street where Yvonne lived in Braybrook. He used to come down to tourist class because there were more women his age. He invited me up to first class on the second night and introduced me to Yvonne and Sam. By then, he had established that Yvonne

---

285 Barry Hirst recalls backing Yvonne after the cruise in floor shows in Geelong. Yvonne attended a cruise reunion hosted by Barry on May 16th 1970. On July 25th 1970 Yvonne subsequently performed at the Collendina Restaurant, Ocean Grove with backing provided by Barry Hirst.

lived in Dodd Street, Braybrook and Yvonne had established that he worked in the car yard at the end of her street.'

Kaye recalls that Yvonne was the star of the cruise ship's evening entertainment. 'She was always very sweet, friendly and kind to people. Even though she was a star, she was never out of touch with reality. She asked me where I was from. I told her I was from Adelaide. She said, "I go to Adelaide often, but I don't know anyone there apart from my agent." As the week went on we chatted more. She told me she was coming to Adelaide shortly after the cruise and she asked if we could catch up then. I said, "That'd be great!"'

Yvonne and Kaye subsequently met up again in Adelaide in mid-April 1970.[286] Yvonne had previously appeared on Adelaide television variety programs such as Ernie Sigley's *Adelaide Tonight* on NWS-9 and on Channel 7's *Tonight With Barry Ion*. Yvonne would vary her TV appearances when in Adelaide. She'd appear on Ernie's show one trip and on Barry's show on her next trip. 'I don't think she ever did both on the same trip,' says Kaye.

Kaye recalls Yvonne and *Till Death Do Us Part* star Warren Mitchell appearing on one of the *Tonight* shows in Adelaide. 'Yvonne and I went to a party in Warren's room at the Hotel Enfield after the show. Yvonne was staying there as well. The menu at the party was champagne and prunes. We stayed for a while, then we went somewhere else because we were both starving.'

Yvonne's Adelaide agent would book her appearances and accommodation, and he'd also drive her to her engagements while she was in Adelaide. Kaye recalls that Yvonne would

---

286 Yvonne flew to Adelaide on April 12th and returned to Melbourne on April 26th 1970.

also make one or two other performances while in the city. 'I remember her performing at the Port Adelaide and North Adelaide Football Clubs. Cabaret was big at hotels in Adelaide on Friday and Saturday nights. Yvonne did a floor show at the Finsbury Hotel and she may have also done some floor shows at the Enfield Hotel. We'd usually end up at a nightclub or the Swinger disco at the Hotel Australia. Sometime after that we'd even go into Hindley Street to the Crazy Horse, which was a female strip club. It was about the only place open in Adelaide at that hour of the night.'

Kaye recalls getting into trouble with her parents when Yvonne was in town. 'I'd get home at ungodly hours and I'd have to get up and go to work the next morning. I was like a groupie in a sense, but I was company for Yvonne. I used to help her carry her bags because she'd have endless costumes that she'd change into. I went to Melbourne a couple of times and I met some of Yvonne's family, including Tricia. She had baby Leisel then. Yvonne was absolutely besotted with Leisel. She was a beautiful child. I remember when we were on the cruise, Yvonne was always shopping for Leisel, never for herself. She'd buy her stuffed toys and things like that.'

Kaye remembers Yvonne being very humble about her singing career. She describes her as being very down to earth and very caring of her family. 'When I first went to Melbourne she wanted to haul me around in this little Datsun 120Y to meet everybody. I met her dad Ted a couple of times at the pub. He was lovely.'

Sam Anglesey enjoyed introducing Yvonne to 'a bit of sporting activity. I barracked for Carlton and Yvonne came to the footy with me a couple of times. She hadn't done that before because she hadn't grown up with that sort of life. She became a sort of Carlton supporter, only because of my interest.'

In 1969 Melbourne's *Sporting Globe* newspaper ran a "Miss Football Quest" competition in conjunction with HSV7's Sunday *World of Sport* program. Every Saturday during the football season, the *Sporting Globe* and HSV7 cameramen were tasked with taking photos of 'pretty barrackers' at random at football games.

Yvonne happened to be at a Carlton game with Sam in early May 1969 when her photo was taken. Her photo subsequently appeared in the *Sporting Globe* on May 14th 1969. As a result, Yvonne won an assortment of prizes including a 'superb dinner' for two at Melbourne's then prestigious Southern Cross Hotel. Yvonne became the sixth finalist in the competition and as such she qualified to compete in the final for the chance to win a fortnight's holiday for two to Tokyo and the Far East. Her lack of football knowledge cost her in the long run, but to quote Sam, 'we cracked dinner for two!'

Sam remembers taking Yvonne to the 1970 Victorian Football League's Grand Final between Carlton and Collingwood. 'In those days they packed them in like sardines at the MCG.[287] Yvonne was just overawed by the crowd and all the roaring. There were people everywhere. I wasn't gonna leave, so I sent her home in a cab at half time because the football was just too much for her.'[288]

Early in the 1971 football season, the local press published a front page article noting that the Sunshine Football Club

---

287 The Grand Final held on September 26th 1970 attracted a crowd of 121, 696.

288 The author was devastated by the result of the game which saw Carlton defeat his team Collingwood by ten points.

had 'won a new supporter' that year in pop singer Yvonne Barrett.[289] 'Attractive Yvonne will be barracking for the Crows[290] this year with her "footy mad" boyfriend 3UZ's Sam Anglesey. "Sam is mad about football," Yvonne told The Advocate reporter. "He will watch a game of footy any time no matter who is playing."'[291]

Sam also loved cricket. 'That's my real love. I'm a cricket tragic! We went to the cricket at the Melbourne Cricket Ground a few times. I mainly took Yve to the Test matches, but we also went to the odd Sheffield Shield cricket match.'

Mick Hamilton recalls being at the cricket with Yvonne and Sam. 'A couple of the guys from The Vibrants and Sam and Yvonne used to go to the MCG and watch the Test matches. Yvonne would always come, but she'd never watch the cricket. She'd unfold a lilo, then she'd put it in the aisle and just sunbake. The guys around us in Bay 13[292] would go ape shit! She had the figure from hell and she had on this tiny little bikini! She probably knew exactly what she was doing, but she paid no attention to anybody. She just lay there and sun-baked the whole day. We'd be watching the cricket and having a few beers, while all the blokes around us would be salivating!'

Yvonne and Sam frequently enjoyed hanging out at the Winston Charles all-night nightclub[293]. Sam recalls that he and Yvonne would go there after finishing work late in the

---

289 Accompanying the article was a photo of Yvonne decked out in a Sunshine football club jumper, football shorts and football boots. The photo showed Yvonne about to kick a football with her right leg.

290 The Sunshine Football Club was also known as The Crows.

291 'Well Stone The Crows', The Sunshine Advocate, April 6th 1971.

292 It is well known in the cricket world that rowdy spectators congregate in Bay 13 which is a section of tiered seating at the MCG.

293 Run by Col Jones in Toorak Road, South Yarra.

evening. 'We had carte blanche there. We didn't pay to go in or pay for drinks or food. So why wouldn't you go! If we took in another couple they were on the house too.

'It was a bit of a muso's hangout, and bands like The Mixtures would come and play live music at midnight or one o'clock in the morning. We got to know a lot of the groups and enjoyed watching them perform. After they'd finish playing a set, they'd come down and sit with us in the audience. At certain times in the night when you were wining and dining, the compere would say "Over in the corner we've got Yvonne Barrett and Sam Anglesey" and they'd shine the spotlight on us, or the compere would say "We've got Johnny O'Keefe here tonight" and the spotlight would move to him. That was the only thing you had to put up with there. That was part of the gig and that's why people went there to meet all the stars.'

Jillian McCandlish worked at the Winston Charles. She remembers Yvonne performing floor shows there from time to time. 'Her outfits were always amazing. Yvonne was a fun girl and I remember her fondly. I recall one funny story involving Yvonne. This happened before she met Sam Anglesey. Yvonne was going out with a truck driver at the time. They went to the drive-in movies in his truck and he parked it in the back row!'

Frank Howson left school at fourteen and got a job as an office boy at Radio 3UZ. He remembers Yvonne going into 3UZ soon after he started at the station. Much to Frank's delight, Yvonne remembered him from their days together appearing in the *Stop The World I Want To Get Off* musical. Frank has never forgotten Yvonne's kindness and her warm heart. 'I don't know how many times I've worked before with someone in this business, and they pretend they don't know who you are later on! That wasn't Yvonne. She remembered me and she always made a fuss of me when she came into the station. It's important to humanise the fact that she was a very nice person. She used to wear all those sexy dresses on TV and everyone thought she was an exhibitionist. Even though she seemed to be very flamboyant, I found her to be very shy and a bit insecure in herself. Maybe that is why she was so kind to other people. I've only got the nicest of memories of Yvonne.'

Radio 3UZ was Melbourne's top rating radio station at the time. Sam Anglesey and Stan Rofe were the station's top disc jockeys. Frank Howson got to know both very well and he has never forgotten the support they gave him while he worked at 3UZ. 'Sam was a great guy. I was only young, but I thought Sam and Yvonne appeared to be very happy and very much in love. They seemed to be two peas in a pod and they always seemed to be laughing when they were together. I thought they were a fabulous pair. I know Sam was very proud to be escorting Yvonne around.'

Sam's 3UZ colleague Stan Rofe was a great champion of Australian music. He went out of his way over many years to help young artists kick their careers off. Johnny Chester, The Thunderbirds, Ronnie Burns and Russell Morris were just some of the artists who gave credit to Stan for giving them advice and direction in the early days of their careers. Russell Morris describes Stan as being 'an exceptional warm man. He was such a big star, but his door would always be open for any sixteen-year-old kid who came into his studio with a record.'[294]

Stan Rofe produced Frank Howson's first record "Seventeen Ain't Young"/ "I Hide and Seek" in 1969. Stan subsequently

---

294 'Final Chord Sounds For Stan The Man', The Age, May 17, 2003.

told 3UZ station's program director John McMahon to put the record on 3UZ's playlist. McMahon was known to get very moody. Frank recalls that McMahon had walked into the studio that day after a long liquid lunch. 'When he saw that my name was on the playlist, he told Stan Rofe to get me off the playlist. His nose was out of joint because I was the office boy at 3UZ and now I was going to be a recording artist.'

Nevertheless, Frank recalls that 'Stan risked his job by playing the record on air. I made the 3AK charts, but the record never appeared on 3UZ's charts because John McMahon kept it off.'[295]

On June 30th 1970, the fifth Australian Pop Awards were held at the Dallas Brooks Hall. The awards were telecast throughout Australia by HSV7 Melbourne. Yvonne was voted runner up to Allison Durbin in the Go-Set magazine national Pop Poll. Top male singer was John Farnham. Yvonne sang "Lu" and "Picture Me Gone" at these awards. Sam Anglesey recalls picking Yvonne up at the end of the awards night. 'She was pleased about her award, but she just took it in her stride. It wasn't any big deal to her. In a way, that was one of the things that attracted me to her. We weren't taking ourselves too seriously. That was something nice we shared together.'

On July 4th 1970 Yvonne was a bridesmaid at her brother Peter's wedding. Later that night she appeared with The Barry Veith Big Band at the Cabaret Stardust.

Yvonne and Sam were invited to Ronnie Burns's wedding to Maggie Stewart on October 21st 1970. Sam recalls that he couldn't attend the wedding because he had a shift at 3UZ that day. He knew that Yvonne wanted to go to the wedding, but

---

295 Frank's "Seventeen Ain't Young" spent five weeks in the Top 40 charts and peaked at No. 35.

she would have been going on her own, so Stan Rofe took her to the wedding. Sam appreciated Stan's kind gesture. 'That's the sort of bloke Stan Rofe was!' Ronnie recalls that Yvonne and Stan joined in the celebrations and well wishing. 'It was great and I was happy that they were there.'

On December 11th 1970 Yvonne appeared in a pop festival which was the highlight of Melbourne's fourth annual "Walk Against Want". The walk finished at the Sidney Myer Music Bowl where more than thirty singers and groups staged a Starlite Concert. The event was backed by the Federation of Commercial Broadcasters and sponsored by Community Aid Abroad, Inter-Church Aid, and the Australian Catholic Relief. Other artists and celebrities to appear included Anne & Johnny Hawker, Johnny Chester, Liv Maessen, Bobby & Laurie, Russell Morris, John Williamson, Smacka Fitzgibbon, Jimmy Hannan, Sam Anglesey, Stan Rofe, and Ken Sparkes. All artists gave their services for free.[296] Later that night, Yvonne drove to Morwell for an appearance at a hotel.

In mid-December 1970, in an interview with a show business reporter, Yvonne denied rumours that she and Sam Anglesey were engaged. 'Sam and I haven't even discussed marriage,' she said. Yvonne went on to say that her 'only plan for 1971 was to finish the year with a big savings account.'[297]

By April 1971 however, Yvonne appeared to have given some thought to marriage. She told a local newspaper reporter that she and 'her boyfriend' Sam Anglesey had bought two acres of land earlier that year in the Riddell Ranges, near Mt. Macedon. She went on to say that 'we won't be getting married until a

---

296 "Footsore To A Pop Festival", *The Age*, November 30th 1970.
297 *TV Times*, December 11th 1970.

house is up and furniture in.' Tricia Barrett remembers the couple talking about getting married. She also recalls Sam often saying at the time 'We're in love! We're in love!'

Although Sam contends that he and Yvonne never discussed marriage, he says 'We just cruised along in our little world, but I guess we did have aims of one day maybe settling down together!'

Sam also claims that he advised Yvonne to invest some money into property. 'I said, "While you're making a few quid, do something with it." We bought that little two-acre property. It was somewhere to go for a picnic or with a few mates. The land was a nice little getaway. I had a Honda trail bike and a GTHO Falcon back then. So we'd just zip up the highway in the falcon or jump on the motorbike. Yvonne wouldn't go up there much on the bike. She'd go up in her car. The trail bikes were more of a blokey thing. They were too dangerous to have someone on the back.' Notwithstanding Sam's comments, it was reported in the press that Sam was giving Yvonne lessons on the trail bike, as she 'hoped to eventually own her own bike.'[298]

If Yvonne wasn't going up to the property, Sam and a few mates such as Russell Morris would travel up on their bikes. 'We were weekend bikers,' says Sam. 'We'd take our trail bikes up there and we'd make a camp fire and hang out together. It was a nice little escape!'

Tricia Barrett believes that the purchase of the land in the Riddell Ranges was a bad investment and a real rip off! 'When they bought the very dense land, they didn't know at the time

---

298 'Well Stone The Crows', The Sunshine Advocate, April 6th 1971.

175

that they wouldn't be able to build on it. They found out later that it wasn't to be cleared.'[299]

Whenever possible during the summer months, Yvonne and Sam would spend a lot of time on Brighton beach. They enjoyed going for a run along the beach before going for a swim. They would bump into Richmond's legendary football coach Tom Hafey on the beach on a regular basis. Sam remembers that 'Tom was a nice guy. He was one of our beach buddies.'

Yvonne loved sunbaking at the beach and at the Barrett family home in Braybrook whenever the opportunity presented itself. When she got too hot she would dive into the above ground swimming pool, which she had purchased and had installed in the family's backyard in 1969. Then she'd sunbathe some more. Being a redhead, Sam didn't like getting out in the sun too much. Yvonne and Sam also enjoyed having a barbeque in the Barrett backyard. Yvonne's much-loved dog Prince would always join them.

Prince was half kelpie, half Labrador. He loved to travel with Yvonne in her car and he often accompanied her to work. Yvonne taught Prince many tricks. One such trick was waiting every day for the postman's arrival at the Barrett home. The postman would initially greet Prince and then place the mail in Prince's mouth. Prince would then hotfoot it into Yvonne's bedroom and deliver her mail. If she wasn't home at the time, he would pass the mail to Sheila Barrett.[300]

Next door neighbours Rhonda and Kevin McCabe recall

---

299 Sam claims he gave the property to Yvonne when they split up. 'I said to her "you keep it."' Tricia recalls that her brother Peter took over paying the rates for the property when Yvonne died. 'He paid them for a while then gave the land back to the council. It was a waste of his money because he couldn't clear the land or do anything with it.

300 'A Prince Among The Mail Men', The Sun, August 10th 1967.

being allowed to swim in Yvonne's pool. Rhonda remembers the pool 'being a big deal back then because nobody else in the neighbourhood had a swimming pool. My girlfriends who lived across the road from me were allowed to swim there as well.' Tricia Barrett confirms that 'Yvonne would let anyone have a swim in the pool.'

Kevin McCabe recalls having 'lots of swims' in the pool. 'I used to run away to next door. I was in there more than I was in my own house. Sheila used to let my mother know I was in there. One time Sam Anglesey, Yvonne and The Field Twins were all in the pool. I was looking at them from over the fence.'

Kevin remembers Yvonne having photos showing her singing on *Swallows Juniors*. He told a couple of his mates from the Braybrook State School about the photo. 'Those two kids came to Yvonne's home to get her autograph. Then about 50 or 60 other kids lined up outside the Barrett's front door. They then piled in the front door and walked out the back door after getting an autograph.'

Yvonne made several appearances in Adelaide during the early 1970s. She appeared at a number of venues during a two week stay in Adelaide in April 1970. She also appeared on Ernie Sigley's *Adelaide Tonight* TV program that same year. Yvonne subsequently made a number of appearances in Adelaide in June 1971 and during the months of May, July and August 1972.

Geoff Mayne was a guitarist in the Adelaide based band Brass Buckle in 1971.[301] He played a key part in the formation of the group which ultimately consisted of Mike McCabe on vocals, Geoff on guitar, John Tamblyn on keyboards, Iain Neilson on drums, John Chamings on bass, Billy Clark on sax,

---

301 Geoff had previously been in a band named "Inkase" for some five years.

and Roger Swanson on trumpet.

Geoff recalls that music in Adelaide was beginning to move from the teenage dances to the pubs and clubs at that time. 'We played all over the place in Adelaide, backing artists and doing our own thing. Our bookings were made through the Central Booking Agency (CBA) in North Adelaide.' The CBA was the most popular booking agency in Adelaide at that time. They would book all the top acts such as Johnny Farnham, Ronnie Burns, Yvonne Barrett, Russell Morris, Ross D. Wyllie and bands such as The Strangers, The Mixtures, Flying Circus, Axiom and Zoot. The list was endless!'

On June 13th 1971, Brass Buckle backed Yvonne at the Combine,[302] a weekly Sunday night dance in Adelaide's Marion Shopping Centre.[303] The Combine was considered to be one of the best run and most popular regular dances in Adelaide.

Robin Malone was a key player in the success of the Combine. He was instrumental in getting together with six YCW[304] branches in the area to initially get the shows going for their members. He recalls that the 'dances quickly grew beyond our imagination. We made good money for our YCW branches. We had over 3,000 people on some long weekends and that was when there was no alcohol available. I, like many people, met my future wife through the YCW. We were from different branches, but she was at the Combine every Sunday night.'

Robin recalls that 'we did most of our bookings through the CBA. All interstate bands and artists, including Yvonne, were

---

302 The club was named "Combine" as six Young Christian Workers (YCW) Movement branches combined to run the shows.

303 Now known as Westfield Marion, it is Adelaide's largest shopping complex.

304 Young Christian Workers.

booked through the CBA. Someone from the Marion shopping centre had to be there to give us access to their administration area for entertaining artists. Peter Schrader was second-in-charge at the shopping centre. He loved the entertainment industry and he was at the club most Sunday nights.'

Robin kept records of the Combine's attendance figures. He recalls that there were over 2,600 people in attendance the night Yvonne appeared at the Combine. 'Yvonne was the main attraction that night. Male and female fans milled around the stage during Yvonne's performance. Issi Dye[305] was also on the bill that night. Brass Buckle also had their own set.' He adds that Chris, his then girlfriend, now wife, had noticed that 'I took a liking to Yvonne. She was so, so nice!'

Geoff Mayne has fond memories of backing Yvonne that night. 'She was very nice, attractive, and very good vocally. She was a wonderfully talented girl and very easy to get on with and a real pleasure to work with. You can't say that about a lot of singers. Our drummer Iain remembers Yvonne being great on the one-off show we did with her. In fact, she left a lasting impression on all of us!'

In late July 1971 Yvonne attended John Farnham's 22nd birthday celebrations at a fancy-dress party that 'rocked on through the night. Many of Johnny's show business friends went along to help him celebrate, but none of them knew where Johnny was until a large woolly bear (aka Johnny Farnham) took off its head.' Yvonne wore a ballerina outfit, as her fancy dress, to the party.[306]

---

305 In the 1960s Issi appeared on TV shows such as "Bandstand", "Kommotion", "The GO!! Show" and "Uptight." He subsequently became a regular presenter and performer on the "Happening 70's" TV Show. He is still performing today.

306 TV Week dated July 24th 1971.

In October 1971 Marc Leon's[307] band The Graduate[308] was chosen to be the opening act at the newly opened The Don hotel in Darwin. The band was booked to play at the hotel for three months during which time they backed a number of floor show artists, including Yvonne, Ian Turpie and Matt Flinders. Yvonne was booked to perform her show for two weeks beginning on November 29th 1971.

Marc was looking forward to meeting Yvonne and to be backing her on stage because of a connection the two had in 1967. That year Marc recorded his first solo single "I Can't Get Enough". The song was arranged and produced by David Mackay for EMI Records. Marc recalls that Mackay recorded the backing to the song at Armstrong's Studio in Albert Park. The Strangers played the rhythm section and the Johnny Hawker Big Band provided the brass backing.

Sometime later, Marc asked David Mackay if he could recall the names of the two female background vocalists who sang on "I Can't Get Enough". 'David told me 'one was Yvonne Barrett.' Marc believes Pat Carroll might have been the other backup singer. Marc says 'It's hard to pick out everything the girls sang on that song, but one of the background bits really stands out. I always liked that sexy "Oooh Baby!" bit!'

---

307 Marc Leon's career began in 1960 as a lead singer in rock'n'roll bands. He subsequently taught himself to play guitar and he started to write songs. In 1964 his band "The D-Men" recorded three successful singles on CBS, featuring four of his compositions. By 1966 Marc's musical interests had shifted towards Jazz, Blues and R&B (Soul). Marc moved to Melbourne in 1968 and joined The Vibrants. After that band broke up, Marc formed "The Graduate". That band survived in various line-ups for ten years. Since then Marc has shared the stage with many international acts including The Kinks, Mungo Jerry, The Bee Gees, Jose Feliciano, Fairport Convention, Burl Ives and Roberta Flack.

308 The group consisted of Marc Leon (vocals and guitar), Glenys Hewett (vocals), Frank Durant (drums), David White (bass), Murray Elrington (trumpet), and John Hossen (saxes and flute).

Sam Anglesey accompanied Yvonne on the trip to Darwin and he subsequently assumed the role of compere of the shows. He introduced Yvonne on stage every night. Marc remembers that 'Sam was really smooth in the way he did it. He had such a cool manner and a great speaking voice to put it over.'

Marc remembers that Yvonne didn't specifically mention any of her favourite singers or groups while she was in Darwin, but he believes her taste and influences would have been very similar to his wife Glenys Hewett's preferences, namely Dionne Warwick, Dusty Springfield, and Diana Ross.

In Darwin, Yvonne sang primarily what is now known as "Adult Contemporary" songs. Marc recalls that Yvonne sang some ten songs in her show. None were from the charts of the time. 'She definitely sang Nancy Sinatra's "These Boots Are Made For Walking", Ike & Tina Turner's "River Deep, Mountain High", Sandie Shaw's "(There's) Always Something There To Remind Me", Dusty Springfield's "You Don't Have To Say You Love Me", plus at least one Burt Bacharach song such as "Alfie" or "The Look Of Love." She liked Petula Clark too so there may have been one of her songs in the set list too. She also sang "Lu." It's a great song and Yvonne did an excellent version!'

Marc, his wife Glenys Hewett and fellow band members found Yvonne to be easy going, loads of fun, and a delight to work with. Marc recalls that Yvonne and Sam hung out with the band a lot of the time. 'We all stayed at the Seabreeze Motel.[309] We were practically the only residents there, so we all partied just about every night after each gig making full use of the facilities, including the bar, BBQ and pool. Yvonne

---

309 The motel was blown away during the tropical Cyclone Tracy that devastated the city of Darwin (the capital of the Northern Territory), from December 24-26th 1974.

and Sam joined in. We all went on a couple of outings together with a ranger who took us down the Adelaide River and to Berry Springs.'

Glenys Hewett and Yvonne got on really well and spent time together sunbaking at the motel's pool. Marc recalls that Yvonne 'had a fantastic tan. She said that she sun baked all the year around, even on cloudy days and in winter.' Glenys loved the short dresses Yvonne wore, particularly a lacy one. Yvonne told Glenys she made that dress and would be happy to make her one like it. Yvonne stayed on at The Don hotel for a couple of extra days after her appearances so as to catch up with Ian Turpie, who followed her as the hotel's next floorshow act. But true to her word, Yvonne sent Glenys the dress she made for her two weeks after she left Darwin. Glenys was over the moon about the dress!

In August 1972 it was reported in the press that Yvonne and Sam Anglesey had opened the "Get Shop" in Wattletree Road, Malvern. The report noted that 'Among the many items on sale are hand woven Poncho capes for children and original 18th century Indonesian etchings. Yvonne designed a two-piece hand-painted calico outfit for the shop.'[310]

Tricia Barrett opines that Yvonne 'was conned' into setting up the shop. She recalls that Yvonne put the money up for the business and Sam Anglesey's mother ran the shop. Tricia adds that 'the shop probably gave Yvonne a bit of an interest for a while, but she wasn't able to be there to do much with it. Mrs Anglesey probably thought she could run the shop, but she wasn't a businesswoman and she didn't run it very effectively.'

---

310 Listener-In TV, August 19th to 25th 1972.

Liz Dennis recalls that Yvonne's mother[311] thought Yvonne was misguided financially at the time. Tricia agrees. 'Yvonne put a lot into that and lost out on the venture.'

In the early 1970s the Sunbury Pop Festival (aka Sunbury Rock Festival) became one of Australia's pop music hot spots and the Australian equivalent of Woodstock[312], albeit on a much smaller scale. The Festival wasn't actually held at Sunbury; rather it was held on a 620-acre (2.5 km2) private farm between Sunbury and Diggers Rest in Victoria on land with a natural amphitheatre.

The Festival ran over the Australia Day long weekend from 1972 to 1975. It was promoted by Odessa Promotions, which was formed by a group of television professionals, including John Fowler from GTV 9 Melbourne. Located 40 kilometres north-west of Melbourne, the then sleepy hollow of Sunbury had a population of around 3,000, but come festival time it used to swell to around 40,000. John Fowler developed the idea of the festival to 'give everyone a good time and promote Australian bands.'[313] Local residents George and Beryl Duncan lent their property for the weekend in return for improvements to fencing and irrigation.

The festival site became what some described as a "hippie playground", although one lacking glamour. Not only did the heat make it an endurable test, but sanitation was almost non-existent. Most portable toilets would soon be blocked, and portable showers were invariably rendered out of action.

---

311 Liz's Aunty Sheila.

312 Woodstock was a music festival held on a dairy farm in the Catskill Mountains, northwest of New York City, between August 15th to 18th 1969. The festival attracted an audience of more than 400,000 people.

313 Sunday Herald Weekend, January 25th 1997.

The tent city would also become a dust bowl. Garbage was piled everywhere. The daily press tended to ignore the music, preferring to focus on the hippies getting back to nature, swimming nude in the creek coiling around the desolate paddock, and zealous drug squad police making numerous arrests of young hippies for possession of marijuana. Surprisingly, drunk and disorderly youths were largely ignored.

Sam Anglesey recalls he and Yvonne spending part of a day at one of the Sunbury Pop Festivals. 'I don't remember if it was the first one[314] or the second[315]. I remember Thorpie was there.[316] We didn't spend the whole day there. Both of us got naked in the river like the rest of them. No one knew who we were and when you're all naked you all look the same!'

Sam recalls being on what was the inaugural flight, and the first international Qantas flight, out of Tullamarine airport in 1972. 'It was a junket so to speak. Everyone on board was a VIP. It was offered to Lewis Bennett, the manager of 3UZ, but he didn't want to go. I was the white haired boy, so I got the nod. There were a lot of interesting blokes on board, for instance journalist Keith Dunstan and cartoonist Jeff Hook. They were on assignment for *the Sun News-Pictorial* newspaper. Jeff was doing his cartoons and Keith was writing his stories. I took them to Candlestick Park to watch the Giants play baseball against the Dodgers. I was away roughly a month. I did the whole San Francisco experience. I spent a whole day with Creedence Clearwater Revival out at their Cosmo's Factory. I made a couple of radio specials with them. I discovered the

---

314 Held on January 29th to 31st 1972.

315 Held on January 27th to 29th 1973.

316 Billy Thorpe & The Aztecs performed at the Sunbury Festivals in 1972 and 1973.

west coast lifestyle of that time and I came back a different person. I became really radical in my politics and attitude towards the end of my relationship with Yvonne.

'I didn't want to hang round Melbourne or mess up Yvonne's career. I said to her, "I'm no good for you Yve!" I let it sink in. I was getting too far out for her. I didn't want to drag her away to follow the life I wanted to live after my life changing trip. I decided I'd take a new direction in life. I'd had enough of radio. I'd been doing radio ten years by then. I went farming in Tasmania. I wanted to live in the mountains and raise sheep and cattle. That wasn't for Yvonne. So I just distanced myself slowly.'

Sam believed that being a solo performer, like Yvonne, was very hard. 'When you do a gig, you don't always know who is going to be backing you till you get there. It could be some scungy local band who can't read music. So you've gotta do an afternoon rehearsal and do the show all in one day with whatever band you've been given.

'Towards the end of our relationship, Yvonne hooked up with Peter Arrowsmith, a piano player and musical arranger. Having Peter going out with her to gigs was great. He could get with the band and show them how to play, and he could play the lead bits anyway. I thought she was in safe hands so to speak. She soon got pretty tight with Peter. I could see that too, so I thought this is an opportune moment to end our relationship.'

According to Sam, their breakup was pretty amicable. 'We were both really madly in love with one another. It was a magnificent obsession and a great love story of two people who hung out together. It was also a bit like a bush fire; too hot not to cool down. We had such fun together. We were always laughing. She was just so easy to get on with. She didn't have a bad bone in her body. We never had an argument or a cross word until the end. I don't have a bad memory, other than my guilt at being a bit of a bastard in the end. To wind it down, I started painting myself as a bad guy. I think I did the right thing, but I'm sad it ended up the way it did. I never saw Yvonne again after that!'

9. JINGLES, RADIO & TV COMMERCIALS & NEWSPAPER ADVERTS

By the mid to late 1960s, pop stars were augmenting their income by working in jingle studios. Yvonne was one such pop star. By 1969 she had been involved in the recording of jingles for four years, as well as appearing in magazine and newspaper adverts and other promotional opportunities. Yvonne could be heard on radio singing commercials for such companies as Pict Peas, Budget Rent-a Car and Baker Boy Bread. That same year Doug Parkinson sang on a psychedelic Coca-Cola TV commercial.[317] He also recorded a commercial for Peters Ice-Cream.

Brian Buggy OAM[318], musical director for J.C. Williamson Theatres, wrote many musical arrangements for jingles in 1969. He also sang jingles that year in a group with Yvonne, Ted Hamilton[319], and Dick Healey who was the alto saxophone

---

317 Coca — Cola proved to be a money spinner for pop singers and pop groups. The Executives had appeared in a TV Coke ad the previous year. Singer / songwriter Brian Cadd appeared in an early 1970s Coke ad, as did Ronnie Burns.

318 The Order of Australia recognises Australian citizens and other persons for achievement or meritorious service.

319 By 1955, eighteen-year-old Ted Hamilton was being hailed as a teenage singing sensation because of his performances in nightclubs and on national radio on such programs as *"The Ford Show"*, *"Calling The Stars"* and *"The Gladys Moncrieff Show"*. He'd also had hit records with "Primrose Lane" and "The Things We Did Last Summer". Hamilton was also the featured singer with Australia's premier swing-band the Bob Gibson Band, and the Australian All-Stars jazz quintet. The arrival of television saw Hamilton featured in variety shows on all channels, including *"The Hit Parade"* (ABC), *"Make Mine Music"* (ABC), *"Bandstand"* (Channel 9), and *"Sydney Tonight"* (Channel 7). In 1961-62, Hamilton was a regular on the seminal variety television show *"Revue 61/62"* produced by MCA (America) for the 7 Network. In late 1965, Hamilton compered *"In Melbourne Tonight"* on Monday nights on Channel 9.

player with the Australian Jazz Quartet. The *Listener-In* TV magazine noted that 'their work could be heard in such things as the Radio 3XY themes, and jingles for Four 'N' Twenty Pies, and ICPOTA.'[320] Yvonne also sang on a TV advertisement for the Ford Falcon that year.

The majority of the group's jingles were recorded in Melbourne at Bruce Clarke's "Jingle Workshop". In 1941, sixteen-year-old Bruce Clarke signed up for guitar lessons, while undertaking a gasfitter apprenticeship. Two years later he was teaching guitar. By 1949 Bruce was a fulltime professional musician working in nightclubs and radio orchestras. He accompanied overseas artists on their Australian concert tours and played in dance halls and ballrooms that were the mainstay of pre-television social life. Following the arrival of television in 1956, Bruce moved into film and television music production and composition.

Bruce established his Jingle Workshop in 1957. It produced advertisements which had music and singing as their main features. It quickly became Australia's busiest commercial recording studio, producing radio and TV themes, film scores and jingles. Bruce knew the key to the jingle business was constant invention, so he was always looking for something different.

In 1969 Ted Hamilton OAM[321] was starring in the very popular Australian television police drama series *Division 4*.[322] He was also working solo and in vocal groups providing radio jingles for businesses such as the Gas and Fuel Gas

---

320 'Hey, Isn't That Voice Familiar?', Listener — In TV, November 1st — November 7th 1969.

321 Ted Hamilton was awarded an OAM for service to the performing arts and to the community in the 2013 Australia Day Honours List.

322 Ted appeared in 227 episodes from 1969 to 1974.

Generation and Reg Hunt-Rhodes car dealership group. Ted was one of the busiest and the most in demand for this type of commercial. Ted also provided the voice and image for some of Australia's most popular and successful commercials, namely Craven A, Mac. Robertson Land, ICPOTA[323], Marshall Batteries, Philip Morris (Oh! What a Beauty), Coca-Cola, Kodak, and Louie the fly.

In 1970 Yvonne recorded numerous jingles and radio commercials over thirty-three days during a ten month period.[324] Primarily they were recorded at Bruce Clarke's Jingle Workshop. Yvonne also recorded commercials at W&G (186 Batman Street, West Melbourne) and at Melbourne's Armstrong's Studios[325] that year. She was involved in recording commercials that same year for numerous clients such as Buttercup, Carpet City, Golden Casket, ICPOTA, Pampas, Scholls, Shell, Steam Rollers, Swan Lager, Toyota, and Tuckfields. Yvonne also recorded radio station IDs for Launceston's radio station 7LA.

Ted Hamilton recalls that Dick Healey did most of the arrangements for Bruce Clarke's Jingle Workshop. Dick and Ted would always engage Yvonne to record jingles with them because they enjoyed recording with her, as Ted remembers.

---

323 ICPOTA was short for "In the classified pages of The Age".

324 January, May, August, September were Yvonne's busiest months recording jingles in 1970.

325 Bill Armstrong has been involved in the Melbourne music industry for over 60 years. He had established three record labels (Paramount, Magnasound and Danceland) by the early 1950s. He and his team began recording jingles and pre — recorded music segments in the 1960s for local music programs such as "Sunnyside Up" and the "GO!! Show". Armstrong and Roger Savage teamed up to establish Armstrong Studios in 1965. Russell Morris's "The Real Thing" and Daddy Cool's "Eagle Rock" were just two of many hit records that came out of Armstrong Studios. Source: 'Bill Armstrong: the most prolific music recorder you've never heard of', The Sydney Morning Herald, November 13, 2015.

'I worked with Yvonne on these jingles from the middle 1960s to the end of 1970.

'Yvonne was a lovely girl. She was very down to earth. She had no snobby uppity things. She was a quick study. She had a lot of talent. She had a good voice and she was a good lead singer for vocal groups. She didn't have to sing harmony and she didn't have any vibrato which a lot of the singers had. They were bad group singers because they wobbled all over the place. Yvonne didn't. What she didn't know in music form, she picked up quickly.'

Ted recalls that the group recorded numerous radio station jingles. 'We used to do a whole series of them. Bruce Clarke used to fly me down from Sydney, if I was working up there. I was the lead group singer in most of the commercials I did for Bruce and Bill Armstrong. I could save them studio time because I sight-read[326] instantly what they wanted me to sing. I could sing three and a half octaves, so I had a hell of a lot to do with it. I also wrote music and composed it.'

Whenever female vocals were required, Bruce Clarke engaged Yvonne's services. Ted Hamilton attests to the fact that Yvonne did so much work for Bruce Clarke. 'Yvonne was on most of them that Bruce did. I can't remember all of them, but he did a lot, particularly for regional television and regional radio throughout Australia. We used to do all those television and radio station identifying commercials, particularly for regional television and regional radio throughout Australia. We also did all the *Herald Sun* newspaper commercials.'

Yvonne and Ted Hamilton had a good working relationship. Ted enjoyed engaging in some banter from time to time with

---

326 This means to play or sing written music the first time it is seen.

Yvonne over her looks. 'Yvonne was a very good-looking girl. She was the full package. She looked great and she used to flaunt it too and she knew how to sell it. She used to wear these skin-tight jeans and she had a great arse and legs. I'll always remember that because I used to say to her, "You've got a great arse baby!" I also used to say to her "It's a shame you don't know you've got a good arse and legs darling. You could show them off if you were more aware of it!" She'd look at me and just laugh.'

Ted recalls that Yvonne had one failing, however. 'She used to wear perfume to the point where it was so overpowering. I had to say to her once "Yvonne darling, you're a beautiful girl, but I can smell you before you get to the top of the stairs at Bruce Clarke's Jingle Workshop. Alf Bean was the sound engineer there and we'd often laugh and say, "Yvonne's arrived!"'

'We all arrived on time, but Yvonne would often be late. You'd smell her coming in because she wore this very strong French perfume. She used to douse herself in it. My God it was strong! We'd all be standing round a microphone and all we could smell was her perfume. It got to the point that I had to speak to her about it. I said to her "Yvonne you can't wear that perfume into a cloistered area like a sound studio." Most of the show business gals either have a good sense of humour or they get out of it. Yvonne was a good gal. She responded, but she wasn't too happy about it for a while.'

Yvonne was also part of another vocal group which was primarily formed to sing commercials. The group included John and Anne Hawker and another male singer. They sang jazz arrangements of songs and old standards as well as pop songs.

Born in Melbourne in 1946, Mick Hamilton began playing professionally in rock bands from his mid-teens. He has worked not only as a sideman, but also as band leader, solo performer, record producer and musical director. He has been a member of The Moods (recording "Rum Drunk"), The Vibrants ("Something About You Baby" and "My Prayer"), The Springfield Revival, and the rockabilly band The Mighty Guys.

Mick recalls doing gigs together with Yvonne and also hanging out together with her. 'We also did a few jingle sessions together at the Jingle Workshop. Studio work was my job at the time. Bruce Clarke[327] was a really good jazz guitar player. He used to do a lot of jingles at his little studio. When I was with The Vibrants, we played on quite a few jingles and Yvonne sang on quite a few with us. She was the lead singer on the stuff she did with us.'

Mick is aware that Yvonne recorded 'a lot of jingles. We used to see her at the Jingle Workshop a lot when she was coming out or we were going in or vice versa. She could have been there in other situations as part of a group doing backings. She probably did backups with Pat Carroll and John Farrar too. John used to do that falsetto thing. Lots of times the girls on some of the Melbourne records were actually John and a girl, such as Yvonne or Pat.'

Mick recalls that The Vibrants backed Yvonne on 'a handful' of dances around town. 'Whenever we backed anyone of stature, I was as nervous as buggery! I just didn't want to screw anyone up, particularly someone like Yvonne who was good and someone I liked. She was one of the sweetest and most natural person I've ever met. So, I'd always be so bloody

---

327 Bruce Clarke was honoured with a Medal of the Order of Australia in 2008 for his services to the arts. He died on July 24, 2008 aged 83.

terrified that I wouldn't fully notice what artists did on stage. I had my head down and arse up trying not to stuff it up. We were all winging it to be honest!

'I remember Yvonne being terrific on stage though. She probably wasn't the greatest singer of all the ones around. Lynne Randell had a great voice and not too many measured up to her. Yvonne was a natural performer though. She had the full package. She was really charismatic and sexy on stage. That wasn't diminished at all by the fact that she had a three inch skirt on! But it probably didn't help me concentrate on the charts.

'Yvonne seemed to be totally unaware of her effect on guys, but I'm sure she wasn't. I'm sure she was totally aware of it, but she didn't seem to be using it as a weapon. She appeared to take it in her stride. She didn't seem to be overly flashing herself around. She knew she looked great and she just went for it. When The Vibrants began to have some success, we probably didn't back her as we tended not to back anybody after that. In later years though when we were on a decline, we started backing people again at venues like the Winston Charles. I can't remember if we backed Yvonne there, but she was certainly there all the time. It was the hangout for Yvonne and Sam Anglesey and all of us.'

As well as performing jingles, Yvonne did a number of newspaper and television adverts. In 1965 she appeared in a photographic magazine advert for what would now be known as a child's laxative. That same year Yvonne appeared in newspaper adverts for Guild Chemists. She was pictured showing make up products to a female customer. Yvonne also appeared that year in a newspaper advert for Dafel Dolls &

Bears.[328] She was pictured showing a customer a brush on a neck chain placed around a fluffy pooch toy.

Whilst appearing on the *GO!! Show* in the mid-1960s, Yvonne was chosen to be the seventh pop star colour pin-up featured on the back of Nabisco's Rice Krinkles breakfast cereal packets. Marcie Jones recalls that 'when we were all doing the *GO!! Show*, we were asked to do many things in the way of publicity. I did a milk commercial, and like Yvonne, I had my picture on the back of a Nabisco's Rice Krinkles breakfast cereal packet.'

In 1966 Yvonne recorded a TV commercial for Cadbury's Milk Tray chocolate. She was shown being driven down Melbourne's Beach Road[329] by a young handsome male in a red convertible. During the drive Yvonne was shown sitting in the convertible eating chocolates. Tricia Barrett recalls that Yvonne ended up eating 'about three boxes of chocolates' before the producers of the commercial were satisfied that they had the best possible commercial. She remembers Yvonne being physically sick that night from all the chocolate she ate.

Tricia Barrett also recalls Yvonne being selected to play the role of "Fancy Nancy" in a television advertisement for the Fanta orange soft drink promotion. In costume as "Fancy Nancy", Yvonne was driven by bus to all the Melbourne beaches and to a number of shopping centres over the

---

328 Dafel Dolls and Bears has been operating as a family run business since 1941. It specializes in unique gifts for children including dolls, bears, collectables and miniatures.

329 Beach Road, is a bayside suburban coastal road running along the south-eastern side of Melbourne's Port Phillip Bay. It starts at its southern point in Mordialloc and ends at the intersection of New St and the Esplanade in Brighton. https://en.wikipedia.org/wiki/Beach_Road,_Melbourne

Christmas holiday season and school holidays. She wore an orange wig and bikinis and beach wear whilst promoting the Fanta soft drink as "Fancy Nancy." She also gave away gifts and products.

At that time Yvonne's Adelaide-based friend Kaye Johnston and her husband Bruce were spending a few days with Yvonne and Sam Anglesey at their apartment in Rathdowne Street, Carlton after honeymooning in Tasmania. Yvonne and Sam had been invited to the wedding, but much to their disappointment they couldn't attend the wedding because of work commitments. Yvonne did the next best thing by sending Kaye and Bruce a telegram wishing them all the very best on their special day.[330]

Kaye recalls that Yvonne was involved with the "Fancy Nancy" promotion at the time. 'I never went with Yvonne to a performance while we were in Melbourne, but Bruce did. They went once to a beach and then to a shopping centre. Bruce came home with a bright orange T-shirt which said "I'm a Fancy Nancy fan." He wore that T-shirt till it fell off him.'

Tricia Barrett recalls that Yvonne also appeared as "Fancy Nancy" on Adelaide's beaches and at the city's shopping centres. 'It was a big gig because it occurred during the summer holidays.'

Sam Anglesey remembers that Yvonne enjoyed all aspects of her work. 'She did heaps of advertising jingles at Armstrong studios and lots of other places. I used to do heaps of voice overs, but I didn't appreciate how good a singer Yvonne was until I realised the demand she was in for doing jingles. The jingles were already written, so you've got to sing them the

---

330 Kaye still has Yvonne's telegram.

way they are written. That was pretty challenging, but that's why Yvonne got a lot of work!'

10. "COME AND HAVE A CLOSER LOOK AT THE WAR"

Little did Yvonne and Pat Carroll know when they returned to Australia in January 1966 that they would be selected to tour Vietnam again in a 14-day concert tour in July 1968. Also selected were singer Johnny Chester, comedian Jack Perry, and backing group Jigsaw,[331] which comprised Denis Tucker (bass), Ron Gilbee (rhythm guitar), Ray "Screamy" Eames (lead guitar), and Ollie Fenton (drums).[332]

Denis Tucker recalls that prior to departure for Vietnam a dress rehearsal was held at an old picture theatre in the Melbourne suburb of Fitzroy. 'We got everything fairly right and then it was time to get all our needles done because there were a lot of things to be caught over there.'

The party was due to fly out for Vietnam on July 12th 1968.[333] At the time, however, a national strike by oil tank drivers, over rates of pay and conditions of work, threatened to delay their departure. Nevertheless, all members of the tour arrived at Melbourne's Essendon Airport at 8am hopeful that they

---

331 The Strangers were to have gone to Vietnam but contracts for other work prevented them from leaving Melbourne, hence the selection of Jigsaw.

332 Sadly Ollie was killed after the Vietnam tour while working on Melbourne's South Eastern freeway.

333 Yvonne appeared on ATVO's "Blind Date" program that same day. The episode had been filmed the previous week.

would reach Sydney in time to catch the last Qantas plane out of Sydney at 1pm that day. A 'fuming' Pat Carroll commented to newspaper reporter John Sorrell at the time, 'Heavens I do hope the pilot hurries. All this waiting is affecting my nerves, and I might even lose my voice!'[334] At 10:15 the relieved entertainers flew out for Sydney in an Electra aircraft. Once there they ultimately caught a Pan Am Boeing 707 flight to Singapore via Jakarta.

After an overnight stay in Singapore, the party flew into the Tan Son Nhut airbase,[335] which was located near the city of Saigon in southern Vietnam. There they were met by amenities officer Ron Franck. The party was then taken by bus to the Embassy Hotel in Saigon. That was to be their base for the next five days.

Denis Tucker recalls that the bus had chicken wire on its windows and the driver had a 'great big Armalite rifle sitting beside his pedal. I said to him, "What's the wire for?" He said, "It's so they won't throw hand grenades into the bus."'

Pat Carroll noticed en route to the hotel that since her last trip to Saigon, 'there were more refugees lying on the pavements and in shop doorways. There were also many war-scarred buildings. We passed the racecourse which was the scene of a major battle against the Viet Cong in February 1968. The police post around the corner from our hotel was a grim reminder of how close the war had come to the centre of Saigon. It was partially burnt out and its walls had been pock marked by bullets and rockets.'[336]

---

334 "Up, Up Away...No, Not Today", The Herald, July 12th 1968.

335 The Tan Son Nhut Air Base was a Republic of Vietnam Air Force (VNAF) facility. The United States used it as a major base during the Vietnam War, stationing Army, Air Force, Navy, and Marine units there.

336 'Singer Writes From Vietnam', Listener — In TV, July 27 — August 2nd 1968.

After the party had booked into their hotel, they all met at the bar on the roof of the building for a briefing about the tour from their escort officer Lt. Peter Nichelson. He outlined what they could and couldn't do while in Saigon and on tour.

Johnny Chester had jumped at the opportunity to join the touring party, but he admits that he 'definitely felt concerned' for their safety on arrival in Saigon. 'The Embassy Hotel was the only multi-storey building left standing in Saigon. On our first night there, a civilian suggested we go out on to the hotel's balcony to have a look at the war. So out we go. It was as if we were looking at a big Cinerama screen. You could see bombs exploding after being dropped by the B-52s, flares dropping around the city outskirts, spotlights flashing, and tracer bullets flying through the air. Occasionally you'd hear a rat tat tat and screams. It was quite unreal. But it was like the guy said, "Come and have a look at the war."'[337]

Denis Tucker remembers they all inadvertently ignored an important piece of advice on their arrival in Saigon. 'They told us don't drink the water, but us people from civilisation brush our teeth in it, don't we? By one o'clock in the morning we've all got the "Saigon Shits" and we're fighting over the dunny. A medical officer came around about two o'clock that morning and gave us this powder to take. I asked, "What is it?" He said, "Basically it's opium to knock off the cramps in your gut, and plaster of Paris to bind ya!" That got most of us to the first concert the next day. Yvonne was very sick that first night. So much to her disappointment, she had to miss the troupe's first show the following day.'

Pat Carroll recalls the first show was held at the home for

---

337 Author's interview with Johnny Chester, February 3rd 1991.

the soldiers who worked on headquarters establishments in Saigon. 'When we arrived, we saw that the front of the building was encased in wire to stop people throwing bottles, stones and grenades on to it. There was a security guard on the gate as there was on every important building in Saigon.

'The show was a great success. Two hundred and four soldiers attended the hour and a half show. The sound of the music attracted U.S. servicemen who were passing the building. Afterwards we had tea and talked with the diggers, signing photographs and chatting about home. It was quite touching to see grown men, who were fighting a war, get so excited over a photograph!'[338]

Denis Tucker recalls that the party's shows went for two to three hours from then on. 'Each singer gave us a batch of sheet music of say eight songs. They'd work out the bracket of songs in the order that they'd wanted to do them on that day, and we'd play each song as they wanted it done. Jack Perry would open the shows by telling a few jokes, then he'd introduce Jigsaw. We'd play some stuff and then the girls would come on and do their thing. As soon at that happened all the blokes out the front of the audience would get their cameras out. I'd never seen so many cameras before. Half these guys were so excited though that they didn't notice that the dust lenses were still on their cameras while they were clicking away.'

Johnny Chester knew he had to play up to the audiences if he was to stop them from calling out for more of Yvonne and Pat. 'They didn't wear a great deal of clothing on stage. Yvonne was wearing a see-through net over a white bikini. It was a bit risqué back then. So, I used to go out and say, "You either

---

338 'Singer Writes From Vietnam', Listener — In TV, July 27th — August 2nd 1968.

listen to me or you go home for a cold shower!'" Those remarks from "Chess" would always win the audiences over. After he had finished his set, all the performers would come out on stage for the closing of the show. Johnny counts himself 'very lucky and fortunate to have done the tour. It was a good little show.'[339]

Johnny had the greatest admiration for both Australian and American troops, but he opined that the Australian soldiers were the more responsive audiences. 'At Nui Dat,[340] I asked for a couple of blokes from the audience to sing "Summertime Blues"[341] with me, and who should come up but a soldier who used to be a member of my original group.' [342]

Denis Tucker recalls that the party performed nine shows for American troops and nine for Australian troops. 'We didn't get paid by the Americans for doing their shows. We were paid something like $200 each by the Australian Government. It wasn't a great deal of money, but it was a great experience.

'Each morning our escort officer Peter Nichelson, a lieutenant in the English army, used to jump all over us to get us on the bus to go to an American PX.[343] We'd have our breakfast there, and then it was down to the airport in Tan Son Nhut[344] and we'd fly out to whatever bases we were going to perform at. Sometimes we did two bases a day. If we had

---

339 Author's interview with Johnny Chester, February 3rd 1991.

340 Nui Dat is a former 1st Australian Task Force (1 ATF) base now part of Ba Ria city in Ba Ria-Vung Tau province, Vietnam.

341 Johnny's version of "Summertime Blues" reached No. 30 on the Melbourne charts in 1962.

342 Author's interview with Johnny Chester, February 3rd 1991.

343 PX was Vietnam War — era jargon for a post exchange / military store.

344 The Tan Son Nhut Air Base was a Republic of Vietnam Air Force (VNAF) facility located near Saigon.

to fly a long way away, we'd leave around six or seven in the morning. It was an experience flying around the place.'

Denis observed that segregation was still rife at that time. 'All the African Americans would sit in one place and all the white guys would sit in another. So, we purposely sat with the African Americans!'

The party mostly flew by helicopter to the American bases. Johnny Chester remembers that their helicopters would generally arrive on time to pick them up. 'But on one occasion our helicopter arrived an hour and a half late. We found out later that the helicopter's gearbox had seized during refuelling. It was one of those twin rotor things and it just tore the helicopter in half. The guy refuelling it had his arm pulled right out of its socket. We felt very relieved because the gearbox could have seized in the air.'[345]

Denis Tucker recalls the party played Nuit Dat[346] twice because of what was happening with the Tet Offensive.[347] 'Half the camp got to see us one day and the other half saw us a few days later. We did all the other ones like the American fire bases and a naval base. We'd fly into a base and we'd play and then have a meal in the officer's mess. To be in that mess you had to have rank, so we were made honorary lieutenants in the army.'

The party had to be back in their Saigon hotel by about eight pm because there was a curfew at nine o'clock. According to

---

345 The United States used it as a major base during the Vietnam War, stationing Army, Air Force, Navy, and Marine units there.

346 Nui Dat is a former 1st Australian Task Force (1 ATF) base now part of Ba Ria city in Ba Ria — Vung Tau province, Vietnam.

347 The Tet Offensive was one of the largest military campaigns of the Vietnam War. It was launched on January 30th 1968, by forces of the Viet Cong and North Vietnamese People's Army of Vietnam against the forces of the South Vietnamese Army of the Republic of Vietnam, the United States Armed Forces, and their allies.

Denis, 'There was shit going on all the time! You'd get shot if you were on the streets after the curfew. If it was too far to get back to Saigon before the curfew, we stayed overnight at bases. If that happened, you'd hear the boom, boom, boom sound of gunships[348] rocketing places all night. It was pretty frightening in some places. We were told if a fight started we would be whisked away in helicopters and our gear would be replaced if it got blown up. We stayed in a group and we were pretty close. If we were gonna die, we were going to die together. I think we were all insured for $25,000 each.'

Denis recalls Yvonne and Pat being 'a little edgy and a bit feisty together because Yvonne used to go with John Farrar. Now all of a sudden Pat was with John, and Pat and Yvonne were on the same tour.'

Jeff Lander and Ron Golding arrived in Vietnam as national servicemen on December 10th 1967 and December 11th 1967 respectively.[349] Both were stationed at 2AOD (Advanced Ordnance Depot) in Vung Tau. Their role was to supply stores, clothing, weapons, weapon parts, ammunition, and equipment to all bases where Australian troops were in Vietnam.

Jeff's first day in the army was February 1st 1967. He spent three months at Puckapunyal doing basic training, then three months at Bonegilla undertaking core training. He then spent six weeks at Moorebank before leaving for Vietnam.

Prior to leaving Australia, Jeff was a regular viewer of Australian music shows on TV. He remembers first seeing Yvonne on the *GO!! Show*. 'I'd admired Yvonne as a performer before she came to Vietnam to entertain the troops. So it was

---

348 A gunship is a military aircraft armed with heavy guns, primarily intended for attacking ground targets.

349 Jeff and Ron left Vietnam in December 1968.

a real thrill when she and Pat Carroll came over to make our lives a little easier. When you have a bunch of blokes living in a pretty well all-bloke environment for a long time, and you have two pretty Australian girls come over to lift your spirits, then certainly they're going to succeed. When it was someone like Yvonne, it just made it ten times easier!'

Jeff recalls seeing the show at the Badcoe Club in Vung Tau.[350] 'This was the first time I'd seen Yvonne perform on stage. Seeing her reinforced how I'd previously thought of her as a performer. She had everything going for her. She was talented, attractive, very friendly, down to earth and she could sing. She held the audience in the palm of her hand. Everyone was taken with her.' Jeff has never forgotten how lovely Yvonne was. 'She was very easy to chat to. That's why I had such a big smile on my face in the photo I had taken with Yvonne.

'Yvonne and Pat Carroll visited our unit after their show. They wanted to meet the boys in their own environment, so they rocked up in the OR's (Other Ranks) mess. They were both happy to talk to us. They quizzed us about our thoughts and feelings. It made us feel that they weren't just doing it as a façade; rather they were genuinely concerned about what was happening in Vietnam.'

Jeff remembers Pat not being as amenable to the photo opportunity as Yvonne was. 'I would have liked to have had my photo taken with her, but she wasn't as approachable as Yvonne. Instead she gave out autographed photos of herself, but they were pre-processed. She was very nice, but Yvonne was friendlier. You can't underestimate the effect this has on people, especially in Yvonne's case, when she was so lovely.

---

350 The club was named after Major Peter Badcoe who lost his life in Vietnam on April 7th 1967. He was posthumously decorated with the Victoria Cross.

She reminded me about everything that was good about home. It was absolutely sensational to find a girl like Yvonne, that you could have met at a local dance. She made you feel so comfortable. It was almost like she had the ability to transport you back to Australia. When you were talking to her, it was just like you were talking to a girl at home.'

Ron Golding placed his name on the list to go overseas because at that time, to get any benefits out of the two years of National Service, you needed to go overseas to be eligible for a war service loan. Ron recalls that 'it was during the end of the national service period, that the then government changed it to a Defence Service Loan which made anyone in the Defence Force eligible to apply for that loan at the time. By going to Vietnam, I became eligible. I was initially eligible for an $8,000 loan to build a new home, but before I finally took the loan up it had risen to $25,000. So that was a hell of a help to me at the time!'

Ron met Yvonne the same day as Jeff Lander. 'We introduced ourselves and she told me a little bit about herself and her background. Yvonne was very friendly, down to earth and lovely to talk to. She didn't hesitate to walk around off stage and have a photograph taken with me. I've kept that photo. At the time, Jeff Lander and I swapped cameras. I took a photo of him with Yvonne and he took one of me with her. I can still picture Yvonne in her little mini dress. It was good to get an Australian female entertainer up on stage in a mini!'

Ron remembers having 'a can of bloody Reece's beer' in his hand when the photo with Yvonne was taken. 'I've never heard of that beer since. I think it was a New South Wales beer. We couldn't get our own beer which was the Swan beer.

It didn't travel well. It used to go off. VB was the main beer, so I acquired a taste for VB.'

Ron and his colleagues looked forward to visits by entertainment groups. 'It was a hell of a thing to receive these people who had volunteered to entertain the troops. Their visits gave us a lift. They spoke about what was happening back home and they were very forthcoming with their positive comments about us being in Vietnam and the job we were doing. They said people at home were very supportive of them coming up there to entertain us.' Ron remembers the whole group being very friendly. 'They weren't there just to do a show. They were there to make us feel comfortable with them after their show as well.'

For one Australian soldier in particular, the troupe's 1968 visit held special significance. Seventeen-year-old Peter James joined the Army in 1966 because he wanted to see the world. Peter was really excited when he heard Yvonne was coming to his 2nd Advanced Ordnance Depot unit in Vung Tau. Like Yvonne, Peter had gone to Braybrook Primary School. Peter recalls that Yvonne was two grades ahead of him and she didn't come to his notice until grade six which was her last year at the school.

Peter remembers that Yvonne sang and danced in a talent show put on by her grade. 'She stood out because she was just so good. I was secretly in love with her. At the time I was about eight and Yvonne would have been about eleven. I had to walk past her house to get to school. She was pretty popular at school and very nice to look at. Even though I was young, I knew she was going to be somebody. I've always remembered her because of that talent show.'

Peter got 'really excited' when he heard that Yvonne was visiting his unit in Vietnam. He told whoever would listen to him that he used to go to the same school as Yvonne. 'As it turned out our unit was chosen to supply lunch during their visit. One of the senior sergeants introduced me to Yvonne as being "Peter James who went to school with you. Do you remember him?" She said, "I think so", but I could see she didn't.'

Nevertheless, Peter was given the job of looking after Yvonne during lunch. 'I asked Yvonne what she'd like to drink. She said, "What have you got?" I told her beer, spirits, and Barossa pearl. She said she'd have a glass of Barossa pearl. She had a few of those. While I was looking after Yvonne, we talked about the Braybrook Primary school, its principal and the show she did which so impressed me years before.'

Peter recalls them being 'interrupted constantly by blokes wanting to have photos with Yvonne. I had my photo taken with her but it got lost over the years. I'm afraid the members of my unit didn't behave themselves very well at lunch. They forgot their manners. They were reaching over us and grabbing handfuls of food. I apologised to Yvonne saying we were not normally like that. She just laughed and said, "Don't worry. We don't get this sort of treatment very often!"'

Peter attended a show at the Badcoe Club a night or two following the unit lunch. He recalls it being a very emotional time for all those who saw Yvonne, Pat Carroll, Johnny Chester and Jigsaw perform that night. 'Seeing them reminded me of home. Having grown up in Braybrook like Yvonne, I felt very emotional seeing her perform for half an hour or so. She was very popular singing the songs of the day and she received much of the cat calling, whistling and thunderous applause. I felt very proud of her that night.'

Seeing Ray "Screamy" Eames playing guitar on stage with Jigsaw also brought back memories for Peter. 'Ray lived in the same street as Yvonne in Braybrook. When I was in primary school he used to drive around in a sky-blue Studebaker. Ray told me that the Studebaker was the best car he ever had.'

Peter James never saw Yvonne again after that night. After his discharge from the Army in 1969, he obtained a part time job at the Ashley Hotel in Braybrook. Yvonne's father Ted was a regular at that pub. Peter recalls that 'we used to call Ted "Snowy" because of his silver coloured hair. We looked after him big time because he was Yvonne's father. Ole Ted was a bit of a drunk, but he was a very friendly character. Everybody loved him.'[351]

Denis Tucker recalls his father Bert and Yvonne's father Ted being drinking mates at the Ashley. He describes them as being 'two ole farts sitting in the corner of the hotel bullshitting to each other!'

John Hosie was a national serviceman who found out in recent years that his birth date was never pulled out in a ballot! 'I had been in the CMF SR (Supplementary Reserve) in the 91st Forestry Squadron RAE and I must have said "Yes" to a question about whether I would join the Nashos!'

Nevertheless, John found himself in Vung Tau, South Vietnam in 1968 serving with 17 Construction Squadron, Royal Australian Engineers. John doesn't remember many performers coming to "Vungers", but the show at the Peter Badcoe Club in

---

351 Peter re-joined the army in 1979, but five years later he was discharged with what is now known as post-traumatic stress disorder (PTSD). 'That was a pity as all I ever wanted to be was a soldier.'

Vung Tau was one he recalls well. 'We didn't see many women for many months, so I was a little overawed with seeing an Australian woman, let alone a singer! Hearing songs of the day from back home performed by such beauties as Yvonne and Pat reminded us how much we wanted to go home. Their performance on stage was appreciated and warmly received.'

The Ninth Infantry Division's weekly publication *The Old Reliable* reported on the troupe's performances at the informal celebration of the 9th Division's 50th Anniversary at the US Army's Bearcat military base[352] on July 18th and 19th 1968. 'Although sponsored by the Australian Forces Overseas Fund, the troupe, which had primarily come to Vietnam to entertain Australian troops, were obtained for special shows at Dong Tam and Bearcat before American forces.

'Emceed by Jack Perry, 51, comedian and TV — radio veteran, the Bearcat show opened with familiar American and British songs performed by the "Jigsaw" band. Next on the program was Yvonne Barrett, 22, a tawny beauty whose songs included "New Orleans", "You Don't Have To Say You Love Me" and a medley of Trini Lopez hits. She was followed by Johnny Chester, 27, a versatile singer with an urbane style who gave hard working renditions of rock'n'roll, country and western and traditional ballads. Pat Carroll, 22, a svelte mini-skirted brunette, was next, performing a medley of Supremes hits.'[353]

Once the tour was over, each performer was presented with a "Department of Defense United States Military Assistance Command, Vietnam (MACV) Certificate of Appreciation"[354] in

---

352 Located near the city of Biên Hòa in Đồng Nai Province in southern Vietnam.

353 '50th Festivities', The Old Reliable: Vol.2, No. 30 Republic of Vietnam — July 31st 1968.

354 Signed on July 26th 1968 by Creighton W. Abrams, General, United States Army Commanding.

recognition of their "outstanding contribution to the morale and welfare of the United States and other free world military assistance forces in the Republic of Vietnam while touring the Command, entertaining personnel of all services. The significant and lasting impression you made enhanced the morale of the fighting forces and reflects great credit upon yourself and your profession."

Denis Tucker remembers his thoughts upon his return to Australia on July 30th 1968. 'Vietnam was a real eye opener. I never thought, "Why did I do this?" It was a good thing to do because the boys were over there putting their lives on the line all the time. I don't know about the others, but the best experience for me was feeling those wheels touch the runway at Essendon Airport again. We were all pleased to get back to peace and to reality. You don't realise how good Australia is till you get out of it!'

When Yvonne and Pat Carroll flew into Melbourne on July 30th 1968, they told a reporter that they had a 'constant "wet nurse", namely a British Army officer, on their fourteen-day entertainment tour in Vietnam. 'The girls said Lt. Peter Nichelson, 23, who is with the Australian Army for five years, "treated us like soldiers." Pat said "He gave us orders and we weren't allowed to do anything without him saying so. He was a wet nurse, mother, father, the lot!"'

Pat Carroll describes the two Vietnam Tours as being really exciting. 'When we first went there, I didn't realise how awful it was. Maybe I was just young and naïve the first time. I think I was optimistic that the war wouldn't drag on for long. I thought it was all Betty Grable and what you see in the movies of her entertaining troops and everything. They treated us very well and I really enjoyed doing it. We definitely had a lot of laughs and fun, and we all loved the performing part of it.'

Tricia Barrett recalls that Yvonne didn't talk much to her about the two tours of Vietnam, 'except to say that they had a couple of scares in a helicopter. She said she got scared when they were fired on. The party had one close call in particular when their helicopter suddenly dived to within twenty feet of the ground to avoid artillery fire.' Tricia remembers Yvonne coming back to Australia from one of the Vietnam trips quite ill. 'She couldn't eat and she'd lost a lot of weight. She never put that weight back on and we never knew what it was. She said they were treated well by the Australians, but not by Bob Hope's manager on the first tour.'

Sam Anglesey remembers Yvonne speaking to him briefly about the 1968 tour of Vietnam on her return home. 'She had a good team of people with her and she said she absolutely enjoyed the experience. She was very personable, and the troops went mad over her. One of my cousins was involved in the war, so she signed all his underdaks with kisses. His mates went wild over those autographed underdaks!'

On her return to Australia, Yvonne was also quoted as saying that she regarded the tour as being 'the highest point of her career so far. The experience could never be equalled!'[355]

From Christmas 1965 to 1971, more than 300 Australian entertainers were sent officially to Vietnam. Although some were big names on the Australian scene, the poor financial rewards and demanding schedules ensured that most were young hopefuls. One of the hoped for results of officially sponsored entertainment was to demonstrate support for the

---

355 "They Gave Diggers A Kick", The Herald, July 30th 1968.

war among those idolised by the young. Unfortunately for the Government, its penny-pinching funding attracted few big names. To make matters worse for the Government, as the war wore on, the young took to the streets increasingly, to demonstrate against the Australian presence in Vietnam.

The Vietnam Veterans' Commemorative Walk (VVCW) in Seymour, Victoria is the only one of its kind in Australia dedicated to Vietnam Veterans. The Walk has been created using symbolic elements of Vietnam and over 60,000 names of every serviceman and servicewoman who served in the conflict are listed. Denis Tucker has his own paver inscribed "Denis Tucker Entertainer July 1968" at the VVCW.

Denis always had a lot of time for Yvonne. He describes her as being 'a beautiful and lovely person. She was serious at times, and fun at times.' In a very kind gesture, Denis paid for a paver for Yvonne to be inscribed "Yvonne Barrett Entertainer July 1968" at the Vietnam Veterans' Commemorative Walk.

In December 1993, Sheila Barrett received a letter from the Commanding Officer of the Australian Army's Soldier Career Management Agency. The letter, pertaining to the "Issue of the Vietnam Logistic and Support Medal", read as follows: "Dear Mrs Barrett, please find enclosed the Vietnam Logistic and Support Medal[356] awarded in respect of your daughter, Yvonne Barrett, for her service in support of the Australian Armed Forces in operations in Vietnam. The award was approved by the Governor General on Schedule VLSM8/93 dated 19 November 1993."[357]

---

356 Yvonne's Vietnam Logistic and Support Medal is now housed at the Australian War Memorial (AWM) in Canberra.

357 xxvii The medal, made of nickel silver, was awarded to qualifying personnel "for service of one day or more" in the area of Vietnam operations.

11. "YVONNE'S EYE POPPERS"

On October 28th 1967, shortly after relocating from Brisbane to Melbourne, Ross D. Wyllie became the host of *Uptight*, a new four hour pop music television show for the ATVO Channel. *Uptight* aired every Saturday from 8am until 12pm.[358] Ross had a No. 17 hit on *Go-Set's* National Top 40 in July 1969, with his cover of the Ray Stevens song "Funny Man". He followed that up with a No. 1 hit, "The Star" in November 1969.

Ross thought very highly of Yvonne. 'Outside of television, I didn't see her that much, but I enjoyed working with her on *Uptight*. It wasn't just me. Everybody across the board thought the same. You just warmed to her. She was lovely. She didn't take herself seriously for a start, and she didn't have a big head. She was quietly spoken and she was never a problem.'

Ross recalls Yvonne being nicknamed Gracie in the *Uptight* days. He doesn't recall being responsible for giving Yvonne that nickname, but he says 'I'll take the blame for it.'

Ross remembers Yvonne appearing on *Uptight* one Saturday morning wearing a tiny green sleeveless top which was held together by a safety pin. 'Yvonne wasn't well endowed in the breast department, and she wasn't one for wearing a bra. So the girls used to band aid her breasts together to give her a

---

358 *"Uptight"* closed in 1969.

bit of a cleavage for television. The safety pin gave way this particular morning and she ended up flashing what very little boobs she had.'

Carmel Chayne[359] first met Yvonne on the *GO!! Show.*[360] She remembers Yvonne being 'a total little stunner! I say that as a woman and as a peer. She was different to everyone else. She was intriguing, a very free spirit, and so sexy. At times we would work at the same dance on the same night. All the guys in the bands and at the shows used to look at her a lot different to how they looked at some of us. They really liked us girls, but "Gracie" had a look about her that was really beautiful!'

Kel Monaghan[361] recalls backing Yvonne 'a lot' as a member of The Bobby James Syndicate.[362] 'In those days, if it was a town hall gig, they'd have three or four bands on, and they'd also have half a dozen solo acts. Carmel might sing three songs, then Little Gulliver might sing three, or Yvonne might come

---

359 Carmel Chayne's singing career began in 1964 with a group called "The Soul Four". Olivia Newton John was also in the group. When that group folded, Carmel formed a folk group which subsequently won "Kevin Dennis New Faces". While singing at the "Tom Katz" dance in Sorrento, the club owner offered to manage her. This led to Carmel being booked to perform on the *"Go!! Show"*. Those appearances led to Carmel being offered a regular spot on *"Uptight"*. Carmel's solo career blossomed and saw her become a regular at dances and discotheques around Melbourne and interstate.

360 Carmel made three appearances in 1966 on the *"GO!!Show"* (May 30th, June 20th and August 8th). Carmel recalls singing "Tar and Cement" and "The Sign Of The Times" on the show.

361 Kel learnt to play the guitar as a youngster. He formed his first band "The Fugitives" at the end of 1964. That band folded, so Kel formed "The Trio Plus One" which consisted of himself, the three other members of "The Fugitives" and Issy Di. Sometime later he became a member of The Bobby James Syndicate. He worked with Ronnie Burns for a year, and then teamed up with John Perry from The Vibrants for a short period. Some time after that Kel formed a group called "Crimson". Carmel Chayne, Kenny Leroy and Gary Howard were also in the group. Over the next few years the group performed in Singapore, Hong Kong, Thailand, Indonesia, Surabaya and the Philippines on six monthly contracts.

362 The band consisted of Bobby James and Carmel Chayne (vocals), Kel Monaghan (keyboards), Darryl Feddon (drums), Doug Sterling (bass) and Lindsay Shah (guitar).

and sing three. I remember there being half a dozen bands at some of the dances. You'd set up all your gear and you'd only play maybe fifteen minutes, then another band would come on. Then a vocalist would come on.

'This would have been at the beginning of 1966. We also worked at the Menzies, Savoy and London hotels a lot. Then we'd play the Swinger dances and that's where we would back acts like Yvonne, Pat Carroll, Bev Harrell, Dinah Lee, Frankie Davidson and other Sydney acts.' Kel and Carmel recall Yvonne singing 'in the same style' as Dionne Warwick, Dusty Springfield, and Cilla Black. 'That's because it was the style of the time. You didn't do anything out of the norm in those days. You played what you were hearing.'

Kel remembers backing Yvonne one particular night in a floor show at either the Menzies Hotel or the Savoy Plaza. 'After the show Yvonne said to me, "Hey let's go and get a coffee together." I thought, "Wow this is really cool!" I would have been eighteen or nineteen at the time and I was absolutely star struck! Yvonne was just the hottest, sexiest, stunning girl around! I don't remember everything we talked about over coffee, except her saying that we should get together the next week and go out. I could tell that she really liked me. But at that time I was just the guitar player in the band and I felt like I was punching above my weight. We probably could have had some sort of relationship, but I felt that was beyond me.'

Carmel Chayne recalls that she really got to know Yvonne when she was a regular on ATVO's *Uptight*. 'Yvonne was on *Uptight* quite a few times when I was on. That's where I really remember Yvonne's stunningness from. She would be the one with the shortest skirt and the little cut outs on her tops. I remember watching the guys go, "Wow, I like this chick!" Yet at the same time, she'd be very classy. Yvonne could be aloof and very intriguing, but I never heard a bad word said about her!'

Carmel never ever felt disrespected by any performer. 'It was a lovely innocent time. We looked forward to seeing each other. The boys cherished us. I never had anything put on me by either bands or promoters. Maybe the guys were like that with the female fans, but they weren't with the female entertainers.' Kel Monaghan concurs. 'There was a very strong camaraderie because it was all so new and so fresh and everyone was finding their feet.'

At the time Lily Brett was pursuing a career as a pop music journalist. She interviewed Yvonne and Carmel for an article she wrote for *Go-Set*[363] about the problems facing female singers. Carmel told Lily Brett that she echoed Yvonne's opinion that one of the difficulties of being a female singer was that the boys couldn't show their appreciation at dances. 'You saw it happening all the time. The boys take a girl to the dance, and they're really frightened to smile or whistle at you. When they try, there is invariably a girl standing next to them, digging them in the ribs and glaring, while the boys are only trying to show you that they like you as an artist.'

Yvonne commented that 'it is mostly girls who buy records. They tend to buy those recorded by groups, or single male artists, unless a girl comes up with a really good sound. I suppose it's because most girls, apart from working or going to school, have got nothing much else to do, except think of boys. So, they become really devoted fans, while boys of the

---

363 Brett wrote for "Go-Set" from May 1966 to September 1968. She ultimately moved to the USA and achieved success as a novelist, essayist and poet.

same age have got many other interests and hobbies, such as cars, football and other sports.'[364]

Shortly thereafter Yvonne discussed her theory, with a show business reporter, as to why females predominantly attended teen shows in Australia. 'Boys,' she said, 'are too preoccupied with their cars and Meccano sets to come to teen shows. Girls have less to do and are reputedly more emotional. And the boys who do come prefer taking out girl singers than screaming at them from the audience.' She added that this was harrowing, particularly for a female vocalist at many "mod" dances, where young girls came with each other, danced with each other, and waited impatiently for their favourite male singers to appear. 'You can guess how I feel coming on after a popular male singer,' Yvonne said, suppressing a shudder. 'It's frightening. You wonder who in this entire female audience is going to cheer you!'

Yvonne had no cause to worry. Girls not only cheered her, they wrote to her, phoned her, and even called at her home in Braybrook. Children from a nearby school visited her almost every afternoon. 'Most times they want autographs,' Yvonne said. 'And one little boy, I've just found out, sells blocks of them. Good luck to him.'

Yvonne went on to discuss her career ambitions. 'I want to get to the top; right up there on top; with a hit record, interstate recognition, and overseas recognition. I'm going to be something someday.' The reporter predicted that based on the way Yvonne said it with those blue eyes simmering, fantasy seemed only one jump ahead of fact! In this instance, it's quite possible that Yvonne was saying what she thought the reporter and fans wanted to hear at that time!

---

364 Lily Brett Reports — 'The Problems facing Girls On The Pop Scene,' Go — Set, August 3rd 1966.

At the time Yvonne was averaging a cool $100 a week. 'That's when I'm singing at only four dances a week,' Yvonne said in some awe to the reporter. He suggested that after adding this to the income she earnt from television shows and commercials, Yvonne was earning a fair living for a teenager. He went on to say 'That's why Yvonne can afford coloured stockings and shoes to match every dress in her wardrobe, slack suits by the dozen, and her most recent purchase, an $80 guitar. She's taking lessons from John Farrar so she will be able to rehearse herself.'[365] By way of relaxing, Yvonne and John Farrar looked forward to the weekends so that they could go horse riding at the Lysterfield riding school.

Yvonne's mother wasn't worried about success coming to Yvonne too soon. 'Mum knows that my idea of a good party is a few people who can talk, dance the frug[366], and enjoy food like oysters, crayfish or just fish and chips,' said Yvonne.[367]

In early November 1968, Yvonne appeared at the Junior Sailor's Club at HMAS Albatross located in Nowra, New South Wales. The club had a reputation for always providing good fun for their audiences. The Navy News magazine noted that 'When well-known singers Yvonne Barrett and Ian Logan paid a visit they were popular; well naturally when you looked at Yvonne.'

Yvonne chose not to wear a daring outfit this particular night as she knew her act was to be followed by 'an extra special attraction' namely the appearance of Candy Barr[368],

---

365 'The Pied Pipers Of Pop — Aiming For a BIG Name — That's Yvonne Barrett', The Herald, September 12th 1966.

366 The Frug was a dance craze from the mid-1960s, which included vigorous dancing to pop music.

367 'The Pied Pipers Of Pop — Aiming For a BIG Name — That's Yvonne Barrett', The Herald, September 12th 1966.

368 Candy Barr's real name was Juanita Dale Slusher.

an American stripper, burlesque dancer, actress, and adult model in men's magazines of the mid-20th century. It was a smart move on Yvonne's part as it was reported the next day that Candy Barr 'put on a real wild performance, which had the boys whistling and cheering. Nobody tried to socialise with her due to a rather large threat in the form of a certain LA handler who warned everybody in no uncertain terms to stay clear of the stripper.'[369]

Yvonne subsequently flew to Perth in mid-November 1968 for two weeks of singing engagements in that city's night clubs. She then flew to Tasmania for more singing engagements before returning to Melbourne to prepare for a three-week cabaret engagement in *Copacabana* at the Lido Theatre Restaurant. Yvonne hadn't previously appeared in a show such as this, so gone were the days of teenage dances, at least for the time being. She would now be swapping her mini-skirts for glittering costumes.

When Melbourne's Tivoli theatre closed in 1966, the genre of erotic performance found audiences in theatre restaurants such as the lavish Lido Theatre Restaurant situated in Russell Street. Millionaire David H. McIlwraith[370] bought the Lido in 1965. He came from a very wealthy plumbing family, so no expense was spared with his productions. He presented revues, in the continental style, with a chorus of showgirls, some nude, and with talent drawn from both television and stage.

McIlwraith's exotic Latin American Revue *Copacabana* ran from January 25th until February 18th 1969. Yvonne sang three production numbers including "Brazil" and "Heat Wave"

---

369 'A Night At Albatross,' *Navy News*, November 8th 1968.

370 McIlwraith had been a dancer and choreographer. At that time, he was known as David Hamilton.

while fronting six shapely female dancers. She also performed several dance routines in the production. *Copacabana* also starred Bill & Fuji, who performed an amazing escape act and acrobatic thrills, as well as songs and dancing from the varied talent of Ron Lees, Antonio Rodgrigues, Nino Palermo's Latin American Music, and The Lido Girls.

Brenda (Long) Halman danced as a performer on the Lido's lush green velvet revolving stage for a time. She observed that David McIlwraith 'was miles before his time. He had a vision and he loved the theatre. When we worked, we had the best of everything, including beautiful costumes. We'd do four different shows at times. Tuppy Downs[371] did all the choreography.'

A day before *Copacabana* opened Yvonne told a reporter that David McIlwraith used to teach her dancing. 'I auditioned for him about six months ago and he said he would remember me if a suitable show came up. I wasn't surprised that I was offered this job. It's impossible to compare my job in *Copacabana* with pub work. I would like to continue in production singing, but unfortunately, it's restricted in Australia to the Lido. After the show has finished its three-week season I shall return to dances and hotel work. These jobs have little prestige but provide a regular income.'

When asked by the same reporter if she would consider performing overseas, Yvonne said she was hesitant about going overseas. 'Why go overseas and starve when there's so much work here!' When pressed further on the subject, Yvonne said she would only go to Europe. 'But before I went, I would want a contract signed and my fare paid.' [372]

---

371 Tuppy Downs was May Downs daughter.
372 'Now It's Cabaret Work For Yvonne,' *The Herald*, January 24th 1969.

Another reporter subsequently noted that the six female dancers in the production were 'young and gay[373] and pretty, and the same applies especially to a young woman named Yvonne Barrett who combines bodily beauty with a clear unpretentious voice.'[374] Yet another reporter noted the 'best of the items' in *Copacabana* was "Heat Wave" sung by Yvonne.[375]

Yvonne subsequently appeared in David H. McIlwraith's lavish American Cabaret Revue *Touch & Go* which ran at the Lido from February 19th to March 5th 1969. The revue starred the incomparable Eartha Kitt, the Fantastic Allisons, Ron Lees and the Fabulous Lido Girls. Born in 1927, Kitt was an American singer, actress, dancer, activist, voice actress and comedian. Known for her highly distinctive singing style, Kitt had U.S. Top 10 hits with "C'Est Si Bon", "Santa Baby" and "Just An Old Fashioned Girl".

After seeing Yvonne's performance in the revue, a reporter noted that Yvonne 'had great potential in cabaret if given the right opportunities and coaching.'[376] Another reporter suggested that, although Yvonne only sings "Heat Wave" in the revue, 'it is a thrill enough appearing with a star of Eartha Kitt's magnitude, and it marks the peak so far in Yvonne's career in show business. It's hard work, and expensive too, if you are as versatile as Yvonne Barrett, whose repertoire includes pop and adult songs and what she describes as "semi adult."

'Immediately following the closure of *Touch & Go*, Yvonne began a short engagement at the Winston Charles nightclub in South Yarra. A holiday is what she hoped for when she finished

---

373 Meaning 'jovial or happy'.
374 'Economy Show But Still Good', The Herald, January 26th 1969.
375 'Hot Rhythms At The Lido', Listener — In TV, January 30th 1969.
376 'Eartha's Back,' Listener-In TV, February 15th — 21st 1969.

at the Winston Charles. But if the demand for her talents continues, she knows that she may have to postpone it.'[377]

That's exactly what happened. Yvonne's plans for a well-deserved holiday didn't eventuate. After completing her engagement at the Winston Charles, she flew to Queensland for appearances in mid-March at Brisbane's Cloudland Ballroom, the Dog Patch cabaret disco in Strathfield, and Ipswich's Damien's Disco and Wonderland Ballroom. She then performed several shows at Bicky's Cabaret in Surfers Paradise.

Show business reporter Tony Underwood reviewed one of Yvonne's performances at Bicky's Cabaret. He noted that 'Yvonne bounced on to the stage in a low cut mini-skirt. Her first number was a powerful rendition of "Always Something There To Remind Me". In her next number "Can't Take My Eyes Off You", she stepped off the stage displaying a tantalising length of leg and provocative hip movements. Following this Yvonne swung gently through the appealing, slow-tempoed "You Don't Have To Say You Love Me." She began very softly through the minor- keyed section of the song, coming on strongly through the beefier middle-eight part of the song, which changes to major and then key-changes up for a thrilling finale.

'Yvonne is a natural vocalist with a wealth of experience in the live entertainment field. To complete the picture, she is gorgeous. One of her best performed brackets was a Trini Lopez one because of the relative simplicity of the backing of these medley numbers. Included were "Gonna Get Along Without You Now", "If I Had A Hammer" and "The More I See You".'

Tony Underwood went on to say that 'Yvonne then introduced

---

377 'The Story of a Star,' Sunshine Advocate, February 27th 1969.

some rather interesting variations on the traditional "bump and grind" normally reserved for a stripper, during the next number. This was "Big Spender" originally recorded by Peggy Lee, and later by Shirley Bassey. One man was completely carried away by Yvonne's presentation. He presented himself, blinking in the spotlight, on stage. He thought he'd received an invitation. A member of Bicky's staff informed him that "stage invitations" were rarely given out and when they were, they were only given to recognised artists. So, the man sat down. Yvonne finished her performance and the crowd yelled for more.'[378]

On April 15th 1969 Yvonne appeared on ATV0's *The Johnny Farnham Special*. The special was compered by Jimmy Hannan and starred Johnny Farnham and guests including Ross D. Wyllie, The Strangers, Yvonne, Carmel Chayne, and The Gingerbread Revue. The highlight for Yvonne was singing a duet of "That Old Black Magic" with Johnny Farnham. The *Herald* reporter Grant Aldous noted that Yvonne's act was polished. 'She looked good and sang strongly!'[379] That same month, Yvonne appeared twice on GTV9's *In Melbourne Tonight*.

Patti (McGrath) Newton recalls doing many duets on *In Melbourne Tonight* with Yvonne and with Pat Carroll. 'They used to get a group of different singers together. We would do a musical comedy number choreographed by Joe Latona. We were often put in these production numbers because we could all sing and dance. We all had our own solo careers as well.'

On May 12th 1969 the Melbourne press reported that former Seekers' guitarist and singer Keith Potger had announced

---

378 'Yvonne is Gorgeous and Entertaining', Gold Coast Bulletin, March 14th 1969.

379 'Johnny's TV Show Looks Like A Hit', The Herald, April 16th 1969.

from London that he was planning to start his own group modelled on the original Seekers. One report noted that Potger and his manager David Joseph were understood to be searching for possible members for the new group. 'Mr Joseph telephoned his office (Jardin Productions) yesterday asking for photographs and tapes of three Melbourne singers to be sent to London as soon as possible. The singers are Yvonne Barrett, Carmel Chayne and Julie Ann Oliver.'

The report noted that Yvonne had said that she was considering the offer to join the new group. "If I joined the group, it would seriously affect my ambitions to become a top dancer," she said. "But I haven't entirely thrown the idea out the window." Carmel Chayne was said to be currently touring Vietnam and couldn't be readily contacted. 'The strongest tip is Julie Ann Oliver of the Greenwood singers.'[380]

Shortly thereafter *TV Week* magazine announced that Yvonne had turned down Keith Potger's initial offer to be the "voice" of a new Seekers-style group he was hoping to form. 'The offer was not concrete enough,' Yvonne told us. But when this edition went to press, further talks were in progress between Yvonne and Keith.'[381]

Two days later, a press report announced that renewed rumours that members of The Seekers were planning to reform the group with a new girl singer were disclaimed by former Seekers' spokesman Athol Guy. 'The rumours started afresh when it was learned that Keith Potger, the Seeker who remained in London, had invited Melbourne singer Yvonne Barrett to join a vocal group he was starting in London. Athol

---

380 'New Seekers', The Herald, May 12th 1969.

381 TV Week, May 15th 1969.

Guy said this week that it was quite possible that Keith was planning a new group. 'But he certainly couldn't call it The New Seekers or anything like that unless more of us were in it,' Athol said.'

The report added that Yvonne had rejected Keith Potger's offer in a phone call to London on Monday night, May 12th. Yvonne was quoted as stating that Keith Potger had never mentioned the possibility of Athol Guy or Bruce Woodley being in the group. 'But he asked me not to disclose the details,' she said. 'I decided to turn down the offer because it wasn't concrete enough. Besides, it was not what I had planned for myself. I am a trained dancer, and I want to work so that I can use that ability.'[382]

Tricia Barrett comments that Yvonne never wanted to go overseas. 'She was a homebody!' Tricia's daughter Martine agrees. 'There's not many of us in the family. I think that's why she didn't want to go overseas. She really appreciated what Nana had done for her, so she wasn't going to leave her.'[383] Moreover Yvonne had a busy schedule in ensuing months, including several appearances on GTV9's *In Melbourne Tonight*, HSV7's new teenage show *Turning On* and *Seven's Club Show*. She was also booked to appear with 'swinging' Miss Frances Faye in David H. McIlwraith's Lido production *Wild Wild West Revue Gay's The Word* from June 2nd to 12th 1969.

The fifty-six-year-old Faye was a cabaret and show tune singer and pianist whose double-entendre songs and throaty laughter made her a favourite on the Los Angeles saloon scene. Reviews of her Lido performances varied, however. One

---

382 'Guy Denies New Seekers Rumours', Listener — In TV, May 17th 1969.
383 Yvonne was Martine's Godmother.

Melbourne reviewer described her as being a 'good pianist and a better singer, but as a comedienne, she is at best a poor man's Phyllis Diller.'[384] The same reviewer noted that Yvonne was what the program said, 'talented and beautiful.'[385] Another reviewer noted that 'the lead up acts Yvonne Barrett and the Lido girls were good, but who remembers? The atmosphere in the Lido was great, but who noticed? Frances Faye dominates her audience and leaves them crying for more.'[386]

To show or not to show, that was the question puzzling Melbourne's HSV7 management in mid-1969. Bringing the bosom back to television was by now presenting problems for the station. 'At least that's the lesson Channel 7 had learnt in the last month or so,' according to show business reporter Rex Lopez. 'Once accused of being too masculine, the station recently revamped its programs to include some attractive shots of girls. Now the station's program planners are in a quandary because viewers have been complaining the channel's birds are showing too much. Special guest Yvonne Barrett showed too much of herself and the ballet girls were immodest in the station's *Seven's Club Show.*'[387]

Another show business critic noted that, as was the case in all forms of entertainment, most TV singers had some sort of a gimmick they hoped would put them above the rest in this highly competitive field. 'Yvonne Barrett's gimmick is daring dresses, shaped and cut in a way that tantalises and excites. It's one gimmick which has paid off for Yvonne as far as I'm concerned. When I heard she was appearing on *In Melbourne*

---

384 'Too Much Corn, Miss Faye', The Herald, June 3rd 1969.

385 Ibid.

386 'Frances Left Them Crying For More', The Age, June 3rd 1969.

387 'To Show, Or Not To Show', The Herald, June 25th 1969.

Tonight last Wednesday I made sure I was tuned in. Yvonne, I'm pleased to report, didn't disappoint me. Her dress was one of the most daring yet.'[388]

Yvonne was now setting tongues wagging over the clothes she chose to wear for her TV appearances. She certainly didn't please everyone with her performance on *Seven's Club Show* on June 20th 1969. The channel was bombarded with phone calls from viewers, mostly women, who protested that Yvonne's dress was far too revealing. But Yvonne had different ideas. She didn't believe she had shown too much of herself. Rather she believed that a shocking sound system had greatly affected her performance that night. A reporter agreed. 'I felt sorry for Yvonne Barrett when the tape she was miming to suddenly went haywire. Even her low-cut jacket was forgotten when the sound became distorted.'[389]

The dress, which caused a storm of controversy when Yvonne first wore it on television, was an embossed organza and the near-topless bodice curved outward and down, all the way to the broad buckled belt.

TV viewers were certainly now seeing 'a lot more' of Yvonne. Too much, according to some irate fans who phoned TV channels to complain about her skimpy clothing. Yvonne explained to seasoned show business reporter Robert Fent that she had nothing against bras. 'It's simply that I can't find one small enough to fit me.' If Yvonne regarded a youthful figure as a problem, it was still getting results while she designed her own clothes.[390]

Yvonne told a *Dolly* magazine reporter that she wasn't

388 'A Gimmick I Like', The Truth, undated article.
389 'To Show, Or Not To Show', The Herald, June 25th 1969.
390 'Yvonne's An Eye Popper', Listener-In TV, July 5th — 11th 1969.

'fussy' about wearing bras. 'It depends on the dress, whether it can take a bra or not. It's the outfit that's suggestive, not the underwear. The public expect me to wear something different, something daring, every time I perform, but I'm a very modest dresser off stage.'[391]

Robert Fent told his readers that "Yvonne's Eye Poppers" was a phrase coined for her clothes by a colleague the morning after his grandfather had fallen from his armchair while watching Yvonne on Channel ATV0. Yvonne wasn't upset by the public's reaction to her clothes. 'Whenever a producer books me these days I am told to wear something low-cut. The clothes haven't changed really. I think it's because I'm getting more work these days that people are noticing.

'I was wearing see-through dresses and all that kind of stuff three years ago. Anyway, I don't think the clothes are any more revealing than anything you would accept in a movie, and I don't think they're sexy. I wear them because they are showy and comfortable. I keep my show clothes strictly for work, but I could easily wear my dresses around the house or to parties.' Robert Fent closed his article by noting that Yvonne wasn't worried about overexposure on TV, 'but she may be in for some heavy colds as the winter stretches on!'[392]

Continued criticism of her revealing clothes did not worry Yvonne in the slightest. In her opinion, there were far too many singers on television wearing the same, drab old styles. 'I want to look different.'[393] In August 1969, *TV Week* magazine featured a colour special of Yvonne 'the pretty young thrush with the peek-a-boo haircut' modelling five controversial

---

391 'To Bra Or Not To Bra', Dolly, November 1970.

392 'Yvonne's An Eye Popper', Listener-In TV, July 5th — 11th 1969.

393 'Yvonne Takes The Plunge', TV Week, August 16th 1969.

outfits which sparked uproar when she wore them on television. 'Yvonne's dressmaker, Biba of Bourke Street, Melbourne whipped up a little confection in one night. No wonder — there was nothing to it! Just a whiff of candy pink polyester chiffon held together by three hand-beaded rings!'[394]

In the laced-up look for Spring, Yvonne also modelled 'a black coffee gabardine jerkin dress kept intact by gossamer-fine gold lacing. A heavenly body in midnight blue is Yvonne wearing a silk velvet micro-mini. The dress features "London Look" long sleeves and the deep plunging neckline is highlighted by an unusual drop pearl brooch. White boucle is the up to the minute fabric in the simple number. A dash of spicy orange extends the down-sweeping line of the bodice, and quilted orange boots complete the ensemble.'[395]

The *Herald* newspaper's fashion reporter Tony Johnston was now describing Yvonne as being 'probably the pop scene's most controversial dresser'. He went on to say that Yvonne loved to shock people. 'Yvonne, attractive and lithesome, fronts the television cameras in short skirts, revealing necklines, cutaway backs and any other style that shows her to the best advantage.' When asked why she wore such outfits, Yvonne told the reporter that she liked to wear anything she knew wouldn't be seen on anyone else. 'That's why I have them cutaway a lot. I have them made in bright colours too. Colours that will look good under any colour lights.'[396]

Off stage, Yvonne was a little more sedate. She preferred to wear casual gear, especially anything that didn't crease. She liked to wear trouser suits with wide legs, boots and miniskirts

394 Ibid.

395 Ibid.

396 'Yvonne Loves To Shock You', The Herald, September 27th 1969.

matched with a sweater. She didn't like wearing hats. The only jewellery she was wearing were rings. She also had a number of watches. When asked by a reporter what a snappy dresser like her thought of other girls her age, Yvonne opined that she thought they dressed rather well, but she didn't think that a lot of their clothes were very well made. 'But that's because they can't afford to have all their clothes tailor made!'[397]

Yvonne kept busy in the second half of 1969 working the hotel circuit and appearing on TV shows such as Graham Kennedy's *In Melbourne Tonight*, Bert Newton's *In Melbourne Tonight*[398], and Jimmy Hannan's *In Melbourne Tonight*. She also appeared on HSV7's *Seven's Club Show*, *The Mike Walsh Show* and the *Turning On* teenage musical program compered by Baby John Burgess. In September 1969, Yvonne performed "The In Crowd" and "Now I'm Gonna Fly" on Brian Henderson's *Bandstand*. She appeared five times [399] on Jeff Phillips's short lived ABC *Sounds Like Us* program singing such songs as "For Once In My Life", "Don't Give Up", "Reach Out For Me", "On The Other Side Of The Tracks", "As Long As I'm Singing", "One" and "Cute," a duet with Phillips.

On November 16th 1969 Yvonne performed "Heat Wave" accompanied by The Fabulous Lido Girls in The Lord Mayor's Command Performance at the Melbourne Town Hall. Jeff Phillips, Lovelace Watkins, Ron Lees, Judith Durham, and The Four Lads also performed on the night. First established in 1947, and patterned on the Royal Command Performance

---

397 Ibid.

398 On July 17th 1969 Bert Newton's "*IMT*" was broadcast live from the Puckapunyal Army base. Entertaining army personnel and the TV audience were Yvonne, Gaynor Bunning, and Tim Evans.

399 On November 6th and 13th 1969, August 31st 1970, and October 6th and 7th 1970.

of London, the event was aimed at raising funds for various Melbourne hospitals and charities.

Yvonne saw 1969 out with two performances at Box Hill's Whitehorse Hotel. She performed in Morwell on New Year's Day 1970. On January 6th 1970 Yvonne and Sam Anglesey were among the 150 or so guests who attended the wedding of John Farrar and Pat Carroll at the Christ Church, South Yarra.

Yvonne continued to steel the limelight at the Lionel Rose[400] "I Thank You" Gold Record[401] function held at the Melbourne Town Hall on January 27th 1970. She wore a daringly low-cut micro-mini dress glittering with white sequins, which was slit high up each side to reveal silver bikini pants. It was little wonder that she received wild applause for the way she belted out her three numbers interspersed with some high-kicking choreography.

Yvonne was now kept busy working at hotels, clubs and private parties, as well as making TV appearances. So it was important that she had an ample supply of outfits to wear. She told a *TV Times* reporter that she sketched her dress designs mainly during long stints of travelling to and from singing jobs. She went on to say that she'll get an idea sometimes when she's driving, so she pulls over to the side of the road and sketches it while the idea is still in her head. She admitted that she got ideas for her outfits by the hundred, but only a few worked.

Yvonne then mentioned that many of her wild outfits that she designed for her stage and TV appearances were minimal in size, and at times the architecture couldn't match the stress and strain of a television appearance. Other outfits started out

---

400 On November 5th 1969 Yvonne appeared with Lionel Rose at the Tottenham Hotel to raise money to assist Sunshine's Aboriginal Youth Hostel.

401 Lionel's record had already sold 50,000 copies by this time.

basically the same as one might find in any modern dress shop, but Yvonne had a way of putting in slits, splits and peekaboo holes that entirely changed their character. She added that she always endeavoured to keep the cost of her outfits minimal. One of her dresses, an outfit of black lame, cost her only $3 for material and making. For another outfit she paid $60 for sequins alone, but that was a rare case of extravagance!

Yvonne expressed the view that female singers only had themselves to blame if they didn't look as glamorous on TV as they should. She regarded her clothes as a very important part of her act. 'Even if they don't like my style of singing, I'm giving the audience something to look at. After all television is a visual medium.' Yvonne admitted that her outfits had raised eyebrows among adult viewers of *In Melbourne Tonight* and even surprised teenage audiences of the *Go!! Show, Uptight* and other TV pop programs. Yet the daring was mixed with decorum, so not even the most anxious producers had asked her to cover up.[402]

For someone who was extremely talented, Yvonne didn't have that strong a belief in her talent. Tricia Barrett recalls Yvonne being insecure to the point of wondering why people would want to see her perform. 'Show business was all she knew. I think she thought that if she was a bit different by wearing revealing costumes, she'd get by because she was a bit out there. That had a lot to do with the costumes. Audiences used to love her to wear something back then that was revealing and stuck on where necessary.'

Tricia recalls that their mother Sheila was a self-taught dressmaker and she made most of Yvonne's costumes on an

---

402 'She's An Eyeful Even With A Three Dollar Outfit', TV Times, April 8th 1970.

old Singer sewing machine. 'At times she sought the help of my ex-sister-in-law and her neighbour Mrs McCabe. They were both professionals and they helped if mum couldn't get a costume to fit and sit properly. Mrs McCabe was marvellous and she was a lovely lady.'

Tricia remembers that, as far as her mother was concerned, Yvonne could do no wrong when it came to her outfits. 'I never heard her criticise Yvonne at all. She was happy to make Yvonne's clothes as revealing as Yvonne wanted them.' On May 14th 1970 Yvonne sang "Meanwhile Back In Real Life" on GTV9's *In Melbourne Tonight*. She wore her latest show business costume made by her mother. It featured a cream sequin jacket open at the sides to reveal a silver lame bikini. Yvonne highlighted it by wearing a high waisted black belt.[403]

Yvonne always took particular care with her on-stage appearance, and she thought more people in the public's eye should do so as well. 'Some people just don't care what they wear or how they look on stage. More people, male and female, should take more care and should think more.' She likened the role of an entertainer to that of a supermarket product. 'Basically,' she said, 'if people have to choose, they will pick the one that looks best.'[404]

At this point in her life, Yvonne felt she would never do anything but entertain, so her only plan for the future was to keep on singing for as long as possible. She believed that one must perform for each particular audience, not just have one act to be used everywhere. She said 'You've got to read the audience, learn to psyche it, in order to play really

---

403 'Swinging Revelation', Listener-In TV, May 1970.
404 'Rag-trader Yvonne', The Sun, August 6th 1971.

successfully. You have to change the act because of many influences, different classes of people, different age groups, even different suburbs.'[405]

On June 30th 1970 the Australian Pop Awards were held at Melbourne's Dallas Brooks Hall. Yvonne was voted runner up to Allison Durbin in the *Go-Set* magazine's National Pop Poll. Top male singer was Johnny Farnham. Yvonne sang both sides of her latest Columbia/EMI single "Lu"/Picture Me Gone" at the Awards and according to *Go-Set* she 'stole the show completely.'

By the late 1960s to early 1970s, Lionel Gell was running four Gell-Dior ladies hairdressing salons in Melbourne. Staff from his salons also attended to the needs of performers backstage at Melbourne's Tivoli, Her Majesty's and The Comedy theatres. Gell had personally attended to visiting overseas stars for some years by this time. His salons were very well known and he gained a great deal of free publicity out of this show business connection.

Gell recalls that Yvonne and Tricia Barrett first came to him in his Victoria Street salon. 'Yvonne was young when she started coming. You couldn't help but take to her straight away. She was so beautiful. She would have looked good in a chaff bag! She had a lovely charming nature and she'd speak to anyone who came up to speak to her, even when her hair was wet. Over the years I saw her quite a bit at the salons and at parties I threw.

'A lot of very attractive girls are terribly up themselves and very difficult to get on with. They want the impossible done. Yvonne was never up herself. Everybody in the salon loved

---

405 Ibid.

Yvonne. She and her sister Tricia were beautiful people. They were always happy with my work.'

On October 10th 1970, *The Penthouse Club* debuted on Melbourne's HSV Channel 7 as a weekly live to air variety program. It was originally hosted by football commentator Michael Williamson and comedian Mary Hardy. The program, which screened Saturday nights from around 8.30pm[406] was a mix of comedy, light entertainment and live coverage of harness racing.

Yvonne made her first appearance on *The Penthouse Club* on Saturday October 31st 1970. Singers Lainie Kazan and Buddy England also appeared on the show. Yvonne was paid $60 for singing one song that night. On December 26th 1970 Yvonne made her second appearance on the show singing a Trini Lopez medley.

Yvonne's then manager Ron Fletcher recalls not having to push hard to get Yvonne on *The Penthouse Club*. 'I was pretty closely associated with Channel 7 because we used to supply prizes for their *Time For Terry* program[407]. So I got pretty close to the producers, including Neddie Payne who produced *The Penthouse Club*. My own band used to appear every two or three weeks doing popular rock'n'roll songs.'

Yvonne ultimately became a semi regular on the program. She had a great rapport with co-hosts Michael Williamson and Mary Hardy. Yvonne also worked with Michael at a number of different venues. He compered the shows and Yvonne sang. Ron Fletcher recalls that the charismatic Williamson and

---

406 The show's starting time varied over the years depending on HSV-7's Saturday night VFL football commitments.

407 *"Time for Terry"* was a HSV7 variety show hosted by English comedian and entertainer Terry O'Neill. It ran from 1964 to 1966.

Yvonne were 'good mates.'

Comedian Mary Hardy liked to have fun when introducing Yvonne on *The Penthouse Club*. Yvonne was regularly on the receiving end of Hardy's wise cracks. She would invariably introduce Yvonne by saying 'I wonder what Yvonne Barrett is nearly wearing tonight!' Ron Fletcher opines that Yvonne wore revealing outfits because she didn't think she was that good a performer. 'Somebody once wrote in an article that she had the best legs in the country. I think she wore those revealing outfits because she had the body, the figure to wear them, and because she wanted to be a little different to everybody else.'

Ron recalls Yvonne upsetting HSV7's general manager Ron Casey one particular Saturday night. 'She was supposed to sing an upbeat party song on *The Penthouse Club*, but instead she sang Michael Jackson's song "Ben". Viewers rang and said it was the best thing she had ever done, but Ron Casey didn't like it because it wasn't upbeat enough. Yvonne had a bit of a falling out with him after that.'[408]

Yvonne was also a regular on ATVO's *Happening '70* which was compered by Ross D. Wyllie.[409] She wore one of her latest show business outfits towards the end of the year. It was a black mini featuring a gold bib front. The top was made of gold metal.[410] Yvonne made semi regular appearances on ATVOs *Happening '71* which was compered by Jeff Phillips.

John Farrar's mother Gladys was annoyed by the level of criticism that Yvonne received because of her controversial outfits. In January 1971 Gladys submitted the following

---

408 Yvonne survived Ron Casey's tirade and she went on to make more appearances on "*The Penthouse Club*".

409 Ross D Wyllie returned to Brisbane in late 1969.

410 'Yvonne Swings in Black and Gold,' Listener-In TV, October 31st — November 6th 1970.

comments to *Listener-In* TV's 'Axes and Orchids' column: 'An orchid to Yvonne Barrett. She is a kind, generous person and a very good friend and very talented. To the person who said those nasty things about her, I am sure they do not know her or they would change their minds. G. Farrar (Niddrie).'[411]

In July 1971 *Weekender* magazine conducted a poll of more than 100 men to name the sexiest woman in the world and the women they really fancied. The answers, if not the ladies, were very revealing. Unexpectedly famous pin-ups of the age, such as Raquel Welsh and Ursula Andress, went to the bottom of the poll, suffering the men diagnosed, from over exposure. Instead, leaping into the limelight as clear winners came two girls who the world in general may not have known, but who the men of Melbourne said they were tops.

'Top of the list as the world's most desirable woman came well-known and attractive pop-singer, Yvonne Barrett. "Her wide large eyes send some men into ecstasies," said one respondent. Another described Yvonne as being "wild and fantastic!" TV personality Judy Banks came second primarily because she "looked sweet and wholesome!"' [412]

In March 1972, Yvonne's last single "No Longer Part Of Your Life"/ "Mr 7654312" was released by Albert Productions. Both songs were written by UK producer Simon Napier-Bell. He also produced both songs for Yvonne during the year he spent in Australia working for Albert Productions. Napier-Bell also produced Alison McCallum and John Paul Young that same year.[413]

---

411 'Axes and Orchids', Listener-In TV January 30-February 5th 1971:

412 'The Girls Who Turn Men On,' Weekender, July 16th 1971.

413 Napier — Bell had also worked with the likes of Dusty Springfield, The Yardbirds, The Move, The Scaffold, Peter Sarstedt, and Marc Bolan.

Yvonne sang "No Longer Part Of My Life"[414] on Dick Williams's ABC *Hit Scene* TV show on Saturday March 25th 1972.[415] In an interview with Dick after her performance, Yvonne surprisingly admitted that she was not that mad about "No Longer Part Of My Life." She then did an about turn by stating that she quite liked the song. She went on to say 'It's growing on me. The more I hear it, I can find nice little things in it.' Dick Williams responded by telling Yvonne that the show's crew had been whistling the tune, 'so its growing on them too.' Yvonne suggested 'they keep whistling!'

Yvonne told Dick Williams that she was kept busy doing personal appearances, mostly at hotels. She added that she was also doing a lot of private male conventions, especially at this time of the year. 'They're good fun too. You can sing anything. I have a separate lot of gear I wear for the fellahs.' Yvonne then mentioned that she was flying to Perth the following night for two weeks of shows. She went on to say 'When I come back, I'm back at the hotels again. I think I'm here (in Melbourne) until the end of May, then I go interstate again to Adelaide.' Following their discussion, Dick Williams invited Yvonne to sing Simon Napier-Bell's composition "Mr 7654312".[416]

In April 1972 Yvonne was described in a magazine as 'being one of television's most daring dressers and whose stunning outfits regularly enhance TV variety and Tonight shows. So who better to model the super winter short shorts designed especially for *TV Times* readers by Coats Patons? Yvonne designs most of her own gear by sketching ideas during long

---

414 "No Longer Part Of Your Life" was the A side of her Albert Productions single.

415 Yvonne also sang "No Longer Part Of My Life" on ATV0's *"Musical Cashbox"* on April 18th 1972.

416 "Mr 7654312" (Albert Productions) was the B side of her Albert Productions single

stints of travelling. Yvonne has no hesitation in giving this winter short shorts outfit her seal of approval.'[417]

In early May 1972 however, Yvonne was quoted in the press as saying that she was going to make changes to her shows and TV appearances. She said she would now be covering up. 'I am not going to make any more cut out dresses. From now on, audiences won't be seeing so much of me. When I first started singing I was the only one wearing such revealing gear. Now everyone does it. So, I'm going to choose more covered up clothes and in floor shows I'm not going to use my clothes as a prop any more. I've outgrown all that.'[418]

Yvonne then added that she was also changing her style of singing. 'Up until now, I've always sung what producers wanted on television. But now I want to sing songs that are true to me, songs that I can actually feel. Lyrics have always been important to me but they'll become even more important. I don't know if it will work, but I know I'll be a lot happier. I want to sing and get my own things going.'[419]

Up to now TV viewers had contented themselves with sitting back and watching Yvonne belt out her numbers, and those who had watched her floor shows had seen a pretty girl in brief gear opening her mouth and singing. 'But there will be more to it than that from now on,' said Yvonne. 'I want people to know, just by listening to what I sing, my whole feeling and my whole outlook. And they'll know my whole motivation of life just by the songs I choose,' explained Yvonne.[420]

---

417 'Knitting For Your Winter Wardrobe', TV Times, April 22nd 1972.

418 'Yvonne Goes For Cover' (You Won't Be Seeing Much Of Me in Future'), Listener In — TV, May 6th — 12th 1972.

419 Ibid.

420 Ibid.

Now that Yvonne had decided to hide her charms, it meant that she'd be using more fabric in her clothes. Yvonne pointed out 'That was one good thing about the brevity of my costumes. They took so little material. There's a guy in Buckley's Dress Materials and I'm sure his jaw is still hanging open from when I went in to buy fabric. "What are you going to make with it, missy?" he asked. 'A dress', I told him. "And how much would you like? Four yards?" I replied, 'No, seven-eighths of a yard will do nicely. I'm making pants to go with it!' [421]

In late May 1972, a mystery phone caller threatened to strip and strangle Yvonne. The threats came after an article[422] announced that Yvonne would be covering up for future shows. Yvonne told *TV Week* magazine 'This man called and said that if I didn't wear sexy gear at the hotel where I was appearing that night he was going to tear all my clothes off and strangle me. I was terrified at the time and immediately slammed down the phone and called the police. When I told them what had happened, they promised to protect me.'[423]

During her weekend engagement at Melbourne's Deer Park hotel, Yvonne was escorted by the police from her home to the hotel. They waited until her act was finished then took her home. 'I didn't know whether the man called again the next day,' said Yvonne, 'because I didn't stay around the house. All I did was nip in for some gear and spend the day with friends. The police escorted me again that night. I don't know what happened to the man.'[424]

---

421 Ibid.

422 'Yvonne Goes For Cover' (You Won't Be Seeing Much Of Me in Future'), Listener In — TV, May 6th — 12th 1972.

423 'Death Threat For Yvonne', TV Week, May 27th 1972.

424 Ibid.

Yvonne was made aware by the police that most crank callers got their satisfaction from making calls, but rarely followed them up. She was also told though that there could always be a first time. 'I was really afraid at the time. I didn't want this to be it. I feel a lot better now, but I was really afraid at the time. Now I shall be applying for a silent phone number.'[425]

Yvonne had weekend gigs at the Deer Park hotel for a few weeks following the threat. Her sister Tricia remembers that 'the police escorted her to and from the hotel on each occasion.'[426]

This wasn't the first time however that Yvonne had received prank calls. 'For a long time, I was managing myself and so my number was in the phone book. That was when I started to get the calls. At that time, I was working on stage and my picture was in the papers a lot. I started to get calls, but in the main those calls were just a nuisance. They were the usual calls, probably from kids in call boxes, so they never worried me very much.'

Yvonne was worried however by a male who called her every night for six months. She recalls the GPO endeavouring to trace the calls. 'I think he was an expert because he always rang off before the trace could be put on. I eventually got rid of him by telling him exactly what I thought of him. He was stopped in his tracks. He apologised and said that he now realised that I was a nice girl and wouldn't call me again. And he didn't!'

The May 1972 incident was different however. It was the first time Yvonne had ever had anyone threaten to harm her. She said at the time that 'It's not a nice feeling to know that

---

425 Ibid.

426 Yvonne never heard from that caller again.

someone was even thinking of doing such a thing, let alone really meaning to do what he said. I haven't heard from the caller since. I just hope the police have frightened him away. In any case I don't intend to switch back to the revealing gear, no matter what any caller says,' Yvonne added.[427]

In early June 1972 Yvonne appeared in a magazine photo shoot wearing what she described as being 'her new cover up look, an ankle length tiered skirt and blouse.' The outfit was a far cry from the chic hot pants and miniskirts she had previously worn for her singing act. She told a reporter at the time that she couldn't make up her mind whether she would wear her new clothes look when she next appeared on *Penthouse Club* on June 10th 1972. [428]

Yvonne was now in demand all over Australia for live performances at hotels, dances, cabarets, clubs, balls and trade conventions. During the last weeks of June 1972, she worked at King Island, and in Perth, Darwin and Launceston. In mid-July she appeared on 'Penthouse Club and then flew out of Melbourne for appearances in Brisbane, Toowoomba, Sydney and Adelaide.

Gavan Anderson was teaching guitar at a Melbourne music store when the opportunity to be Russell Morris's guitarist came up. 'I worked with Russell for about four months until his "Wings Of An Eagle" single took off and he had to go to the UK. Russell told me Yvonne needed a guitar player, so I got handballed over to Yvonne in late 1972.'

Gavan recalls Yvonne having charts for the songs she performed on stage. 'I was her "musical director" on the gigs.

---

427 'Death Threat For Yvonne', TV Week, May 27th 1972.

428 'From Top To Toe', Listener — In TV, June 1972.

Most of the bands couldn't read music, but they could read chord charts. So I would learn Yvonne's songs and give them to the band and hope to God I could remember them. The band relied on me to give them the right chords and right notes to pitch off. It was also my job to hold the rhythmic part together when the band couldn't. That certainly happened quite a lot, but it was a lot of fun.'

Gavan recalls that, as Yvonne didn't have any hit records of her own, she sang songs like "Secret Love". He remembers her singing a great version of that song, 'but she had trouble getting the top note. So I said to her, "Why don't we drop it by a semitone and it'll make it easier?" She said, "It doesn't matter. No one out there knows. So long as you belt out that note and make it look good, they'll think it's fabulous!" That was pretty true!'

It really depended on what the crowd was like, but Yvonne was generally on stage for around seventy five minutes. Gavan recalls that successful artists such as Normie Rowe, Yvonne and Marcie Jones could all go on stage and patter away to the audience and keep them engaged because they had initially learnt their craft at rock'n'roll dances. Gavan recalls that Yvonne was certainly good at that.

Gavan has vivid memories of an early incident that convinced him that Yvonne had the ability to deal with hecklers. 'She had great everything else, but she wasn't exactly endowed bust wise. We were playing at the Tarmac Hotel in Laverton[429] one night when a woman stood up and said "I don't know why you are wearing that outfit. You haven't got any tits!" Yvonne quick as a flash said, "Why don't you sit down. No one wants

---

429 Laverton is a western suburb of Melbourne.

to see your new dress which is several years old anyway!" The audience just burst into laughter.'

Yvonne and Gavan worked at the Yallourn East Hotel quite frequently. Gavan recalls Yvonne walked into the hotel's foyer and dropped her bag one particular night. 'She had a bag of dope in it and it fell out on the floor in front of everybody. She just picked it up and winked at me and said as quick as a flash "I'm a vegetarian!" We used to smoke dope and drink Southern Comfort. She always had a bottle of that with her in that period.'

Gavan found Yvonne to be 'really lovely' to work with. 'She was not up herself at all. She would have been very aware of her own limitations as a vocalist. Any musician who worked the amount that all of us did is always aware of their limitations.'

Gavan also remembers Yvonne having a beautiful heart. 'We played at the Deer Park hotel one night. It was one of the last gigs I did with her.[430] I was dosed up with pills because I had the flu. I had a fever of 101 and I passed out in the band room before we went out. I couldn't do the floor show with her, but she paid me anyway. She didn't have to do that. It was just a beautiful thing to do!

In 1973 Margie Bayes saw Yvonne at a gig at a Mordialloc hotel. She recalls going to the hotel with a group of friends, not knowing in advance that Yvonne was performing there that night. Margie caught up with Yvonne after her performance. 'I'd stopped singing by then because I'd had a poisoned throat. We'd lost touch once I stopped singing. I went to the side of the stage when she finished her performance. I started to follow her into her dressing room, but I was stopped by a security

---

430 Gavan worked with Yvonne for approximately six months.

guard. I said to him "If you tell Miss Barrett that Margie Bayes is here I'm sure she'll say show her in." Well she did.

'I wasn't driving that night, so we had a few drinks together. I forgot that my friends were waiting for me when Yvonne got into a big ole conversation. She seemed as good as gold and we talked about old times. All of a sudden, Yvonne said, "Margie I should have left here an hour and a half ago because I had another gig half an hour ago." Then she said, "Stuff 'em! It doesn't matter." So we just drank on.'

That was the last time Margie saw Yvonne. She remembers being surprised that Yvonne forgot she had another gig to go to. 'We knew each other inside out. She knew if she'd said to me "Margie thanks for coming backstage to see me. I'm glad you did, but I've got another gig." I would have said, "It's been beautiful to see you Von." Then I'd have given her a kiss and said "I've got friends waiting for me, so I'll go and let you get on with what you've gotta do." But she didn't. It was like she really didn't care!'

12. 'IF I CAN'T HAVE YOU, NOBODY ELSE WILL'

Tricia Barrett believes that Yvonne contributed to the breakup with Sam Anglesey. 'I think Yvonne was a little bit naughty there. She was working with Peter Arrowsmith and she fell for him. My memory is that Sam caught Yvonne with Peter and that's why he broke it off with her.' Tricia liked Sam. She recalls that Sam never put Yvonne down and he never spoke badly about her, even when they broke up. 'Yvonne did the wrong thing, but Sam still did the right thing by her. He was a good man!'

Yvonne first met Peter Arrowsmith in Tasmania in the latter part of 1972. At the time Peter was playing the piano in Wendy Stapleton's band[431] at the Wrest Point Hotel in Sandy Bay. Every week pop stars such as Ross D. Wyllie and a number of Sydney based nightclub artists, such as Lovelace Watkins and Delilah, were flown in by Federal Hotels[432] to appear at the Wrest Point Hotel. Federal Hotels were very big on floor shows.

Much to Wendy's delight, Yvonne was booked to do a weekend of shows at the Wrest Point Hotel with backing to be

---

431 Back then the band didn't have a name.

432 Now known as the Federal Group.

provided by Wendy and her band. Wendy takes up the story. 'I first met Yvonne when both of us were students at the May Downs School of Dancing. Yvonne was some eight years older than me. Back then I was a little kid who looked up to her as what we called "one of the big girls!"

'When Yvonne arrived at the hotel, she realised it was me from the dancing school. We rehearsed with Yvonne on the Thursday for shows that night and Friday and Saturday nights. Instead of finishing each night and going to her hotel room, Yvonne would come back to our place. She hung out with us the whole weekend.

'The four band members, all in their mid to late 20s, were really fabulous musicians. All had been in the Navy band in Perth, except for the bass player. By the end of the weekend Yvonne and our very good pianist Peter Arrowsmith[433] were in love with each other. Peter, who was about the same age as Yve, left the Navy after some thirteen years service, to play in Tassie with us.'

Wendy and the band had a six months contract at the hotel. So over that period of time Yvonne would fly to Hobart to be with Peter every chance she got. Once their contract had expired, Wendy and the group returned to Melbourne. Yvonne and Peter subsequently decided to move in together. 'We were firm friends by then,' recalls Wendy. 'I lived in Moonee Ponds and Yvonne and Peter lived in a block of very nice units at 258 Ballarat Road, Footscray.[434] We spent the next few years virtually living in each other's pockets. Yvonne

---

433 Peter hailed from Geraldton, a coastel city 424 kilometres north of Perth, Western Australia.

434 Peter's sister Anne moved to Melbourne at some point and she lived in the unit with Yvonne and Peter for a time.

was the life of the party. She was incredibly funny and she'd have you in tears. It was nothing to finish work at one am and drive to their place and sit there talking till four or five in the morning.'

Eventually life began to change for Wendy and Yvonne. Wendy recalls not seeing Yvonne and Peter as often as they had previously. 'They became quite reclusive in the last years of their relationship and I started getting busier with bands and I was touring in different states.'

By now Peter Arrowsmith had become Yvonne's full time musical director and pianist. As well as performing on the big floor show circuit, Yvonne and Peter performed as a duo at some of Melbourne's top hotels including The Windsor and The Savoy. Melbourne's President's Motor Inn, located at 63 Queen's Road, was another venue where Yvonne and Peter performed a number of times. Peter engaged the services of a drummer and a bass player for these performances. Yvonne noted in a letter[435] to her friend Kaye Johnston that 'the boys, that's Peter and a drummer and bass player, do dinner music and I go on stage about 9 o'clock.'

Yvonne's repertoire at this time included such songs as: "Always Someone There To Remind Me", "Anyone Who Had A Heart", "Ben", "Big Spender", "Can't Take My Eyes Off You", "Don't Go Breakin' My Heart", "Downtown", "Fever", "For Once In My Life", "Goin'Out Of My Head", "Happy Together", "He's A Rebel", "How Sweet It Is To Be Loved By You", "I Feel The Earth Move", "I Just Don't Know What To Do With Myself", "I Know A Place", "I'm Gonna Make You Love Me", "I Only Wanna Be With You", "I Say A Little Prayer", "I Started A Joke", "I Will Survive",

---

435 Letter dated July 3rd 1974.

"I Wish You Love", "Killing Me Softly", "Little People", "Love Will Keep Us Together", "Lu", "Misty", "Moonlight In Vermont", "One", "Quando, Quando,Quando", "Steam Heat", "Tar and Cement", "The Girl From Ipanema", "The Look Of Love", "The More I See You", "To Sir With Love", "Walk On By", "Wishin'& Hopin'", "You Don't Have To Say You Love Me", and "You're My World".

Kaye Johnston recalls that she and Yvonne kept in touch until about the mid-1970s. 'We'd always exchange gifts and catch up in some way for our birthdays. Peter came to Adelaide a couple of times with Yvonne for performances. He was lovely. He was entirely different to Sam Anglesey. I really liked Sam, but I thought Peter was more Yvonne's type. He was more of a kinder and gentler soul, and a bit more of an average guy, whereas Sam was quite alternate.'

Yvonne's niece Martine Barrett saw Yvonne and Peter perform on stage 'a couple of times in the 1970s. Peter was a very talented musician. I was young at the time, but I remember Peter better than anyone else she performed with. He was a very warm and sweet person. Whenever I was around him, I felt safe.'

By now Peter and Yvonne were getting jobs right around Australia. They performed together all the time, either as a duo or in floor shows with a house band. Prior to their performances with a house band, Peter would always rehearse with the band so as to ensure that everything was right with the songs that Yvonne was going to sing.

Wendy Stapleton recalls that Yvonne was still doing TV appearances, but as the years went on that became less and less because the whole age thing changed. 'Countdown started, so unless you changed or went overseas, you were almost put into another basket. Everyone had to face it. You went from being a pop star to cabaret star. You never lost your status as an entertainer, but you lost a lot of work for the simple fact that as you got older different hotels wanted different things. Then disco came in. The whole scene changed and you just had to cop it and make the most of what was around.

'Yvonne did that very well. A lot of people from that scene basically couldn't stay in it. Although they could sing, they didn't have the personality to be able to pull off doing the floor shows that Yvonne did. She was an all-round entertainer. She was very affable and funny. She had a lovely voice and she could dance and she'd been through theatre and television. People like her could do floor shows. Whereas once others were put out of the pop scene, they were fish out of water and they couldn't pull it off.'

In March 1975 the *Truth* newspaper reported that Yvonne had gone into semi-retirement. It was said that Yvonne had stopped nearly all live appearance work because she was fed up with the shoddy deal handed out to artists around Melbourne's pub circuit. In the future Yvonne planned to stick to making occasional TV appearances. She was quoted as saying 'There are good agents and good hotels to work, but there are also a lot of bad ones. I'm just tired of poor bands, bad agents and shocking conditions and I don't particularly like some of the audiences.'

Yvonne's comments rang true with the *Truth* reporter. 'Sadly, I must support Yvonne's depressing allegations. The deal handed out to artists by these glorified swill houses is nothing short of shocking, and I'm sure most Melbourne performers will agree.'

The reporter went on to note that Yvonne's big hope now was to get regular work at an intimate restaurant where she could sing with her group performing the songs she liked. 'But don't worry about missing her from your TV screens. She's definite that she will remain on TV as long as producers continue booking her. With looks and a voice like Yvonne's, that will be for a long time.'[436]

Tricia Barrett remembers there being speculation at the time within the industry that Yvonne was retiring from show business. She didn't believe that Yvonne planned on doing that however. Rather Tricia contends that Yvonne saw this as a good time to finally have a good break from singing. 'It wasn't a case of Yvonne hiding, dropping out or running away. Yvonne had never gone on a proper holiday. She always worked over Christmas and New Year's Eve. She'd stay with us for a few days when we took our caravan to either Barwon Heads or Torquay and we'd go to the beach every day.'

Yvonne subsequently made several TV appearances in 1975 on such shows as *Penthouse Club*, *The Ernie Sigley Show*, and *The Graham Kennedy Show*. She sang such songs as "The Last Blues Song"[437], "Never Can Say Goodbye"[438] and "Everybody Gets To Go To The Moon".[439]

Mid-1975 saw Yvonne making regular appearances at the Stardust Showroom, which was located near the St Kilda Beach. A reporter from the *Toorak Times* saw one of Yvonne's performances. He described Yvonne as being 'the sexiest

---

436 'Yvonne Quits The Hotel Circuit', Melbourne Truth, March 29th 1975.

437 Written by the great songwriting team Barry Mann and Cynthia Weil and first recorded by Helen Reddy.

438 Written by Clifton Davis and first recorded by the Jackson 5.

439 Written by Jimmy Webb and first recorded by Thelma Houston.

singing chick in town. I caught up with her the other night in the Stardust Showroom where she fronted a swinging three-piece group. Gee she looks great and sounds it too.' He went on to say that 'Yvonne sings regularly with the Stardust Room dance band which comes on stage right after the main show at about 11pm and rocks on till 3am in the morn.'[440]

In 1976 Yvonne virtually disappeared from television screens. This enabled her to achieve her dream goal of working regularly in an intimate restaurant where she could sing with her group performing the songs she liked. Yvonne was now working as a regular artist at the Little Reata Mexican Restaurant at 68 Little Collins Street, Melbourne. She sang nightly from 11pm to 2am during the period 1976 to 1977.

Yvonne left the Little Reata around mid-1977. She was quoted in *The Scene* magazine as saying 'I went there because I just wanted to get down to singing. I'm singing a lot better now. I had been there so long I felt I had to move on.' Yvonne also believed working late hours from 11 PM to 2AM at the restaurant interfered with too many things in her life. 'I couldn't do television for instance.' Ron Moore, the owner of Little Reata, was sorry to see Yvonne leave his restaurant. He comments that 'Yvonne was a great talent. She had something special!'[441]

Shortly after Yvonne quit working at the Little Reata restaurant, the producers of *The Don Lane Show* contacted Yvonne and finally persuaded her to make her first TV appearance in some eighteen months. Yvonne told a reporter that she thought 'it was odd that after all these years, television

---

440 'Yvonne Barrett', Toorak Times, August 1st 1975.

441 Moore says that he 'never got over Yvonne's tragic death. Luck didn't go her way!'

producers still want me to dress up in "sexy" clothes. She added 'I'm no Maria Venuti!'[442] The reporter noted that Yvonne was somewhat on the thin side. He went on to say that Yvonne refers to her 'skinny chest as being quite pathetic really. But the public remembers Yvonne from years ago when she was known for plunging necklines and bare midriffs.' That was the image *The Don Lane Show* producers asked for when she reappeared on the show in late 1977.

Yvonne insisted at the time that there was 'a big difference between me today and me the singer even a year ago and I want people to see it. But they asked me to wear the sexy gear. I don't mind that. I just want them to be happy. But sexy clothes are old fashioned. I've got some lovely, interesting, new outfits. Fortunately, I've still got some of the old ones put away.' Eventually the TV audience saw Yvonne on the Lane show in a bra top, bare midriff, and long skirt, and singing that old standard "Hallelujah I Love Him So." 'They wanted me to do a well-known song, rather than something that was a bit challenging,' she said.[443]

Yvonne's last appearance on *The Don Lane Show* saw her go out in a blaze of glory. With superb backing provided by the magnificent eighteen-piece "Don Lane Orchestra" led by GTV9's Director of Music Graeme Lyall (AM), and with great backing vocals supplied by Neva Phillips, Sandy Watsford and Helen Cornish, Yvonne floored the studio audience with a spine-tingling version of "Hallelujah I Love Him So". It was a performance to remember!

Yvonne's friend Lesley Kirk saw Yvonne for the last time at

---

442 The voluptuous Maria Venuti AM is noted for her work in cabaret and supper clubs.

443 'Me? Sexy?', Listener In — TV, 1977.

the second of two of Yvonne's shows she attended in 1972. She hadn't spoken to Yvonne for some four years, so she decided to ring her in 1976. 'I rang her Mum's number and told her Mum who I was. She said, "I remember you. Yvonne's here at the moment." So Yvonne came to the phone and said "Oh my God, it's so good to hear from you!"

'We had a great ole conversation. She told me she was living with her pianist Peter Arrowsmith. She then said, 'We're going to Perth to live in a couple of months. We'll get you over and have a barbie before we go.'" That was the last time Lesley spoke to Yvonne. She subsequently learnt that Yvonne and Peter left for Perth sometime later. Lesley recalls that 'something came up to do with a job, so they went to Perth fairly quickly. I don't remember how I heard that, nor do I know what happened over there.'

Tricia Barrett also recalls Yvonne and Peter leaving for Perth in a hurry. She is not certain of the timing of their departure, but it is thought that they left Melbourne in the latter part of 1977 after Yvonne made her last appearance on *The Don Lane Show*. Tricia opines that 'they could have left because of a job in Perth. She did a few jobs as "Yve Frances" and that might have been in Perth. I think once they got over there, something went wrong between Yvonne and Peter and they broke up.'

Tricia doesn't know why Yvonne and Peter broke off their relationship. 'I thought Peter was the love of Yvonne's life. He had been her musical director and pianist for a long time. He was the most fantastic pianist!'

Tricia recalls that Yvonne stayed with Lesley Walker following the breakup. 'Lesley was a very old friend of Yvonne's. She used to cut Yvonne's hair. They had become very close friends when Lesley lived in a unit in Essendon. She had been married to Terry Walker of The Strangers. That's how Yvonne met her. Following her divorce from Terry, Lesley returned to her home city of Perth to be closer to family members.'

Wendy Stapleton recalls that Yvonne cut contact with most of her friends when she and Peter left Melbourne for Perth. 'She cut ties with everyone, except for her mother, her sister Tricia, and a mutual friend named Ray. We eventually heard from Peter's sister that Peter was in Perth.' Wendy believes that Peter went there because of the 'massive connections between he and all the guys he'd been with in the Navy.'

At some point Yvonne met Paul Reid in Perth.[444] Paul, who was a few years younger than Yvonne, wasn't in show business. It was a quick romance and it wasn't long before they became engaged. Sheila and Tricia Barrett flew to Perth to catch up with Yvonne and to meet Paul and his mother who had a business importing Morten Bay Bugs to Perth. Shortly thereafter, Paul's mother flew to Melbourne to speak with Sheila and Tricia about plans for Yvonne and Paul's wedding. Tricia recalls meeting Paul a second time when he and Yvonne flew to Melbourne for a brief visit. Tricia remembers that 'Paul was a very good-looking young man.'

Sheila and Tricia both felt that Paul's mother was going too fast for Yvonne. Tricia recalls that she and her mother then went to Perth at Paul's mother's request to talk more about the wedding. 'Paul's mother was a nice lady but everything had to be done her way. She was really pushing for them to have a big wedding at her home. She even had a big archway growing in her garden in readiness for the wedding. We came back home

---

444 Details of when, where and how they met are not known.

and the next thing we knew the wedding was off. I don't know who broke it off or why they broke up, but they parted.'

Yvonne subsequently met Hoang Van Truong on the rebound not long after that in a Perth club. Not much is know about the details of Truong's background. He is believed to have been born in Vietnam on July 1st 1951, making him exactly five years younger than Yvonne.[445] Truong came from an academic family. His father was a dentist. He had two brothers, one a headmaster and the other a teacher. His only sister was also a teacher.

Truong was training to be a dentist before he was called up to serve in the Army of the Republic of Vietnam (ARVN) during the Vietnam War. After the War was over, Truong migrated to the United States, but soon found it wasn't to his liking. He then joined his family who had migrated some years earlier to New Zealand. He ultimately became a New Zealand citizen. While living in New Zealand, he married and had a daughter, but the marriage didn't last. It is believed that Truong travelled to Perth from New Zealand sometime during 1983.[446]

At the time Yvonne was living with her friend Lesley Walker in a big apartment block close by the Cottesloe beach. Yvonne worked for a time as an usherette in a cinema managed by Lesley. 'She would have done that to get a bit of cash because she didn't do any singing in Perth,' recalls Tricia. 'When I visited Yvonne in Perth before their wedding she

---

445 By some quirk of fate, Truong shared the same birthday as Yvonne.

446 The Australian and New Zealand Governments have had arrangements in place since the 1920s to facilitate a free flow of people between the two countries. The 1973 Trans — Tasman Travel Arrangement allowed Truong, as a New Zealand citizen, to live and work in Australia, without the need to apply for authority to enter Australia.

wasn't working. She seemed happy with Truong. They'd go off shopping together hand in hand.'[447]

Yvonne had only known Truong for a few months when she married him[448] in a Perth registry office, two days after Christmas 1983. Yvonne wore a short simple white georgette dress with a drawstring top across the shoulders. A small reception followed in a friend's home. The guests included Lesley Walker and script writer Bevan Lee's mother who was a very close friend of Yvonne's.

Tricia and Sheila Barrett met Truong for the first time on the day of the wedding. 'Mum and I accepted him because Yvonne was marrying him. I didn't hear him speak Vietnamese. He spoke very good English from the get go. I have to say he was charming. He seemed harmless at the time and he adored her. He knew nothing about her musical background. He didn't even know she sang. In fact, he knew nothing about her really.'

Tricia had cause for concern however about the future of the marriage when Yvonne shared a very private thought with her just prior to the wedding. 'Yvonne and I called each other "Darl". It started out as a joke and it became the norm. On the day of the wedding, we were going to the hairdressers and she said to me, "Darl, I don't know why I'm doing this." My words back to her were "Don't do it! You don't have to do it!" She said, "But everybody is here now!" She then said Truong had been kind to her, whereas she'd had problems with other men who had taken money from her. "This one was kind"

---

447 Tricia Barrett opines that Lesley Walker would be the only one who would know exactly how Yvonne met Truong and where. 'After Yvonne died, Lesley never made contact with us. So things could have gone on in Perth that I wouldn't know about.' Efforts to locate Lesley have not been successful.

448 Yvonne didn't take the name Truong. She remained Yvonne Barrett.

were her exact words. So things weren't good right from the beginning. He wanted to get married, so she married on the rebound. I don't think she was excited about it at all.

'Yvonne could perform. She made it a good day. I was the only one in the family who knew what was really going on. My mother never knew. As far as she was aware, Yvonne was happy.[449] Yvonne wasn't happy about it at all, but she just went with the flow and made the wedding a good day. Lesley Walker would have known that too. She was very much a part of Yvonne's life. She signed the marriage certificate as an official witness.'

Yvonne had travelled to Melbourne from Perth on her own for her brother Peter's 40th birthday on November 13th 1983. Looking back years later, Tricia now believes that things weren't going well between Yvonne and Truong at the time of Peter's birthday. 'To this day, except for her empathy and sympathy for the Vietnamese, I don't know what made her marry Truong. I thought their marriage was never going to be any good after that, so I choose to forget the wedding ever took place!'

Marcie Jones recalls Yvonne telling her that Truong really loved her and so she thought she might as well marry him. Marcie remembers saying to Yvonne 'But you're not in love with him!' She replied, "What's love?" Tricia Barrett agrees that Yvonne would have said those things to Marcie.

Whenever Pat (Carroll) Farrar or Olivia Newton John returned to Australia, Marcie Jones would arrange lunch, a

---

449 Tricia contends that "Yvonne's role was to bring happiness for my mother, whereas I could never do that. The only happiness I gave my mother was having two daughters who she adored. She adored her grandchildren. She was brilliant with babies and kids but not so good with teenagers and adults."

few drinks, and some catch up usually at her home. Marcie remembers having a phone number for Yvonne in Perth. 'Yvonne must have given it to me. So I'd say, "Let's ring Yvonne!" She used to apologise when we rang her. She'd say, "I can't believe you guys are ringing me!" I'd say "Oh shut up! You'd be here, if you were in Melbourne." This happened a few times and everybody there would get on the phone and chat to Yvonne.'

Marcie remembers Yvonne telling her all about Truong during one of those phone calls. 'I asked Yvonne why she married him when she wasn't in love with him. She said, "He really loves me, so I thought I might as well marry him." I totally got that as I did that too!'

Wendy Stapleton ultimately caught up with Yvonne when she and her band went to Perth to promote her album "Dazed For Days". Wendy recalls that she and the band stayed in a big apartment block overlooking the sea in Cottesloe. Unbeknownst to Wendy at the time, Yvonne happened to live in a block of flats opposite that apartment block. Wendy says Yvonne was very cagey. 'She wouldn't give her phone number out. So someone passed on my number to Yvonne and she called me. We were so excited to be speaking to each other. She said, "I've gotta see you!"

'It was so bizarre that Yvonne happened to live in a block of flats opposite my apartment block. I ran over and she took me straight into her flat. As I entered the flat I noticed a Vietnamese man washing a car. 'I said, "Who's that?" She said, "That's Truong. He's my husband!"' I said, "What!"'

Yvonne's revelation stunned Wendy for a few moments. 'I told her I was in shock. Yvonne proceeded to tell Wendy that she'd only known Truong a short time before they married.

'She said he was sweet, but there was no use bringing him in to meet me because he couldn't hold a conversation.[450] I said, "How do you get on?" She said, "We just work it out."

Yvonne told Wendy she hadn't done any singing in Perth. She said she stayed out of pubs and clubs where anyone could recognise her. She just wanted to disappear and to be left alone. She told Wendy that she worked as an usherette in a cinema. She liked doing that. No one knew her. She'd just turn up, put a uniform on, guide people in with a torch, get her pay and then go home.

Wendy insisted that Yvonne accompany her and her band to all their gigs during their five days in Perth. 'We picked her up every night and she came to my jobs. Once she was out with us, it was all about having a good time. My band was from a different era. They were in their 20s. They didn't really know who she was, apart from the fact that she was a famous singer from the 1960s and the 1970s. She had a ball with them. They loved her because she was such a character. She was very funny. She was laughing and she kept saying "I'm having the best time I've had in ages."'

Before Wendy left Perth, she and Yvonne promised to keep in touch with each other. Wendy subsequently returned to Melbourne and continued her promotional tour. Then she went to England for quite a while doing tours, so they didn't keep in touch.

At some point after their wedding, Yvonne and Truong travelled to Melbourne to visit family members. Tricia's daughter Martine recalls meeting Truong for the first time.

---

450 Tricia Barrett contends that Truong spoke very good English from the outset. 'I didn't hear him speak Vietnamese.' It appears that Yvonne didn't want Truong to meet any of her friends given that she regretted her marriage to him.

She describes him as having 'a moustache and longish hair. He wasn't a sharp dresser. He was standard and nondescript. He was fairly aloof and didn't go out of his way to impress Yvonne. We were very accepting of him, but there was something about him that nagged at me. With Yvonne everything was music, animals, beach and family. I would have expected Yvonne to have been with someone musical, artistic, or at least a beach lover. I'm curious now as to what his actual passion was.'

Brenda (Long) Halman lived next door to Sheila Barrett in Braybrook. She remembers Sheila being stubborn, very strong willed, hardworking and very frugal. 'Her house and her garden were immaculate. She was very religious and went to church every Sunday. Yvonne had a pretty hard time with her mum being a very strict catholic.' Notwithstanding that though, Brenda opines that Yvonne was the light of Sheila's life.

Brenda remembers Yvonne having a zest for life. 'Yvonne had a lot going for her. She was vibrant, very beautiful, very talented, and she had a great sense of humour. She also had a good heart. She was always kind. She loved animals. She would visit her dad Ted and look after him. She didn't give up on him, no matter what. Unfortunately, she didn't see her inner beauty. She had low self-esteem and would put herself down.'

Yvonne and Truong moved from Perth to Sydney. In May 1985 Tricia and Martine Barrett flew to Sydney to spend two weeks during the school holidays with Yvonne and Truong in Neutral Bay. Tricia recollects thinking that 'things weren't good then and Yvonne was planning on leaving.'

Martine Barrett noticed that Yvonne's relationship with Truong had changed since she had seen them together back home in Melbourne. 'They weren't as affectionate towards each other. There was just a peck on the cheek and a hello. They didn't lean in to each other when they watched television.'

Nevertheless, Martine remembers Truong being happy to have them there. 'He took us and Yvonne out for lunch and introduced us to some of his friends and their wives and girlfriends.' Tricia recalls that she had met the friends previously in Perth. 'His brother Long, who was a headmaster in New Zealand, was also there. He was a very nice man.'

Tricia and Martine were both very pleased when Yvonne took them to see two of her music gigs at the Beef Steak and Bourbon bar in Kings Cross.[451] Yvonne was still working as a cocktail waitress, but she was always happy to get an opportunity to sing. Martine recalls that Yvonne was backed by a guitarist and pianist at both gigs. 'She looked great on stage wearing long hippie type outfits. She sang popular songs that the audience were happy to listen to.' Tricia is not aware if Yvonne had previously appeared at the Kings Cross bar or if she made further appearances in ensuing months.

In July 1985, Yvonne paid for Truong to fly back to his family in New Zealand. Tricia speculates that she was trying to end the relationship. She planned to move house once he was in New Zealand. So, while staying with Yvonne in Neutral Bay, Tricia helped Yvonne quietly pack her belongings. 'I went back to Sydney in August. Yvonne had moved by then into a flat in Birchgrove, a suburb in Sydney's inner west. But everything she owned, as well as a suitcase of my clothes, got left behind in her Neutral Bay unit.'

At the time Balmain's inhabitants were a mixture of retirees,

---

451 On both occasions Truong was working in the gambling casino.

manual workers, artists, thespians, musicians, restaurant workers, left wing lawyers, trade unionists and assorted "colourful" and shady characters. Pubs were many and they had live music played by local musicians.

Yvonne was happy she had moved to Birchgrove because she had met Robert Driver, a local barrister. 'I met Yvonne in July 1985 when she moved into our flats[452] at 36 Louisa Road, Birchgrove,'[453] Robert remembers. 'I strolled home this particular day from work and I called into my friend Toni's flat on route to my flat. Yvonne was there. She had just moved in. I took one look at her as she was rolling a joint with a drink in hand and I thought what more could a bloke want!

'One of the first things I did was give her one of my, what I thought to be very expensive, business cards. It was embossed and all very fancy like. I was feeling very pleased with myself. I go and have a leak and I come back and here she is with a bloody pair of scissors cutting up the card to make filters for her bloody joint. I was aghast! But there was no malice. She taught me how to roll the perfect joint. No one had ever used filters that I'd come across and I'd known a lot of people who'd smoked a lot of dope over a lot of years at that stage. My rage was tempered by the thought "Shit what a good idea!"' Suddenly Robert twigged. Rather than have his business cards destroyed, the better option would be to compromise by ripping out the side of a cigarette packet. That became the filter.

Robert and Yvonne hit it off immediately. 'I had grand

---

452 Robert had moved into his flat some two years earlier.

453 The 1960s apartment building consisted of 32 old fashioned dwellings, some of which suffered from not having natural light or ventilation. Nevertheless, it allowed the less wealthy, a privileged position in the street that had always been significant within the structure of Sydney's urban fabric.

visions of Yvonne being the woman for the rest of my life! She was my kinda girl. She drank, smoked, and had sex. She was the full blonde! But in the back of my mind I think she saw me as a bit of a toy boy. Maybe I was moving too fast or getting ahead of myself.'

Yvonne's small flat was three floors above Robert's flat. Yvonne's flat, which could best be described as a bed-sitter, consisted of one room containing a kitchen, bathroom, and a bedroom. Yvonne also had a great view of the harbour from her flat.

Yvonne and Robert went shopping at Woolworths soon after they got together. Robert recalls being like 'the little puppy that didn't want to let her out of my sight. We're walking along the aisles and Yvonne said to me, "What colour toothbrush do you want?" I always used blue toothbrushes, but I said, "Don't worry I've got plenty of tooth brushes."' Nevertheless, Yvonne purchased a blue tooth brush for Robert. 'Our physical relationship had already started before she gave me the toothbrush. But that's when I knew I had more than a foot in the door. You don't buy some bloke a toothbrush if you're pissing him off tomorrow. I saw that as evidence to some degree of permanency settling on my world.'

Yvonne was still working as a part time waitress in the Kings Cross casino. Robert was not into gambling, but he decided to visit Yvonne's casino one night. 'The attraction for me was free booze. I thought it was going to be like I was at a party or a pub, so I'm chatting away to people standing around a table. But they soon got pissed off with me, and quite rightly so, because they were trying to concentrate as there were thousands of bucks floating around.' That proved to be

Robert's one and only visit to Yvonne's casino. 'I was gently reminded by Yvonne that perhaps my place was at home. Whatever talents I had, they weren't ideally suited to casinos!

'The work in the casino wasn't like a 9 to 5 legit job. The dough she would have got would have been cash in hand. Whatever she was earning, she was living a pretty basic and fairly nomadic existence. In her flat she had a nice enough double bed and a couple of chairs and a table. She didn't seem to spend much money on herself, other than on cigarettes. She didn't have an expensive wardrobe of clothing either.'

Robert was five years younger than Yvonne. 'Our perspectives on the future may not have been aligned, but in my mind at least, she was my future. I think she was happy with the way things were. I would never have thought to marry Yvonne because I would never have thought to marry anyone as I'd been married before. But I wanted to spend the rest of my life with her as she was all I could want.'

Robert recalls that he and Yvonne were of a similar mind. They both supported left wing politics and Yvonne laughed at all of Robert's jokes. If he was out of line, Yvonne would pat him on the head and gently point out the error of his ways. There was never any fighting or arguments, except for one day when Robert didn't get his own way. 'I was sulky and shitty. She pulled me out of that by just laughing at me. With her, everything ended in laughter.

'She could take the piss out of me like no one else could. She would say some little bon mot and diffuse the whole thing. She was confident in her own skin. Her time with me was just magic. Ninety per cent was perfect, but I didn't get my way with the other ten per cent when I thought I should have. I can't remember a single thing where Yvonne made me angry, other than she didn't like jumping to attention.'

It was Robert's impression that Yvonne was resigned to what she was doing. She wasn't bitter or weeping into his arms because of anything. She was happy go lucky and she was having a good time living a quiet life in Sydney suburbia. She laughed a lot and she didn't take herself too seriously. There were numerous people around who Yvonne was simpatico with.

'Yvonne had a job and a bit of a toy boy, so things were fairly sweet,' says Robert. 'If I'd gone all romantically involved it mightn't have been as tranquil. I would have been a dope not appreciating that her experience with men was unfortunate. Why stuff it up by getting obsessively involved. Rather than being smart enough to appreciate the brilliant wicket I was on, I could have screwed it up by talking her to move in with me. It was great the way it was.'

Robert spent all his available spare time in Yvonne's company, but at no time was he aware that he was with a famous person. 'She told me she was a singer, and she might have shared an anecdote or two with me, but I pretty well knew bugger all about her history.'

Robert doesn't recall Yvonne talking to him about a music comeback. He expects that was because Yvonne knew that he wasn't into music of that particular era.[454] 'My impression was that she wasn't going back into music. But this is a thought, not a definitive statement. She wasn't one to sit around and wonder what might have been kind of stuff. It was like, here we are now, let's get on with it! I just think she was happy doing her thing.'

---

454 Robert was a fan of The Beatles, The Rolling Stones and Rod Stewart.

When Tricia Barrett arrived in Sydney in August 1985 to stay with Yvonne, Robert initially thought his idyllic life was in jeopardy. He expected that Tricia was going to cramp his style somewhat. 'But then I thought "What's the bloody problem!" Tricia used Yvonne's flat and we had my flat.'

Robert quickly saw Tricia as a good ally. 'She talked about us as a couple visiting them in Melbourne. She also seemed to be more impressed that I was a barrister than Yvonne was. Whatever reason Yvonne had to do with me, had nothing to do with the fact that I was a barrister. As far as she was concerned, I could have been a garbo!'

Tricia admits that she cramped Robert's style somewhat. 'Robert was genuine and I thought highly of him. He adored Yvonne and he wanted to get to know me. I was happy that Yvonne had met him and I was happy for their relationship, but I just wanted it to slow down a bit. I thought she was rushing into another relationship. I was guarded and being protective because I thought Yvonne had been through a lot with Truong. I think she would have had a good life with Robert.'

Tricia recalls Robert talking of taking Yvonne to Las Vegas. 'He wanted me to go with them too.' Robert remembers talking about such a trip. 'Las Vegas is one of the most amazing places I've been to. It's also the tackiest, but there's something compelling about it!'

Tricia also recalls Yvonne working on a Dusty Springfield act with a male performer in Sydney. 'I don't know his name because she never said who it was. She said it wasn't to be publicized at that time. I thought it would be good if she got back to singing, but nothing came of that.'

In late August 1985, Wendy Stapleton performed a number

of gigs in and around Sydney. Wendy was aware that Yvonne was now living in Birchgrove and she hoped to catch up with her while in Sydney as it had been sometime since they had last seen each other. Wendy wasn't able to contact Yvonne however, so their reunion didn't eventuate. But by a strange quirk of fate, Wendy ran into the person she least expected to see in Sydney.

'I was walking along the main street of Kings Cross on the way back to my hotel from a city nightclub when I heard someone call out "Wendy, Wendy". I turned around but I didn't recognise the person who had called out to me. When he mentioned he was looking for Yvonne, it clicked who he was. I'd seen Truong in Perth, but I'd never met him, so I was surprised that he knew me. Then I realised that he obviously knew who I was from photos of me and Yvonne together.'

Truong hadn't stayed long in New Zealand. He returned to Sydney unexpectedly after spending some six weeks with his family.[455] Wendy wasn't aware of this. Moreover, she knew very little about Yvonne's life and movements at this time, as she had been busy months on end touring throughout England and in recent months throughout Australia. Wendy was relieved when Truong accepted her truthful explanation that she hadn't seen Yvonne for a few years because of her extensive touring, nor did she have contact details for Yvonne.

Meanwhile, unaware that Truong was back in Sydney, Tricia Barrett decided she better be home in Melbourne, in order to 'save drama in the home camp' on Father's Day which fell on Sunday, September 1st 1985. 'I went home from Yvonne's

---

455 "Tragic end for Yvonne", Scene — August 16th — 22nd 1986.

on the Saturday (August 31st) with a letter from Yvonne for Ted[456] for Father's Day.'

Tricia knew that Yvonne loved flowers, but she didn't like them to be floppy. She loved gerberas because they stood up and were happy looking. Yvonne was always buying Tricia flowers, so as daffodils were in season, Tricia bought Yvonne a bunch of daffodils just before she flew back to Melbourne. 'So the last flowers she had were daffodils, and that's what I take to the cemetery when I can visit Yvonne's grave,' says Tricia.

Unbeknownst to Tricia at the time, Truong had by now discovered where Yvonne was living,. He drove to Yvonne's Birchgrove flat unexpectedly some time on Sunday September 1st 1985.

Tricia believes that Yvonne quickly fabricated a story that Truong couldn't live with her because she had signed a sole tenant agreement with the building's owner. Having said that to him, Yvonne then asked Truong to leave. Truong insisted that he had nowhere else to go, and Yvonne agreed to him staying that night.

Yvonne's neighbour and friend Chrissie[457] happened to be with Yvonne at the time of Truong's arrival. She observed the discussion between Truong and Yvonne, and stayed for a few drinks with them before leaving some time later. It is thought that Yvonne and Truong had a meal together cooked by Yvonne in the flat that evening. About midnight, concerned for Yvonne's safety, Chrissie made the last phone call ever

---

456 Tricia is referring to her father Ted Barrett.

457 Chrissie's surname is not known. Attempts to locate and interview her for this biography were unsuccessful.

made to Yvonne. She thought Yvonne seemed subdued during their brief conversation.[458]

Early on Monday morning September 2nd 1985, Yvonne put on a pair of rubber gloves and began washing the previous night's dishes.[459] As she did that, she told Truong to leave. Truong picked up a wine bottle and hit Yvonne on the back of her head with it as she washed the dishes, thereby knocking her to the floor. The bottle smashed and Yvonne cut her hands as she tried to protect herself. She then lost consciousness. As Yvonne lay unconscious on the kitchen floor, Truong removed his belt from his trousers and strangled her with it. Truong then covered Yvonne's body with a doona before leaving her flat.[460]

Yvonne's friend Chrissie woke early that morning. Still concerned about Yvonne, she knocked on Yvonne's door. There was no answer. Chrissie then noticed that Yvonne's flat window was still shut and that her cats were still at her window. Chrissie thought it strange that Yvonne hadn't let her cats out to get some fresh air by then. [461] Sensing that something was seriously wrong, Chrissie hurried to the caretaker's flat.[462] He was not available, so Chrissie spoke to

---

458 "Yvonne Barrett: A Senseless Tragedy", TV Week dated August 30th 1986.

459 Yvonne was found wearing green rubber gloves.

460 Tricia Barrett recalls that the police took the wheels off Truong's abandoned car and 'left it there in the parking lot at Birchgrove. They took the wheels so nobody could drive it. I don't know whatever happened to the car.'

461 Tricia remembers that Yvonne had always loved cats. 'When she died she had three cats. The police station took "George" named after George Benson. One policeman took home "Anna" named after Anna Pavlova, and I bought "Sammy" home with me. I'm not really an animal person. I didn't like cats, but I had to look after "Sammy". As kids we always had animals, but they weren't mine. They were my brother Peter's and Yvonne's.

462 The caretaker collected rent every Saturday and undertook all repairs needed in the block of flats.

his wife who was a nurse. The nurse and Chrissie then rushed to Yvonne's flat and opened her flat door with the caretaker's duplicate key. After finding Yvonne's lifeless body covered in the doona, the nurse immediately rang the local police station.

The Barrett family learnt the news of Yvonne's tragic and brutal death when police rang Yvonne's brother Peter. He then broke the dreadful news to Tricia and his parents. 'It was the biggest shock of my life,' Tricia says. 'I grieve for her and for everyone who misses her. Yvonne was always such a happy person and so friendly and gregarious. Everyone thought she was wonderful. She didn't deserve to go that way. At the time the police weren't sure of what time she died..' Sheila Barrett said at the time that she used to think Yvonne had a sad life. 'Show business was all she knew and all she ever wanted to do.'[463]

Yvonne had rung her father Ted on Father's Day. Tricia asserts that this was the last time any of the family heard from Yvonne. 'She often rang at the weekend, but she used to ring me every Tuesday without fail for a chat. I kept thinking she'd ring any moment that Tuesday. I tried to ring her a bit later that day, but I didn't get an answer because she died on the Monday.'

Following Yvonne's death, Tricia went through a stage where she felt very angry with Yvonne. 'She could have told me how things were with Truong. I could have stayed with her an extra couple of days, but there are a lot of those ifs and buts. Yvonne didn't tell us her problems. I actually leant on her more than she leant on me."[464]

---

463 "Yvonne Barrett : A Senseless Tragedy", TV Week dated August 30th 1986.
464 "Tragic Finale for Yvonne", The Sunday Press, July 27th 1986.

Maureen Elkner first met Yvonne when Maureen's Melbourne singing group The Chiffons appeared on the *Happening 70* television show. Maureen recalls meeting Yvonne again when she moved into the Louisa Road, Birchgrove flats. 'I wasn't a friend of Yvonne's. I was an acquaintance, but when I heard she'd moved into our street, I went to her flat and welcomed her to the street. She was very sweet. I don't mean that in a condescending way. I mean it more in a vulnerable way. She was also very frail. She weighed about 48 kilos or something like that.

'She told me she was trying to get her life back together again, and she wanted to resurrect her career. I wanted to protect her because I saw there was some kind of pain there. She'd obviously been through a lot, but maybe she hadn't told too many people about that. I just wanted to wrap my arms around her and tell her that everything was going to be okay.

'My brother and I were to have dinner with her that week. Sadly, we never had the chance to have a really good chat with her. I was asleep when about three o'clock that morning a guy raced in and said, "My God they've killed Yvonne! They've killed Yvonne!" You don't expect stuff like that to happen to such a really sweet, delightful, gentle and talented person.'

Robert Driver had previously had goods stolen from his flat. As a result, he feared that thieves could also break into Yvonne's flat. He recalls chastising Yvonne every day for leaving her flat window open because of some seedy characters, who not only lived in the flats, but were visited by their seedy mates. 'Yvonne's window was at waist level, so any ten-year-old could have climbed into her flat easily. But like everything else, she smiled sweetly and left the window open so that her cats could get in and out of her flat.'

Robert was going off to work on Tuesday September 3rd 1985 which was the day after Yvonne's murder. He noticed that Yvonne's window was closed. 'I had this uneasy feeling or premonition where you see the same thing every day for weeks on end, and then one day it's different. I didn't knock on the door because we'd had a disagreement on the night she was murdered. I'd gone off to my flat in a huff because I didn't get my own way over something or other. What I wanted to do is so inconsequential that I can't remember, but all was not well between us. I didn't know Truong had been around. I thought he was in New Zealand, and that she was never going to see him again. When I got home after work that day, there were cops and weeping people everywhere.'

13. 'SUCH A WASTE OF A BEAUTIFUL SOUL'

n 1985, Clarrie Lemme and Jeff Ahern were working in Sydney as a team in the Homicide Squad. At the time, Clarrie was a detective sergeant 2nd class, bordering on 1st class, and Jeff was a detective senior constable. Early on in his career Clarrie had worked in Homicide, prior to being transferred to the armed hold up squad in Sydney. In 1976 Clarrie was assigned to Melbourne's Armed Robbery Squad on interchange duty at the time of the Great Bookie Robbery.[465] 'I did two months down there and a couple of weeks in South Australia and Western Australia. Then I graduated to Homicide, which in most states is the elite squad.'[466]

Prior to becoming a detective in the homicide squad, Jeff Ahern had gained experience in the scientific branch of the police force. He was good at photography and looking at crime scenes, car accidents, and murders. He subsequently moved into the field of homicide investigation. There he was able to better use his expertise in photography and in searching crime scenes.

---

465 On April 21st 1976, the "Great Bookie Robbery" was committed by a gang of six people. It is widely believed that some $14 to $16 million was stolen from bookmakers in the Victoria Club, which was located in Queen Street, Melbourne.

466 Clarrie eventually moved into other areas of the police force. He was involved in undercover work for three years, before becoming a pioneer in phone tapping and bringing that into the digital age of recording surveillance.

Clarrie recalls getting called out to investigate a suspicious death in Sydney's inner-west on Monday, September 2nd 1985. He was told that uniform police had found a deceased female on the floor of her flat at 36 Louisa Road, Birchgrove. Clarrie takes up the story. 'Jeff Ahern picked me up and we went straight to the flat and started our investigations. We learnt from the uniform police who initially attended the flat that the deceased woman Yvonne Barrett had come to Sydney from Perth and was working in a gambling casino in Kings Cross.'

Having acquired this information, the two detectives immediately secured the crime scene. This involved restricting people from walking through the crime scene, thereby enabling Clarrie and Jeff to establish what they thought was the cause of death. Clarrie recalls that an examination of Yvonne's body revealed 'injuries to the head, marks on the side of the neck and the throat, and small blood vessels in the eyes. When you looked at a body you could always tell from strangulations, or fixations or no breathing, or the cutting off of the person's breath supply, that a lot of times blood vessels will appear in the eyes because of the pressure. Being strangled also gives you the same blood vessels in the eyes. That was one of the issues we looked at and discussed at the time.'

After examining Yvonne's injuries, Clarrie was almost certain that he knew how Yvonne had died. 'I'd say an argument started. Yvonne might have turned her back on her killer and he has hit her over the head with a wine bottle. She's gone down. He didn't know whether she was going to die or not and he has strangled her in the meantime because things weren't going his way. She may not have been prepared to change her lifestyle by having him back, so this all happened. No doubt he was rejected and that caused him to do what he did.

'Photographs were taken of Yvonne's body, the blood, the broken wine bottle and the strangulation marks on her neck. A forensic person with a medical background attended on the coroner's behalf. She established time of death and whatever else we wanted to know.'[467]

Local detectives assisted in the investigations by speaking to neighbours to establish what they might have heard or seen, and what they possibly knew about Yvonne, so as to assist Clarrie Lemme and Jeff Ahern in narrowing down who they were looking for. A "running sheet" containing relevant information was prepared and subsequently passed to Clarrie and Jeff. Clarrie recalls that he and Jeff 'didn't know anything about Yvonne Barrett at the time of the murder, apart from what the uniform police had established. We had no idea she was a singer, or that she had originally come from Melbourne. We didn't learn that until such time as we made further enquiries and established who her family was.'

By the following day Clarrie and Jeff had established that Yvonne had been drinking with her estranged husband Hoang Van Truong on the day of her murder. 'Truong was the only suspect at this time,' recounts Clarrie. 'Everything pointed to him, but we didn't know where he was. We'd established

---

467 Clarrie says 'Things have changed since those days with DNA and forensic science. Forensic specialists attend straight away now. In our day you called the scientific specialist and the coroner, and established time of death and maybe the cause of death at the particular time. You'd take photographs in situ and indicate where these things were, so they weren't lost. The coroner or someone acting on their behalf can give evidence to the fact that when they go to do the autopsy, they can understand from where the body was, and how it was laid out, or how the body was found, that it coincides with the possible cause of murder.'

from a neighbour that he was trying to convince Yvonne that they should get back together. That neighbour had drinks that afternoon with them. Later that day the neighbour grew concerned when she noticed that Yvonne hadn't let her cats out. She also discovered that the light was on in Yvonne's flat.'

Not knowing his whereabouts, the detectives circulated Truong's description which they'd obtained from one of Yvonne's neighbours. Clarrie Lemme says 'We described him as best we could. We couldn't say at that time that he was wanted for murder, so we stated that he was wanted for interview.'

Clarrie believes that Truong was obviously depressed because he took a number of serepax tablets and then slashed his wrists, and across and down his arms. But he only cut veins rather than an artery. He realised what he'd done and got himself to a nearby hospital. There he was treated by casualty nurses and a doctor who subsequently rang the Burwood police station.[468]

Clarrie recalls that 'a young cop from Burwood raced up to the hospital and grabbed Truong. He was doing his job, but he should have called us first. Truong made some admissions to the young cop, so he arrested him and took him to the Burwood police station. He was going to take a statement from Truong, then put him in the dock and charge him. We had to intercept the cop and take him, together with Truong, back to the Balmain police station where all our information and running sheets were. We interviewed Truong and presented him with evidence that made it a more positive and stronger case. Truong then admitted to committing the murder.'

---

468 Tricia Barrett remembers being told by the police 'that if Truong had run into the Vietnamese community, they would never have found him.'

Hoang Van Truong was charged with Yvonne's murder on September 5th 1985. Clarrie Lemme recalls Truong being full of self-pity at the time. 'To make sure he wasn't a risk to himself from self-harm, Truong would have been looked at by psychologists and welfare people the whole time he was in remand awaiting trial.'

On September 6th 1985, Truong was refused bail when he made a brief appearance in Sydney's Balmain court. In a case of very poor timing, Truong was returned to the Balmain police station at the same time as Tricia Barrett was at the station. Tricia noticed Truong in the next room and she panicked. 'I didn't know where to go. I spotted something on the desk and I went to pick it up. I don't remember if it was a gun, a knife or what, but I was ready to attack him. Clarrie Lemme was a big man and he and another huge policeman picked me up like a bag of apples and carried me to another room. They apologised for Truong being at the police station at the same time as me. That should never have happened.'

Clarrie and Jeff Ahern hadn't previously had a murder case where there was no family member living in the city where the murder had occurred. Tricia remembers being looked after 'wonderfully well' by Clarrie and Jeff. 'At the time I felt like I was in and out of police stations all the time. The police subpoenaed me to identify Yvonne's body, so I flew to Sydney for the identification. They paid my airfare and my accommodation for that trip. Jeff Ahern and Madelaine, a young policewoman, picked me up at the airport. She looked after me while I was in Sydney.'

Tricia subsequently flew to Sydney several more times, namely for the autopsy, the coroner's inquest, and then to organise Yvonne's flat, her coffin, and the release of her body. 'When I went back to Sydney to bring Yvonne's body home for her funeral, the police put me up in a hotel. They kept moving me so that no one, like newspaper reporters, could find me and harass me.'

Tricia contends that the autopsy was a 'dreadful thing to go through because of the pretty horrific things they do to the body. I know they have to do it, but I can't see why it's necessary in cases like that where the cause of death was obvious.' That said though, Tricia concedes that 'they had to check to see if there were drugs or poisons or anything else in Yvonne's system.'[469]

Tricia, Yvonne, and Martine Barrett had been to the hairdresser a few days before Tricia and Martine returned to Melbourne for Father's Day[470]. Tricia recalls that 'Yvonne's hair had been blonde and curly. She'd had a body perm in it and it was just gorgeous.' Tricia got a huge shock when she saw that Yvonne's head had been shaved at the autopsy. 'That really freaked me out!'

Sam Anglesey recalls being on air doing the afternoon drive show on Adelaide's 5AD radio station when he learnt of Yvonne's death. 'It was coming up to the news at the end of the hour when up comes on my monitor the news that Yvonne had been murdered. What a shock! Then I had to go back on air and be all smiley and chirpy and crack jokes when I've just

---

469 Yvonne's Death Certificate doesn't list her injuries. Tricia says 'details of the injuries came out in the autopsy.' She adds that the official death certificate states that Yvonne died 'about September 2nd 1985. They never really had an exact time of death because she wasn't found until September 3rd. My mother always had that date as her remembrance because that's the date when we were told of her death. But she actually died on the 2nd, so I do my remembrance on my own on the 2nd.'

470 Sunday September 1st 1985.

heard of her death.' Sam opines that 'Yve would have been a soft touch. She didn't have a bad bone in her body. It must have been hard on Yvonne's family. They all loved her. She was the apple of their eyes. Yvonne's coming from a working-class family is what I loved about her. She never lost her working-class roots!'

Kaye Johnston heard of Yvonne's death when a friend rang to tell her that she had seen the news of Yvonne's death on the front page of the *Adelaide News* afternoon newspaper. 'I couldn't believe it! Yvonne gave a lot to the soldiers as an entertainer and she did what I would call compassionate work on behalf of some of our soldiers when she came back home. She made phone calls to their partners and I know she even met some of them.'

Kaye had developed a warm friendship with Sam Anglesey and Yvonne during the 1970 cruise on the Achille Lauro. Kaye recalls ringing the 5AD radio station and asking to speak to Sam urgently. 'I knew he would have heard the news via the newsroom and not had anyone to share it with because no one in the newsroom would have known Yvonne. We talked each other through the tragedy in between his radio broadcast.'

Jan and Lyn Field had lost touch with Yvonne when she moved to Perth. They recall receiving the news of Yvonne's death over the phone. They were both totally stunned upon hearing the news. 'We couldn't believe it,' says Lyn. 'It was a big shock. We felt guilty that we'd lost contact with her.' Jan remembers Yvonne helping them in the early days of their singing careers. 'We were quiet and shy and she was outgoing.'

Close friend Ian Turpie opined that it was 'awful and just not fair that it should happen to someone like Yvonne. She was a beautiful girl with a top sense of humour, and she was a great singer. She had everything. I hadn't seen her for eight years. I thought she was in Perth. I wish I had known she was here in Sydney.'[471]

Yvonne's former manager Brian de Courcy noted that there were 'quite a few people who are shattered around town at the moment. Yvonne never said an unkind word about anybody and her murder is a real tragedy.'[472]

John Vallins was living in Sydney when he heard of Yvonne's death on the radio. 'I couldn't then, and still can't understand, how someone with so much life in her could die in such a horrible way.'

Tricia Barrett recalls receiving cards and flowers 'from all around Australia, the U.S. and the U.K. Bert and Patti Newton sent flowers, so did Olivia Newton John and Pat Carroll. And Olivia rang twice to talk to us.'

Margie Bayes has never forgotten the day she heard the news of Yvonne's death. 'My mother died unexpectedly of a heart attack that same day. When I heard Yvonne had been murdered, I just couldn't believe it. I nearly threw up. Yvonne's friendship meant everything to me. I loved her from the minute I met her until the last time I saw her. I was always proud of what she did and I think she in turn was proud of what I did.'

Frank Howson described the news of Yvonne's death as being 'a shocking way for a very nice person to go.' Yvonne's former manager Ron Fletcher recalls getting 'a terrible shock' upon hearing the tragic news. 'I would imagine that had Yvonne lived, she'd still be a bloody good performer. She was

---

471 'Murder Shocks Showbiz World', unsourced press clipping.

472

quite a funny girl. Once you got her out of her shell, she was funny as buggery. I imagine she would have been doing stage shows, but sadly we'll never know.'

Ted Hamilton had been living in America for ten years when he received a call from Dick Healey to say that Yvonne had been murdered. Ted remembers getting a huge shock upon hearing that terrible news over the phone. 'When people are murdered your senses are aroused to indignation. Yvonne had a lot of talent. She was a lovely girl taken too soon unfortunately by the vileness of life. She was very down to earth. She wasn't snobby or uppity. She was a nice-looking girl and she had a lot of talent.'

Carmel Chayne was living in Sydney at the time of Yvonne's death. She had recently returned from living overseas for a number of years, so she wasn't aware that Yvonne was also living in Sydney at that time. 'I found that out when I heard about her death on the radio. It was devastating news. You can't begin to think that's going to happen to someone like Yvonne, especially as she had entertained our troops on two tours of Vietnam. I felt really sad for someone I had known in the past.'

Denise Drysdale was devastated when she heard of Yvonne's death. 'You don't want anybody to go like that, but especially not Yvonne because she was such a lovely girl. To find her in such an abusive situation was so wrong! Mrs Barrett was a lovely lady. She came to a couple of my shows after Yvonne's death. She still hadn't gotten over Yvonne and how she went. To lose a child, like that, is just horrible. She said it nearly killed her!'

Mick Hamilton was horrified by the news of Yvonne's death. 'I hadn't seen her for years, but I just couldn't believe it. I was pole axed. It was just a shocking bloody thing!'

Terry Walker recalls that all members of The Strangers group were shocked upon hearing the news of Yvonne's tragic death. 'You can't explain that happening to someone like Yvonne. I had a great affection for Yvonne. She was a lovely, friendly, happy and delightful person.'

Lesley Kirk heard of Yvonne's death from a friend who heard the news on the radio. 'I was devastated. I hadn't spoken to Yvonne for about nine years but I still considered her a friend. I rang John Farrar's mum the next day. She too was devastated. She'd rung John in America to tell him. He then rang three times the next day to see if she'd heard from Yvonne's parents.'

Family tributes were paid to Yvonne in Melbourne's *The Sun* newspaper. They included the following:

"Yvonne Frances. Loved you always, prayed for you always. God bless. Love you. Mum."

"Yvonne, loved daughter of Ted. To me you were so beautiful, like a brilliant star in the sky. But my darling Yvonne, we never said goodbye. I will always remember the times we had together. But my little sweetheart, I cannot understand. I will always love you until the day I die. Your loving father Ted."

"Yvonne Frances. Dearly loved sister of Tricia, loved sister-in-law and friend of Alan, adored aunt of Leisel and Martine. We'll remember the good times. Love you. Rest peacefully Staish."[473]

"Yvonne Frances. We cried a thousand tears for you Von. And we feel this pain inside. To see someone we really love. To leave us far behind. But we still have love and memories of

473 viii Ibid.
ix Staish was a family nickname.

fun we had together. We will always be your little girls. The ones who will love you forever — Leisel and Martine."[474]

"Yvonne Frances. Dearly loved sister of Peter, loved sister-in-law and friend of Jan, adored aunt of David and Karlie. We love you "Cock."[475]

More than 200 mourners attended Yvonne's funeral on Monday September 16th 1985. The Requiem Mass at the Christ the King Catholic Church in Churchill Avenue, Braybrook was said by parish priest Father Rom Murphy. In his homily, Father Murphy admitted that he didn't know Yvonne personally, but he remembered her name. He opined that the many mourners in attendance indicated 'the affection and esteem in which Yvonne was held. The pages of tributes in *The Sun* newspaper, from friends and family, indicated that there was something very special about her. You don't have that many friends unless you are a wonderful person!'

Father Murphy went on to mention that Yvonne had been a student at Christ the King College. He then briefly summarised her career noting that her talent as a dancer was first recognised as a child at the May Downs School of Dancing. He then mentioned her success in Swallows Juniors, stage musicals and pop concerts. He also noted that Yvonne had toured Vietnam twice entertaining Australian troops during the Vietnam War, and he added that Yvonne also helped put the western suburbs on the map. He concluded his homily with the statement 'Yvonne used her talents to bring pleasure and enjoyment to so many people.'[476]

There were no pallbearers at the funeral. Tricia recalls her

---

474 x Leisel and Martine were Yvonne's nieces.

475 This was another family nickname.

476 "200 mourn murdered pop star", unsourced press clipping.

sister-in-law Jan telling her that the coffin was left on the trolley 'because no one could do it. My brother Peter was looking after his wife Jan and their children Karlie and David. My husband was looking after my mother and my girls. My girlfriend's son Grant Jones looked after me. He was wonderful.'

The funeral director and his staff subsequently carried Yvonne's coffin from the church and placed it in the hearse following the Requiem Mass. The funeral cortege then proceeded to Altona Memorial Park for Yvonne's burial in the Lawn Cemetery.[477]

Yvonne's funeral was 'very hard' on Ted Barrett as Tricia recalls. 'Yvonne loved him very much. He collapsed at the church and was gasping for breath. We thought he was going to die. A doctor, who was friend of the family, tended to him. He was alright after that.' Ted's brother Bill's daughter in law was at the funeral with two of her children.

Patti Newton recalls learning about Yvonne's death while she and Bert were holidaying with their family in Fiji. 'June Bronhill happened to be there. She told me what had happened. We were about to leave Fiji to come home. We got there in time to go to the funeral.'

Wendy Stapleton attended the funeral with several mutual friends of Yvonne's. Tricia's daughter Martine was deeply affected by Yvonne's death. She contends that 'if it wasn't for Wendy staying with me on the day of the funeral, I don't think I'd be here today. I threw myself in the back of the hearse when the coffin went in. Wendy pulled me out and she came up to my house afterwards.'

Marcie Jones recalls there being a number of entertainers

---

477 Yvonne was buried in Section AX, Row NN, Grave 94.

at the funeral. 'I can't remember them all as I was pretty upset. I went with Joy Lemmon who was another good friend. The Field Twins were there too. We were all in shock. It was horrible.' Marcie wrote in her autobiography that 'it was a terrible time for all who loved Yvonne, especially her family and such a waste of a beautiful soul.'[478]

Yvonne's cousin Liz Dennis recalls Yvonne's funeral being one of the saddest funerals she's ever attended. 'Everybody was in shock. We were like zombies! Yvonne was taken so early and the way she was taken affected all the family. All of us just loved her!'

Ronnie Burns recalls Yvonne's death being 'such a shock' to he and his wife Maggie. 'It was a tragedy for a young, very beautiful and absolutely charming person like Yvonne to have such a dark ending.'

---

478 Marcie Jones, 'Marcie Jones: Runs In The Blood', Network Creative Services Pty Ltd, Melbourne, 2008, p.96.

14. 'HAD HE NOT BEEN FOUND GUILTY, I WOULD HAVE GONE TOTALLY BERSERK'

The ten months between Yvonne's death and the trial of her ex-husband was a difficult time for Yvonne's family and friends.

Sometime after Yvonne's funeral, Ronnie contacted Tricia Barrett and invited her to his home for lunch with him and his wife Maggie. Tricia recalls that Ronnie spoke to her at length following lunch. 'He had a huge painting in the dining room and he sat me in front of it to try and get this aura of things. He was trying to help me be peaceful and accept what had happened to Yvonne. From the way he spoke, Ronnie certainly gave me a bit of peace. How long it stayed with me I don't remember, but I'll never forget him. He probably did more for me than any counsellors or anyone else had. I have never forgotten Ronnie for that. He is a beautiful person!'

Marcie Jones remembers that Yvonne never thought she was good enough. 'She had a beautiful soul. I loved her. She didn't have a big ego. I never did either. I was what you see is what you get. She was the same. She was very approachable. I keep going back to the fact that she was a Cancerian. Like

Yvonne I'm a Cancerian, but I've got a Capricorn Moon and an Aries Rising. Yvonne was a Cancerian Dog. She was born in the year of the dog.

'They wear their heart on their sleeve and Yvonne wore hers big time. She was a big beautiful softy. She was too loyal for her own good. You give them a little pat and scratch and they roll over and go okay. Pat her head and she'd be "Isn't he wonderful", even if he was kicking her up the backside.

'It was a shame that Yvonne never got the opportunity to have children, because she would have been a great mother. She craved to be loved, but she didn't meet a man who would really love her and look after her. I think we all pine for that. As little girls we want the picket fence and the knight in shiny armour, but unfortunately Yvonne was a bit used and abused. Me too! So were Joy Lemmon, Lynne Randell and a lot of other women.'

Marcie has friends who are clairvoyants and she says her grandmother was very clairvoyant. 'There are a lot out there who are not good at it and they'll take your money. But the ones I know are not like that. I get very strange feelings. I dream things and I see things. My grandmother was the same.

'Not long after Yvonne's funeral, I went to see a clairvoyant I knew. She said "There's a woman here and she's crying for a lost love." She then said some other things. All of a sudden the penny dropped and I thought "I bet this is Yvonne! She never got over John Farrar." When she said some more things, I knew it was Yvonne. I said "I know who this is. Tell her I understand." The clairvoyant then said to me "She's saying she didn't feel anything when she was killed!"'

Wendy Stapleton recalls that even though Yvonne loved

Peter Arrowsmith, 'she always told me that she never got over John Farrar leaving her for Pat Carroll. The distance probably helped things heal, but she never stopped talking about it. Even when I saw her in Perth, she still said she never got over John. But Yvonne never said a bad thing about either John or Pat. They remained her friends.'

Robert Driver remembers being distressed after Yvonne's death for 'six months or so. I went through the five stages of grief.[479] Yvonne was a standout in my life. She ticked all the boxes! No one from the flats went to Yvonne's funeral. One of the reasons I didn't go was because I thought I'd contributed to Yvonne's death. As I understand it from Chrissie[480], the catalyst was my toothbrush! Chrissie believes Truong saw the extra toothbrush and put two and two together. But for that toothbrush he wouldn't have known about me.

'I was extremely surprised that the cops never spoke to me. I'm not saying I aided and abetted a murder. But it's kind of ironic that the thing that was most significant to me in our relationship turned out to be the thing that was possibly most significant in ending it. This is the way I felt at the time and I still think that. The significance of the toothbrush will live with me forever! I'm not saying it was all my fault. That lay with the guy who killed her. They may have been stoned and probably pissed and things spiralled out of hand. It was a trigger and somebody's still got to pull that trigger.'[481]

At long last Yvonne's murderer was put on trial. Tricia Barrett recalls Jeff Ahern being her 'lifeline' during the ten

---

479 The five stages are: Denial, Anger, Bargaining, Depression and Acceptance.
480 Chrissie lived in the same block of flats.
481 Tricia Barrett asserts that she certainly didn't hold Robert responsible in any way for Yvonne's death.

months wait for Truong's murder trial. 'He rang me nearly every day, much to my husband's horror, to tell me what was happening, what to expect next, and what I had to do. My husband became very jealous because of those phone calls. That was ridiculous! It was a very tough time for me. I don't think I'd ever been in a courtroom before that, so I had no idea of what I was going to face. Plus, I was in a strange city. Jeff Ahern, Clarrie Lemme and Madelaine, the young policewoman, were marvellous to me. I could not speak highly enough of them.'

Jeff Ahern looked after the welfare of civilian witnesses, making sure they were picked up from the airport and dropped off at their hotels, or collected from their homes or hotels. Clarrie Lemme focused on making sure that witnesses for the day arrived in court on time to go through their evidence in the order requested by the Crown or the Defence. Clarrie recalls that it could be pretty involved when you got to court. 'There's empanelling of the jury. You've got to challenge the jury panel. You might get to twenty-four jurors and you only want to take twelve. The Defence has the right to challenge or the Crown may want to challenge. This all takes time.'

Justice Mervyn David Finlay[482] presided over Hoang Van Truong's weeklong trial in the NSW Supreme Court in mid-July 1986. Joseph Xavier (Joe) Gibson Q.C. was the Senior Crown Prosecutor. Snr Public Defender Bill Hosking Q.C. defended Truong. A panel of twelve jurors was subsequently chosen.

Clarrie Lemme states that 'Joe Gibson was an excellent prosecutor. He was very astute. You couldn't have asked for a

---

482 Justice Finlay was admitted to the Bar in 1952. He practised as a Queen's Counsel in New South Wales (NSW). He was a NSW Supreme Court Judge from 1984 to 1994.

better judge, instructing officers, or senior counsellors. They were all very professional!'

Clarrie, Jeff Ahern, scientific and forensic science experts, a representative of the coroner, Hoang Van Truong, and Yvonne's neighbour Chrissie[483] were among the witnesses who testified at the trial. Tricia was subpoenaed to testify in court that she had flown to Sydney, accompanied by her then sister-in-law, to formally identify Yvonne's body at the morgue.

During the trial Tricia stayed in accommodation provided for her by the casino where Yvonne had worked. She attended court by herself because she didn't want to subject her mother to the trauma of the trial. Understandably Tricia found the trial very traumatic. She recalls being physically ill and having to leave the court 'a few times' because she was 'throwing up.'

Clarrie Lemme remembers Truong being very solemn throughout the trial. 'He was very quiet. He just sat there with his head down and he didn't say anything apart from giving his testimony. No character witnesses appeared in court for him either.'

The prosecution fought the case on the grounds that Truong went to Yvonne's flat with the distinct purpose of getting back together with Yvonne. In describing Yvonne's death, police evidence was given that Truong had punched Yvonne in the face and smashed a bottle of wine over her head. Yvonne immediately lost consciousness. Not knowing if that blow to the head had really killed Yvonne, Truong then removed his belt and strangled her with it. Press reports noted that Truong had allegedly said to Yvonne "It's better that we die together."

---

483 Chrissie's surname is not known.

But his attempted suicide by slashing his wrists and taking sedatives was thwarted when he recovered in hospital.[484]

Tricia recalls getting 'a bit cross at one stage' during the trial because it seemed to her that Justice Finlay was sleeping. 'I remember getting real angry thinking how could he close his eyes!' Clarrie Lemme duly advised her that Justice Finlay would have been listening to the evidence, and he would read the transcripts once all the evidence had been heard.

The Supreme Court was then emptied so that the jury could consider their verdict. The jurors were then charged with the responsibility of deciding whether, on the facts of the case, that Truong was guilt or not guilty of the offence for which he'd been charged. The jury was also informed by Justice Finlay that they must reach their verdict by considering the evidence introduced in court, and the directions he had given them.

It took the jury of eleven men and one woman a little over an hour to find Truong guilty of murder. As the verdict was handed down, the jury all turned and looked at Tricia. The guilty verdict was a relief to Tricia. 'Had he not been found guilty, I would have gone totally berserk. I would have torn the place apart and probably would have ended up where he was sitting.'[485]

On August 5th 1986, Truong was sentenced by Justice Finlay to life imprisonment without a non-parole period. Life at that time in New South Wales was fifteen years. Justice Finlay said he accepted psychiatric evidence that Truong had killed Yvonne because of feelings of hurt and rejection. In handing down his sentence however, he rejected a submission by

---

484 'Tragic end for Yvonne,' *Scene*, August 16th — 22nd 1986.
485 'Tragic finale for Yvonne', *The Sunday Press*, July 27th 1986.

the Senior Public Defender, Bill Hosking, QC, that Truong was 'suffering from a disease of the mind that impaired his responsibility for the crime.' Justice Finlay also rejected Bill Hosking's claims that Truong's war service, tragic life, ingestion of marijuana and alcohol at the time the offence occurred, together with the rejection of his desperate pleas to get back together with Yvonne, had diminished his responsibility for the crime.

According to Clarrie Lemme, Bill Hosking, QC was a good Defence Counsel. 'He was very open and very fair. He tried to do the best for his client by requesting a psychiatric examination of Truong to support his application to have diminished responsibility introduced.[486] Defence Counsel would have had access to the psychiatric report and would have sought advice, as necessary, from the appropriate medical people. Justice Finlay would have taken the psychiatric report into consideration, but diminished responsibility was certainly not something I would have talked about at the time. It was straight out murder!

'Justice Finlay was an extremely intelligent and diligent man and he would have looked at the evidence as it was. The facts and the evidence were so strong that he obviously felt Truong went there to do the wrong thing and he did it. He hit Yvonne, then before he took off, he made sure of it by strangulation!'

Tricia Barrett had been quite ill at the time, but she was in court for Truong's sentencing. 'When his sentence of life in prison without parole was released, I was numb. I

---

486 Diminished responsibility exists as a statutory partial defence in most Australian jurisdictions. The defence is only available in cases of murder and serves to reduce the offence to manslaughter.

was thinking it's not bringing her back. I didn't know a life sentence was only fifteen years in New South Wales at the time. In my naivety I thought life meant life!'

Tricia recalls Truong's oldest brother being in court when Truong was sentenced. 'I'd met him previously. He was a lovely man. He and the family sent flowers to the funeral along with a lovely letter to me and my mother. He wanted to see me at the court, but I didn't want to see him or any of them. He left a message saying he wanted to apologise. It wasn't his fault. They were dealing with it too.'

On her return to Melbourne after Truong's sentencing, Tricia Barrett told Patrice Fidgeon, the Deputy Editor (News) at *TV Week*, that the previous year had been an 'absolute nightmare' for the Barrett family. 'It destroys your whole life. You read about tragedies in the paper every day, but you never really know what someone is going through until it happens to you. I not only lost my sister. I lost my best friend. I didn't know how I was going to cope. I had to go on sleeping pills to which I'm now addicted. You wonder how much you can take before you snap. I've cried so much. I haven't got over the grief. I don't know if I ever will."[487]

---

487 "Yvonne Barrett: A Senseless Tragedy", TV Week dated August 30th 1986.

15. AFTERMATH

Some thirty years after Yvonne's death, Tricia revealed just how devastating Yvonne's murder had been. 'It changed my life. It contributed to my marriage break up. I became addicted to prescription drugs Therapax and Rohypnol. I needed them to cope. I was hospitalised four times to get off those drugs. I had two different psychiatrists and I lost weight. The last drug I was on had certain food restrictions and these restrictions were previously foods that I ate. So, I couldn't eat much and I went down to 40 kgs (88 lbs). I spent a month getting off the prescription drugs at the Vauclause hospital in Melbourne. I threw up for years and ended up having stomach surgery for the reflux.

'I didn't go outside for about four or five years. I had no social life, no nothing! I was just under the doona as we say. It changed my daughter Martine's life dramatically too as she and Yvonne were very close. She ended up with a lot of problems. Yvonne's death had a terrible effect on us. It still does! At the time you just have to live with it, but it doesn't make it any easier. I miss her just as much as 34 years ago.'

Tricia believes that Yvonne's role in life was to bring happiness to people. 'She was always bright and happy. She could always make people laugh. When she rang my mother, she'd make her laugh. She'd do funny things, like wiggling her toes when she was singing. You'd laugh and people would wonder why you were laughing. Then someone might want to take a photo of her and she'd put her head down and cover her face with her hair. Or if my kids were with her, she might walk backwards to be funny. I've never heard anyone say a bad word about her and I can't either as her sister.'

At some point in the early 1990s Tricia was contacted by Yvonne's former full time musical director and pianist Peter Arrowsmith. 'Peter rang me out of the blue! It was very sad. He could hardly talk, but he wanted to contact me. He adored Yvonne and he was still devastated by her death.'

During Truong's imprisonment he was treated for a cut finger by a female nurse in the prison's infirmary. Truong and the nurse subsequently had an affair and they were ultimately married in jail. Shortly after Truong had served ten years in prison for Yvonne's murder, Jeff Ahern contacted Tricia and notified her in advance that Truong was being considered for parole. Tricia was horrified by that terrible news, but she wasn't afforded the opportunity to voice her objections to Truong's release.

Truong's wife stood up on his behalf at his parole hearing and said that she would support her husband. Despite objections from the NSW Police Force, the parole board subsequently approved Truong's release from prison.[488] As he was a naturalised New Zealander, Truong was immediately deported back to New Zealand with the stipulation that he would never gain entry to Australia again.

Tricia Barrett still misses Yvonne. 'I miss her badly

---

488 The exact date of Truong's release from prison was not made available by the parole board. It is thought that he was released from prison in late 1995.

because she was the happiest person I've ever met!' Tricia looks at a photo of Yvonne every day and admits that she cries every time she talks about her, despite having had hypnotherapy to stop this. She takes comfort in the fact that Yvonne didn't have to turn 70 and get ill. 'But I'd still rather have her around to see if she was a cranky 70-year-old. I know she was loved and she was very loving. I just wish she was still here.

'Yvonne dreamed impossible dreams. She attracted people around her. She smiled at strangers because they might be lonely. If she saw someone sitting down, and he or she was on their own looking lonely, she would say, "Come and join us." She would soon have them laughing. She was just gorgeous, happy, and funny. She loved people and flowers. She loved to laugh and have fun. She would ring my mother, and my mother's neighbours Vali and Beryl, and she would have them laughing, whereas if I'd ring them, it wouldn't make any difference. Yvonne just had that infectious happiness.'

Tricia also recalls Yvonne being generous to a fault. She shared clothes and costumes with Tricia and with friends and neighbours, like the McCabe girls and other neighbours, for them to dress up in. She used to wear Estee Lauder Youth-Dew. She'd use half the bottle and then give the rest of the bottle to Tricia. She'd then buy herself another bottle. 'Back in the 1960s, Yvonne bought me my one and only Chanel cream boucle suit. Later on, she bought me a black tuxedo which I loved to wear to the ballet. I was talking to my ex-husband's niece Robyn at Christmas a few years ago. She had a watch on that Yvonne had given her. Robyn was only a kid when she said to Yvonne "That's a beautiful watch!" Yvonne took it off and gave it to her. If you said you liked anything she'd say, "Here take it."

'Yvonne and I got on well, I think, because of our five year age difference. I loved seeing her and I was so proud of her. I thought she was so good. I wasn't ever jealous of her. My brother Peter and Yvonne were fairly close, but not as close as Yvonne and I were.'

Tricia only remembers having one fight with Yvonne. 'Because I worked at Dyecraft, we used to get fabric given to us every week. We had a dressmaker in South Road, Braybrook and we used to go to him every Thursday with our fabric. We'd go back the next week to pick up our dresses and to leave the next lot of fabric. All the girls had dresses made every week. We had fabric coming out of our ears, so I always had a lot of clothes. My mother had no money, but she sewed. She was always extremely well dressed.

'I came home from work one day and found that Yvonne had gone to Sydney for a show and she had taken half of my street clothes with her. She said, "You can get more." I did of course, but I was going out that night and whatever I wanted to wear was gone. I think they were the only cross words we ever had!'[489]

---

489 Tricia recalls that Yvonne wore a pink lace dress when she did her first interview after that on the "In Melbourne Tonight" TV show. 'It was a bridesmaid dress which my boss at Dyecraft brought in for Yvonne to wear.'

16. APPENDIX

The following tributes are a sample of those paid to Yvonne in Melbourne's The Sun *newspaper.*

Family tributes included:

"Yvonne Frances. Loved you always, prayed for you always. God bless. Love you. Mum."

"Yvonne, loved daughter of Ted. To me you were so beautiful, like a brilliant star in the sky. But my darling Yvonne, we never said goodbye. I will always remember the times we had together. But my little sweetheart, I cannot understand. I will always love you until the day I die. Your loving father Ted."

"Yvonne Frances. Dearly loved sister of Tricia, loved sister-in-law and friend of Alan, adored aunt of Leisel and Martine. We'll remember the good times. Love you. Rest peacefully Staish."

"Yvonne Frances. We cried a thousand tears for you Von. And we feel this pain inside. To see someone we really love. To leave us far behind. But we still have love and memories of fun we had together. We will always be your little girls. The ones who will love you forever — Leisel and Martine."

"Yvonne Frances. Dearly loved sister of Peter, loved sister-in-law and friend of Jan, adored aunt of David and Karlie. We love you "Cock."

The following are a sample of the tributes paid to Yvonne by entertainers and friends:

"Barrett — Yvonne. To my dear friend Gracie — The soul lives forever, as it will in our hearts. For all the good times I'll miss you. Nothing will ever hurt you again. Deepest sympathy to Mr and Mrs Barrett. — Marcie (nee Jones) and Michael Barnett and family."

"Barrett — Yvonne Frances (suddenly). Dearly loved friend of Lesley and Ron Fletcher. Godmother to Kylie Jane. Deepest sympathy to Mr and Mrs Barrett and family. Although Grace has gone, She's not forgotten. God's taken her afar, And as she was right here on earth, in heaven she will be a star. Although to us her soul is lost, Her memory will always stay. Until we get our curtain call, And we'll meet again that day. Rest in peace Grace."

"Barrett — Yvonne. The hills will always be alive with music when we think of you dear Yvonne. Sincere sympathy to a dear old friend Sheila and family. — Sandra, Alex (Sister Rosalind, Papua New Guinea), Danny and Catherine Cairns."

"Barrett — Yvonne. Wonderful times and memories shared. — Pat and John Farrar and the Carroll family."

"Barrett — Yvonne, So beautiful, so kind. For now, just the very thought of you and the whole world turns Misty Blue. Love John." [490]

"Barrett — Yvonne. Loved friend of Gladys Farrar and family. Deepest sympathy to her family. Forever in our hearts."

"Barrett — Yvonne. A loving tribute to lovely Yvonne. Loving memories. Olive, Albie Farrar and family."

"Barrett — Yvonne. Wonderful memories of a very wonderful lady, who will always be remembered. — Lesley Kirk (nee Zimmermann, Frankston)."

"Barrett — Yvonne Frances. Will always remember you Sis. A true friend sadly missed. — Lyn and Jan Field."

"Barrett — Yvonne. I won't forget you. Farewell old friend. — Joy Lemmon and family."

"Barrett — Yvonne. Deepest sympathy to Mr and Mrs Barrett and family. Yvonne, always a joy to work with, will treasure your warm friendship and great humour. Sadly missed. — John Hennessy."

---

490 The Field Twins attest to the fact that their favourite song and Yvonne's and John Farrar's favourite song was "Misty Blue". They and John Farrar's cousin Lesley Kirk believe that this is definitely John's tribute to Yvonne. Tricia Barrett agrees. 'There was no surname given, but I think if it had been any other John, he would have put his surname in the paper.'

"Barrett — Yvonne. Sincere condolences to Ted on the sad loss of his daughter Yvonne. — Management and Staff, Ashley Hotel, Braybrook."

"Barrett — Yvonne. — Deepest sympathy to Mr and Mrs Barrett. Once a flying swallow who flew to be, A shining star in the sky.- Kaye and Patti."

"Barrett — Yvonne. You will always be in my living memories. All my condolences to the Barrett family. — Lionel Gell."

"Barrett — Yvonne. Loving memories of a happy and caring person.- Val and Les McCabe."

"Barrett — Yvonne. So dearly loved and deeply mourned. — Don and Beryl Sutherland."

"Barrett — Yvonne (Gert). Yvonne to me you were my daughter. The happiness, the comfort and love will never be forgotten. May your soul rest in peace. — Always Beryl."

"Barrett — Yvonne. In fond memory of a lovely girl. The McGrath family (Matt, Eun and Patti) were proud to know and love her. Deepest sympathy to Sheila and the family. R.I.P. — Eunice McGrath."

"Barrett — Yvonne. In loving memory of my lifetime riend, Yvonne. What wonderful times to remember of growing up together. Till we met again Bert and I offer deepest sympathy to Mrs Barrett and family. — Patti Newton."

"Barrett — Yvonne. "Gracie" — the lady of style and personality. Full of fun. I will remember all the good times — the late nights at Winston Charles where we laughed until closing time over a few bourbons. I'll just keep asking myself why you? I'll always remember you. — Denis "Sallsu" Sullivan."

"Barrett — Yvonne. (Tragically taken). Fond memories of a childhood neighbour. Our deepest sympathy to Mrs Barrett and family. — Rhonda, Judith and Kevin McCabe and families."

"Barrett — Yvonne. Loving memories of a happy and caring person. — Val and Les McCabe."

"Barrett — Yvonne. Fond memories of you and your growing up years. Deepest sympathy to Sheila, Ted and family. — Friend and neighbour George and Lorna, Julie and Sandra Crees."

"Barrett — Yvonne. Loved by all who knew her and dearly loved friend of Madeleine, Dionne, Grant, Brandon, and especially Keeli. Heartfelt sympathy to Yvonne's family."

"Barrett — Yvonne. Yvonne, a star throughout life. Now a shining star in God's heaven. Always fondly remembered — Brian de Courcy."

"Barrett — Yvonne. Words are few, feelings are deep. Memories of you are ours to keep. — Dot Compton and family."

17. 'AFTER WORDS'

On the first anniversary of Yvonne's death (September 2nd 1986), Sheila and Ted Barrett and Tricia Barrett paid tribute to Yvonne. Sheila and Ted's tribute read as follows:

In Memoriam: Barrett — Yvonne (Tragically)
In loving memory of our dear daughter,
What can one write to ease the pain?
When it hurts so much to say your name.
And I know now and for ever more,
We will not see you come in the door,
With a happy "Hi" and a lovely smile.
A year has passed since you went away,
We still don't know why you could not stay.
Others are taken this we know,
But you were so special and we loved you so.
And a beautiful person loved by all.
Our hearts are broken with your parting.
Millions of tears can't bring you back.
We know because we've cried.
Yvonne what hurts us most of all is you could not say goodbye.
So dearly loved, so sadly missed.
R.I.P. — Mum and Dad

Tricia's tribute read as follows:

"Barrett — Yvonne Frances" — "The day you were taken away was not just a Grey day for me. It was the end of the Summers — "Darl".[491]

On the second anniversary of Yvonne's death (September 2nd 1987), Sheila and Tricia Barrett again paid tribute to Yvonne. Their tributes read as follows:

"Barrett — Yvonne. Died (tragically) September 2nd 1985. Wishing God had spared you for just a few more years. Heartaches in this world are many, but to lose you Yvonne was worse than any. God bless you — Mum."

"Barrett — Yvonne Frances. Whoever said the pain heals in time, never had a sister and friend like mine. — Darl."

Ted Barrett passed away aged 89 on June 28th 1994. Tricia Barrett attributes his passing to a combination of lifestyle, working conditions and old age. Ted was buried adjacent to Yvonne in the Lawn Cemetery at the Altona Memorial Park on what would have been Yvonne's 48th birthday. Ted's brother Bill and his wife Dorrie had died some years earlier.

Tricia's daughter Martine lived with her grandmother in Braybrook for the last few months of her grandmother's life. Martine recalls that Sheila was very Catholic. 'I was by her bedside three times when a priest was giving her the last rites.'

Brenda (Long) Halman lived next door to Sheila Barrett in Braybrook. Brenda attests to the fact that she and Sheila 'had a

---

491 Tricia and Yvonne always called each other "Darl".

very good relationship. My daughter Kadriye and Mrs Barrett were very good friends too. Mrs Barrett was hard working. Her house was almost immaculate. Everything was so clean, including her garden. She had a very bad heart. She'd be there by herself. The next minute the ambulance would be there. She wouldn't tell anyone. Off she'd go in the ambulance. This happened umpteen times. She had quite a few operations.'

Brenda contends that Sheila was not to be messed with at times. 'She was chopping down trees the day before she died. I had built my fence up. She said she was going to rip it down because she didn't like it. The fence was taken down. Sheila died of pancreatic cancer on May 25th 2001 aged 83. When she died, the fence was put up again. She and I were pretty good mates, except for the fence!'

Sheila Barrett's funeral was held on May 29th 2001, which was the day before what would have been her 84th birthday. Tricia Barrett recalls that Sheila had a heart condition for twenty years. 'We only found out two weeks before her death that she had pancreatic cancer.' Sheila was buried in the same grave as Ted Barrett at the Memorial Park Lawn Cemetery, North Altona.

In more recent years, Tricia wrote the following tribute to Yvonne:

'She filled my house with flowers
And I helped her look for rainbows
She understood so many things
The importance of laughter
And that each moment is forever
She dreamed impossible dreams

Smiled at strangers
Because they might be lonely
And loved music, cats and beaches
I'll think of her on sunlit days and
I see her smile in every flower.

The author's tribute to Yvonne:

Yvonne loved her family. She had compassion and empathy for people. She didn't seek recognition for that. She was generous to a fault. She lent clothes and costumes to friends. Her sister Tricia attests to the fact that Yvonne never said a bad word about anyone.

Yvonne died far too young. Like many of Yvonne's fans, I was devasted when I heard the news of her horrific and brutal death in a case of domestic violence. During her life she gave a great deal to her fans and the world of music. She is greatly missed by her family, friends, colleagues, and her many fans. Her death reminds all of us that life must be lived to the fullest every day, because while its end can be expected; it cannot be predicted!

Yvonne, you have left us with some truly wonderful memories. I feel privileged to have been able to write your life story. With the help of those who knew and loved you, I have made it as accurate as possible. I hope that readers will have learnt how talented, and how special a person you were, and in our hearts, you still are.

I hope this biography will ensure that Yvonne Frances Barrett will always be remembered for her contribution to the Australian music and show business industries. RIP Yvonne. I will never forget the day I met you. Forever in our hearts!

LIST OF IMAGES

1. Yvonne's parents on their wedding day
2. The Barrett siblings
3. Yvonne and Patti McGrath at a dancing competition held in Ballarat
4. Yvonne and Pat Carroll in matching costumes on the Swallows Juniors
5. Promotional photo of Yvonne
6. The last known photo of Yvonne
7. Gravestones of Yvonne and her parents